Criticism, Theory, and Children's Literature

Criticism, Theory, and Children's Literature

Peter Hunt

Basil Blackwell

Copyright © Peter Hunt 1991

First published 1991

Basil Blackwell Ltd
108 Cowley Road, Oxford, OX4 1JF, UK

Basil Blackwell, Inc.
3 Cambridge Center
Cambridge, Massachusetts 02142, USA

British Library Cataloguing in Publication Data

A CIP catalogue record for this book is available from the British Library.

Library of Congress Cataloging in Publication Data

Hunt, P. L. (Peter L.)
Criticism, theory, and children's literature/Peter Hunt.
p.   cm.
Includes bibliographical references and index.
ISBN 0-631-16229-1 (hardback) – ISBN 0-631-16231-3 (pbk.)
1. Children's literature–History and criticism–Theory, etc.
I. Title.
PN1009.A1H76   1991
809'.89282–dc20   90–39269
                                                              CIP

Typeset in 11 on 13 pt Garamond Stempel
by Graphicraft Typesetters Ltd., Hong Kong.
Printed in Great Britain by
Billing & Sons Ltd, Worcester

Contents

Acknowledgements

Some parts of this book have appeared in earlier versions in *Signal, Children's Literature in Education. Studies in the Literary Imagination, The New Advocate, Children's Literature Association Quarterly*, and *Styles of Discourse*, ed. Nikolas Coupland (Croom Helm, London, 1988). I am grateful to the editors and publishers for permission to develop the material in the present book, and to Julia MacRae Books for permission to reprint an extract from my novel *Going Up*, and from Janni Howker's *Isaac Campion*.

I have always regarded acknowledgements pages as opportunities for authors to back modestly into the limelight by mentioning their more famous acquaintances. In my case, it is a matter of admitting the debts I owe to my friends. It will be clear that I have been greatly influenced by writers as diverse as Aidan Chambers, Margaret Meek, and Brian Alderson, although they may well not subscribe to the way in which the ideas have been developed. I would like to thank them, as well as my many friends in the children's literature world in Britain, the USA, Australia, and New Zealand, who have made learning about children's books so pleasant.

Two people require special mention: Nancy Chambers, who has taught me more about high standards in critical writing than anyone, and Tony Watkins, who has taught me a great deal about high standards of teaching, and who on many occasions has allowed me to try out my ideas on his Diploma and MA students at Reading. I would like to dedicate this book to Nancy and Tony, if they are willing to split the dedication five ways with my three eldest daughters, Felicity, Amy, and Abigail, who have not had much practice on the word processor over the last few months.

Introduction: A Map of Criticism

But theory is not criticism. Its purpose is not to offer new or enhanced readings of works, but precisely to explain what we all do in the act of normal reading, with unconscious felicity.
                    Seymour Chatman, *Story and Discourse*

Critical theory may not seem to have much to do with children and books; but it is, as Alan Garner's *Granny Reardun* says of Smithing, 'aback of everything'.[1] Good work with children's literature depends, ultimately, on coherent and thoughtful criticism, and good criticism depends on coherent and thoughtful theory. It is not simply that studies of children's literature should make use of all available disciplines, nor simply, as Anita Moss puts it, that 'if we believe ... that children's literature occupies a place in the traditions of all literature, we owe it to ourselves to explore what is going on in the field of literary criticism, even if we decide to reject it'.[2] We cannot 'decide to reject it', because new theories in time change our habits of thought, and become the norm.

Theory is an uncomfortable and uncomforting thing, for by seeking to explain what we might otherwise have thought was obvious, it draws attention to hidden problems. We usually get along quite well by assuming things to be true that we really know to be quite untrue; for example, that we know how people read, and what happens when they do; that the perceptions and reactions of children and adults are much the same; that we know how and why stories work. Theory may not solve any of those problems directly, but it forces us to confront them.

Having said that, criticism has a great deal to answer for in positively restricting the pleasure derived from texts. As it developed in the early part of the twentieth century, it established two things, both of which have been, and are, largely incomprehensible to the vast majority of the population. It has then spent vast amounts of paper on arguing against these strange creations.

The two incomprehensible things were 'practical criticism' – the idea of treating a text without a context (*all* texts *always* have contexts), and the idea of a 'canon' or literary hierarchy. In some senses, the first was a reaction to the second. The 'literary hierarchy' – indeed, the whole idea of literature – was based on the idea that some texts are intrinsically better than others. This, of course, means that someone has to make a first judgement on this; and so there grew up a kind of literary priesthood, the idea of good and bad readings, better and lesser books. In a democratic response to this, 'practical critics' suggested that anyone, given the tools, could be a critic.

Now, both these ideas spring from basic human needs. Unless we are true practisers of Zen, or mystics, we generally need to discriminate. If a culture is to be ordered, it needs power relationships. More practically, if fiction and poetry are to form part of the education system, they need to be assessed in some way.

But all this has led to confusion: to the idea that there is an *intrinsic* value system which places, say, Shakespeare above all others, rather than a cultural/power system which finds it expedient to place him there. It has led to the idea that personal response is less valuable than generalized response in education, rather than the admission that we cannot award marks, on a scale, to anarchy.

Children's literature confronts these things. Both the children who read the books and most of the adults who deal with them either know nothing of decontextualized reading or literary value systems or cannot understand the point of them, seeing them as illogical and threatening. But criticism is changing. It has many valuable elements which can help us to understand how we understand; help us to work with texts and with people.

The first chapter of this book examines the relationship between criticism, as it is becoming, and children's literature. The second examines the present state of children's literature in general. The third, in order to clarify what we are about, looks at definitions of 'children's literature'.

Having defined our field of study, we now need tools with

which to study it. 'Criticism' is perhaps an unfortunate term: it has, in the past, been applied to everything from analysis to prescription, and it commonly carries a pejorative overtone. That is not what we are about here. We are concerned with understanding what happens when we read, and how we can perceive and talk about a book or make a reasoned selective judgement. (And we are talking about how *real* readers read – not students or critics or others who deliberately read in a deviant way.)

But because the most diligent research has yet to come up with a clear explanation of what happens, we must work from a series of hypotheses.

How is meaning made? What happens in our encounter with a text? We need to see what happens when we read, and at each stage to quality what is happening with what may be happening with a child.

I do not, therefore, propose to analyse books in the way in which many of us have been taught to do – by separating plot, character, scene-setting, style, and so on. Apart from the questionable possibility that such a procedure may enable us to see the book more clearly, I have never been able to see the point of it. It can only be to reduce the experience of the text to a series of analytical moves; and, if you wish to test people's analytic abilities, it would be better to use practical, non-flammable materials. It also carries a lot of freight; for most readers, forced to do it at school, it is likely to destroy whatever it is that people gain from absorption in a book.

So, let us take it in this way. I would like to sketch in an approach, and to suggest, in the following chapters, ways of fleshing out the skeleton. I would emphasize that this is only one method, and not even a methodical method. The critical approach which I would like to suggest should allow a reader to approach texts at least in the knowledge of what is happening.

We begin, then, with the two elements which make meaning: the reader and the book, and begin with two questions which are usually not taken as the province of criticism: What does the book look and feel like? What does the reader feel like? Then, going deeper into both: What is the background of the book? What is the background of the reader? What skills does the book demand? What skills must the reader bring? What is the circumstance of reading the book? This last takes us into the relationship of the child to the book.

As the book is at least fixed in its marks upon paper (even though their meanings change around them), we can then look at the *peritext* – that is, the written (and graphic) material that 'surrounds' the story: the publisher's 'blurb', the typeface, the layout, for example. For real readers, all this makes a difference.

Now we can actually look at the text: first the style of the text, next the structure, and then how these are read, how meaning is made from them. At all points we shall consider how the reader relates to these elements: how genre affects the text, and how knowledge of the conventions of text affect meaning. Then we can turn to the relationship of the meaning made to things 'outside' the text: the ideological implications of the children's book – indeed, the implications of reading at all.

This approach sets the book in the world, but pushes to the end things such as the 'lives' or the psychology of the characters, or how much we are absorbed in fictional events. It also leaves aside practical applications: the role of children's books in socialization, acquiring reading skills, how a particular book might be taught, and the like. It does no more than glance at the history of children's books, or the virtues of specific books or authors. The bibliography supplies sources for all these things; but it must be said that, with few exceptions, books about children's books are grounded on the ambiguities of criticism.

This book is about theory in the sense that it tries to give the individual an understanding of ways of reading texts, so that she or he can then evaluate or use a text in whatever way seems most useful or valid.

1

Criticism and Children's Literature

I have often wondered why literary theorists haven't yet realised that the best demonstration of all they say when they talk about phenomenology or structuralism or deconstruction or any other critical approach can be most clearly and easily demonstrated in children's literature. The converse of which is to wonder why those of us who attend to children's literature are, or have been, so slow in drawing the two together ourselves.

Aidan Chambers, *Booktalk*

This book uses critical theory and practice to help readers to deal with children's literature, and children's literature to help readers to deal with literary theory.

Both these fields are comparatively new to the literary world; both are on the fringes of conventional academia; both are particularly important for the development of literary studies. Just as critical theory now concerns itself with everything in and surrounding the text, from personal response and political background to language and social structure, so children's literature is a field which takes in every genre of writing. Literary theory has pushed back the boundaries of what was once thought to be appropriate to literary/textual studies into philosophy, psychology, sociology, and politics. Similarly, children's literature is usefully studied by educationalists, psychologists, and folklorists, and by students of popular culture, graphic art, psycho- and socio-linguistics, and so on.

The two broad fields also share the dubious distinction that they are regarded by academics and laypersons alike with some suspicion. To the academic, literary theory often seems to challenge conventional views too radically, to be of little practical use, to be too self-serving and nihilistic. To the layperson, it seems to be pretentious and irrelevant. It may be replacing the liberal-humanist 'conventional wisdom' of exclusive criticism with something more democratic, but it often seems to be replacing one set of arbitrary values with another, and that other is elitist. It is seen as over-complex theory, or frightening uncertitude.

Similarly, to the academic, children's literature (which, as we will see, defines itself, uniquely, in terms of an audience which cannot itself be precisely defined) is a non-subject. Its very subject-matter seems to disqualify it from serious adult consideration; after all, it is simple, ephemeral, popular, and designed for an immature audience. It is not, as a university academic once put it to me, 'a fit subject for academic study'. To the layperson, to link the warm and friendly business of educating and entertaining children with theory of any sort seems like destroying the pleasure of it and taking it away from 'real' people.

This book works on the Addisonian premise that there is much to be said on both sides, most of it positive. Literary theory has certainly had a tendency to take on the worst of academic pretensions and to use obscurantist and elitist dialects.[1] Of course, this is partly because it tends to wander into the astrophysics of thought, as it were. But that does not mean that, without being overly reductionist, ordinary mortals cannot take from it much that is useful – in the sense that there is much that can change their attitudes and reveal new and stimulating ways of thinking. Perhaps its most positive contribution has been to see talking about texts as an ingenious and pleasureable game.[2] On the verges of the philosophical swamps are firmer tracts, where we find the major *consequences* of theory: the use and involvement of feminism, politics, narrative theory, linguistics, cultural studies, psychology, even fractal geometry: useful, fresh methods of looking at texts.[3]

Children's literature, as a subject of serious, but not solemn, study, has grown from a highly eclectic and involved 'practitioner' world, which tends to be highly intuitive and dedicated, but frequently anti-intellectual. Just as the advances of critical thought can be, and have been, adapted for use outside academic citadels, so those who work with children and books might benefit from an insight into what is happening in texts, or what is happening with texts. There is no shortage of booklists, selections, and bibliotherapeutic aids.[4] The Children's Literature Association of America has even published a suggested 'canon' of Children's Literature: *Touchstones: A list of distinguished children's books.*[5] All these, either commercially or altruistically intended, certainly save time and allow pressurized librarians, teachers, and other 'users' to make 'informed' choices. However, it might be argued that they also pre-empt and restrict thought. What is needed is a way of approaching children's literature which helps us to make informed choices from first principles, as it were.

By suggesting ways of understanding what texts do and how they work, I hope to help practitioners to cope with the vast output of texts for children. Equally, I would like to bring the pleasures and difficulties of children's literature to a wider audience of both practitioners and academics. But after years of talking about the subject with many remarkable people all over the world, I have concluded that we simply cannot proceed without some reference to literary theory.

Such an idea is not popular, even among the best writers on children's books. Elaine Moss, for example, who won the Eleanor Farjeon Award in 1977 for her distinguished services to children's books as reviewer, librarian, bookseller, and lecturer, has frequently rejected the label 'critic'. This is, she writes, 'largely because it has about it a negative, cutting-down-to-size kind of ring ... I have begged to be considered a commentator rather than a critic ... because I am happy, very happy to leave literary criticism to those who work in universities or polytechnics and who write for a committed and learned audience in respectable specialist journals. This is where real criticism belongs.'[6]

This view encapsulates the division between 'book people' and 'child people' identified by John Rowe Townsend[7] which runs through the now considerable amount of writing for children. Aidan Chambers' sardonic comment that the formulation of a poetics of children's literature is 'but an academic's sinecure away'[8] suggests a deep-seated suspicion.

One reason for this is that, unlike any other form of the arts, children's literature is *available* to criticism, as well as to amateur writers; people are not afraid to comment, to censor, and to be

involved. It might be more accurate to say that the two factions
are those concerned with children and books and those concerned
with books and adults (where the subject-matter just happens, at
some stage, to have been designed for children). Another reason
is that children's books are commonly judged in terms of their
use. As Hugh Crago remarked: 'That the *dulcis et utile* criterion
survives in the criticism of children's books so long after its
virtual demise elsewhere is a pointer to the fact that we are
dealing with the preservation of "tradition" in an outlying area of
culture.'[9]

Rather more obviously than with peer-texts, authors must
necessarily stand in a position of power (whether or not this is
malign, as Jacqueline Rose suggests, or benign is a matter for
debate).[10] Since many disciplines are involved this has tended to
mean more factionalism, as well as a rich intermixture of con-
tributions. This is why we need to consider the first principles of
encountering a text; the context of its use is a separate issue.

The critical revolution of the last fifteen years has meant that
the relationship between the text and the reader has been rethought. Plurality of meaning – which has always been quite
obvious across major cultural boundaries – is now being recognized as obviously applying to all readers.

But it is not always recognized that there is a major cultural
boundary between adults and children, nor that children's book
'practitioners' find little new in this critical revolution. Because
the books they work with are uncanonical and the audience
unfranchised, these practitioner are one step further away from
the 'obvious' interpretation of texts than feminists, whose situation is in some ways similar.[11] (The literary/critical world is, after
all, arranged like a nuclear family, with the patriarch more important than the female, and the female more important than the
children.) Thus children's book people have to do what workers
in almost no other discipline have had to do: to continually reconsider fundamentals: to define, to ask just what is this subject –
and this is where critical theory may help.

Working with children and books, we cannot assume the kinds
of agreed-upon values which exist in academia – for instance, that
Leavis is (or is not) a baseline of values. Who, the question is
likely to be, is Leavis? Neither most children nor most practition-

ers are interested in abstractions. Anyone attempting to develop a coherent 'poetics' of children's literature consequently has to justify the task to both strangers and sisters. Anyone working in any way with children's books must justify her or himself constantly to a huge range of different people, and to fight for status of various kinds.

The most common approach has been that adopted with mixed success by, for example, the Children's Literature Association in the USA: to meet other disciplines on their own ground by producing scholarly journals, articles, and books, all the academic apparatus that so easily alienates those not used to it, but which creates the climate for more books and more courses. This approach, which asserts the parity of children's literature with other literatures and then builds more or less conventional literary criticism upon that assertion, sits rather uneasily with the 'holistic' alliance of benevolent specialists. However, the burgeoning of literary theory has significantly shifted the balance of critical approaches to the point at which such assertions of parity are not relevant.

Literary theory acknowledges the importance of something that most of us secretly recognize anyway: the role of the reader. Much of this change in emphasis from an assumed single meaning and value, whose legitimacy was not questioned (because it was part of the pervading cultural norm), to a very flexible text-and-author-based meaning and value was heralded by Roland Barthes's concept of the death of the author, a concept already well satirized by Malcolm Bradbury. Bradbury quotes Barthes: '. . . the text's unity lies not in its origin but its destination . . . [The book's] source, its voice, is not the true place of the writing, which is reading', and goes on:

> This obviously touched many chords . . . It was particularly popular with publishers, who quickly realized that, if you said that authors wrote books, you had to pay them, whereas if you claimed that readers did, they had the habit of paying you, a much more effective commercial arrangement. It also had considerable appeal for British critics, who had always taken the view that all authors were dead anyway, or if they were not then they should be. There was therefore little wonder that Barthes' book achieved massive sales. Unfortu-

nately because of the nature of its argument he was unable to claim
the royalties, and... was rumoured [to be] begging in the gutters and
the tunnels of the Metro....[12]

This in itself indicates the status of theory, in that it is sufficiently
established to be satirized.

However I should stress that Barthes is one of the few theoreti-
cians (apart from Bradbury) whom I propose to mention by name
in the main body of this book, for the simple reason that the only
point in mentioning a critic by name is that the name acts as a
shorthand reference to a group of ideas. Very few readers can
actually make the necessary associations, and so the use of names
frequently becomes either a weapon or a rather unhealthy totem-
building activity. The division into, say, 'textual' criticism,
'deconstruction', 'Leavisite ...', etc. is very much for the convenience of academic historians, and bears virtually no relationship to the experience of reading. Of course, it would be idle
of me not to acknowledge debts to the writers and thinkers who
have revolutionized critical thought, but Barthes and de Man and
Norris and Leavis and the rest appear here incidentally or in the
guide to further reading. It is their ideas and the possible applications of their ideas that are important.

I prefer, then, to proceed pragmatically. The positive consequence of literary theory is that criticism has broadened to involve
evidence about the reader, and therefore to take in all those wide
disciplines that the children's book world already represents.
The insights of the teacher are no longer 'inferior' to those of
the 'academic'. All specialists now contribute vitally, rather than
peripherally; the scales of values and status have been totally
upset (if not yet the pay-scales). In fact, after the great assault on
the edifice of academia from without, we find the fortress crumbling from within.

And so the academic and the nursery school teacher cannot
really any more afford to ignore each other. They may regard
each other rather patronizingly or quizzically, but both ignore
the findings and practice of each other at their peril.

Critical theory meets children's books at many other points. It
has been concerned, for example, with politics and power, reader

response, and deconstruction, structures, and myths. As Chambers has observed, children's literature is a uniquely important testing ground for literary theories. Recent work by Chambers, Benton, Kelly-Byrne, Cochran-Smith, Crago, and others have tackled the question of child-as-critic.[13] This may seem to some academics a trivial educational exercise; rather, it is confronting the problem of making articulate the responses and the receptive processes of non-peer-readers, which is a useful way of emphasizing that *there is really no such thing as a peer-reader*! Equally important, and equally un-obvious, is Crago's suggestion that 'Children's responses to literature probably do not differ in any significant way from adults' responses, *given that the comparison is made between individual children and adults whose articulacy and sophistication are roughly equivalent*.'[14] What does differ, as we shall see, is the response at different developmental stages and at different skill levels. Again, it is not clear why, in peer-criticism, equal skill and allusion levels are assumed. The criticism of children's literature is forced (as so often) to take on board difficult logistic concepts (such as the non-universality of perception) which 'adult' literary criticism conveniently ignores.

Associated with this is the question of exactly what constitutes the meaning taken from a text. Is it, as Frank Smith suggests, a 'state of zero uncertainty',[15] or is such a state possible or desirable in a 'literary' text? This has been explored widely by reading experts, making use of children's books as tools and exemplars, or by linear empirical and classroom observation.[16]

Interestingly, this question of meaning is complicated by the fracture between the reader and the writer on the one hand and the reader and the buyer on the other. It is likely that child-readers, who are in the process of learning societal and literary norms, will read against societal norms, and be ready to misread or identify the blindnesses of the text.[17] The central problem of the relationship between the adult and the child reflects the problems of power relationships within texts in general. Equally, linguistic/stylistic criticism is particularly adapted to a literature that is constantly adapting itself to the supposed needs and skills of its audience.[18]

If children's books are a proving ground for these theoretical considerations, the theory must be taken on in the context of what is, for many practitioners (and traditionally educated critics), the most disturbing consequence of this change in critical thinking. If the reader is primary, then what happens to values? What happens to accepted canons? What happens to the culture? What happens to Taste? After all, we know what is good, don't we? As one of my students said recently, clearly in despair at the prevailing perversity of *not* coming to judgement, all this reader-power is all very well, but Jane Austen is still a better writer than Judy Blume.

The consequence of the revolution in critical thinking (as well as the pragmatics of dealing with – rather than imposing ideas upon – children) is that we are forced to ask: Why? Why is she better? In what specific, definable ways that can be agreed on she 'better' – and to reject any circular answer: 'because she is'. Jane Austen's language may be more complex in some ways (although, as a stylistician at heart, I would go no further than saying that it is different), and her characterization more extensive. Moreover, a lot of people in the past have read her, or believed her to be good, but does this make her intrinsically better? (A lot more have read and been influenced by Judy Blume.) And the consequence of this is that we cannot talk about an abstract 'better', only about differences. In other words, the status of a text, what gives it its 'quality', is now seen not as something intrinsic, but simply – or complexly – as a question of group power: a text is a text, and how we see it is a question of context. When dealing with children's literature, the question of group power is inescapable.

Recently, I read a response from a mature undergraduate who had just taken part of a course on literary theory. He wrote, 'I haven't got any patience with this modern criticism rubbish. It seems ill thought out, and won't help me in any way to teach "standard" English courses'. Certainly a different mode of thinking is involved; but I would argue that theory does help, even if one's conception of teaching 'standard' English courses is to reiterate the judgements of a previous generation and to confirm certain ideological patterns.

The difficulty with children's literature is that because it is available to all, because there is no 'canon', and because the primary readers are not involved in a literary game, there is little room (except, and this decreasingly, in an examination context) for 'standard' interpretations. Children (and most of their mentors) have no time for the imposed 'right answer', although children are more likely to recognize that this is what they are dealing with.

I hesitate to think what that student would have said to the view that to introduce a child to literature in the way that it has been defined until now is to narrow, not broaden, his or her life: it is to cut the freedom of the equality of all texts to the acceptance of the codes of *some* texts – and those of a privileged minority.

If this seems to be going too far for some, I can only appeal to the experience of most of us who have taught, or been taught, literature. I came to critical theory virtually from the moment that I stopped being a graduate student and began to teach. I had to teach authors I didn't much like: Wordsworth, D. H. Lawrence, Thomas Hardy.... And I had to answer the question from students, why should we read this? In my day, it never occurred to us to ask such impertinent questions. The question then (and, in some schools now, again) was not, what do I do to learn to think, but what do I do to pass?

Consequently, the answer 'Thomas Hardy's prose is good because I say it is', or even because the dominant culture says it is, isn't good enough – at least, not for me and those students who are learning to think for themselves. Why should any student – be it a woman or an American or an East African or a child – give any credence to standards established years ago by old, British, upper middle class, white, university-based males?

Therefore, the 'canon' becomes just another set of texts, liked by a certain set of people, and we are (or should be) free to accept or reject their value systems and the judgements based upon them. Pleasure, mind-expansion, knowledge, socialization – whatever you personally use books *for* – becomes a function of all texts. You may or may not find those things in canonical works – and you are no longer required to.

We need to look at texts, therefore (and this expands, necessarily, to involve non-written texts), as anything but a series of totems before which we sacrifice generations of students. So this critical revolution is not an arcane thing. It is basic, and with children's literature even more so than with other literature.

Equally, children's literature cannot escape, even if some of its practitioners would wish it to, from ideology, past or present. Because the text is intended for supposedly 'innocent' readers, it can scarcely be expected to be innocent of itself. Therefore, fundamental questions have to be faced. What exactly is being controlled in a text? What can, or should be, censored, and by whom?

If children's literature can benefit from contact with critical theory, it must be said that it has its own problems. The central division between current children's literature and past children's literature – can it be called children's literature at all, if it is not 'alive'? – complicates matters. Children's Literature has to be defined in terms of its two elements, children and literature. The criticism that is developed has to be tailored to its special features; children's literature is different from, but it is not lesser than, other literatures. Its unique features require a unique poetics. In 1979 Aidan Chambers put forward the dictum that 'Any comprehensively useful criticism of children's literature must incorporate a critical exploration of the questions raised by the problem of helping children to read the literature'.[19] That now seems to me to be not so much a necessity as an unavoidable fact.

There is another, rather less solemn, consequence to the change in critical approaches: that we can now look at what we like, rather than what we are supposed to like – or, in the case of children's books – what we suppose other people should like. We can respond at a far more personal level, openly and legitimately, than before. Hence, it is important for us to understand where our judgements are coming from, what makes them, and what influences them. If we are honest, we are continually measuring our personal responses, personal likes and dislikes, against 'good' taste, *against* the 'canon', or, rather, the 'canon' against our own private 'canon'. It might even be true that all the theoretical or practical justifications we make for our critical stances are rooted in our own, personal, idiosyncratic concept of what a good children's book is. At a recent conference of the Children's Literature Association in the USA, I asked participants to name their *own* best five children's books: not the best five as prescribed by the 'canon', not the best five for a child, or a class, but best for them.

It is a revealing personal exercise, as well as a revealing public one (and works in the same way for books in general). If there are 'great books', universally rewarding books, then one might expect the lists of many people to have many similarities. But from just over fifty *anonymous* replies, I was given over two hundred different titles, many of them very obscure. The roots of discrimination are very wide and very personal.

The importance of examining the bases of our personal judgements, and of not equating them with either some absolute standard or what the literary/educational establishment prescribes, is accentuated by the fact that most readers of this book are likely to be – or will be forced into the position of being – judges or prescribers, people with a power position over children, as writers, publishers, teachers, or parents. There is, I think, a tension between what is 'good' in the exploded abstract, what is good for the child socially, intellectually, and educationally, and what we, really, honestly think is a good book.

This, then, is the context of this book. I want to emphasize the great richness of children's literature, from the classics to the enormously influential figures of 'popular' culture, from metafiction to experimental mixed-media texts to the latest ephemeral texts, including picture books, fairy tales, and anything else that can *usefully* be taken into the reckoning. It is not a survey or a history or a guide to educational practice; but it partakes of all these and attempts to recommend the best sources to which readers can go. Most of all, it does not try to establish a 'canon' to stand up against literature itself (althought it is possible to do so). Rather, it attempts, by the discussion of a wide range of texts, to provide readers with a personal armoury to allow them to understand children's books better, and to understand their own understanding and the understanding of child-readers. In coming to a better understanding of the judgements which they themselves make, they may then be able to make different ones.

The body of this book is about how meaning is made from a text and the problems specific to, or best demonstrated by, children's books; how they may be interpreted, and how they may be talked about. It therefore begins with the readers: what they bring to books, how they read, what their contexts are, and how these affect the meanings they make with books. We then move into the books themselves, beginning not with the meanings which might be paraphrased out of them, but with the way in which language works and the way in which it works in relation to the reader.

Thus far, we will, of course, have taken in much on the politics of children's books, as well as on the theory and practice of reading, and dealt with it in terms of psychology and stylistics. Then we will consider the way structures work in books and the importance of narrative.

In terms of children's books, I shall be advocating a new critical approach: 'childist' criticism, as a parallel to 'feminist' criticism, although this is in no way intended to imply a them/us division.

Finally, I would like to look at illustration, some of the difficulties associated with the production of children's literature.

But, what exactly is it?

2

The Situation of
Children's Literature

Why Study Children's Literature?

The best answer is: because it is important, and because it is fun. Children's books have, and have had, great social and educational influence; they are important both politically and commercially. Children's books have been a recognizably discrete 'type' of text since the mid-eighteenth century (although, as we shall see, some critics argue for putting the date back much further.) The present output in Britain alone is estimated to be 5,000 new books each year, with 'about 55,000 titles in print'.[1] (The actual figures are hard to establish, because of reprints, re-cycled texts, and of course, the problem of definition.)

From a historical point of view, children's books are a valuable contribution to social, literary, and bibliographical history; from a contemporary point of view, they are vital to literacy and culture and are at the leading edge of the trend towards image-and-word, rather than simply written word. In conventional literary terms, their numbers include acknowledged 'classic' texts; in popular culture terms, they are central. They are probably the most interesting and experimental of texts, in that they use mixed-media techniques which combine word, image, shape, and sound.

For example, in 1986, a new 'classic' was published, a cult phenomenon among children (and adults), one which is a genuine nudge forwards for the possibilities of the children's book. This is Janet and Allan Ahlberg's *The Jolly Postman, or Other People's Letters*.[2] This is an inspired collection of letters, complete with envelopes and their removable contents, between nursery-rhyme characters. There is a letter from Little Red Riding Hood's lawyers to B. B. Wolf, Esq., calling on him to cease the harassment of grandmothers. There is a catalogue from Hobgoblin Supplies for the Witch in the Gingerbread House, a postcard from Jack to the Giant, an apology from Goldilocks to the Three Bears, and an advance copy (with its own ISBN) of Princess Cinderella's memoirs from the Peter Piper Press. As Nancy Chambers commented, 'The Ahlbergs plainly believe that children deserve every ounce of their talent, intelligence, inventiveness, and care.'[3] As a cross-media, multi-referential object, it requires serious thought; as a book with a very wide allusive base, which has sold around a million copies in hardback, in several countries, there must be special pleading if it is to be ignored.

Children's literature has unique genres within it: the school story, texts designed for single sexes, religious and social propaganda, fantasy, the folk and the fairy-tale, interpretations of myth and legend, the picture-book (as opposed to the illustrated book), and the mixed-media text. The re-telling of myths and legends is little found elsewhere. Narrative dominates.

Of course, there is often a sceptical sub-text to the question 'Surely there is nothing worth studying?' There are two useful answers. The first is that children's literature can be justified *on the same terms* as adult literature; a 'canon' of great books which can stand beside *the* 'great books' can be complied, from Carroll to Mayne.[4]

Indeed, there are several contemporary writers for children, people such as William Mayne or Alan Garner, who could reasonably be evaluated in the same breath as any contemporary writer. When Mayne was put forward for the 1975 Hans Christian Andersen Award, for example, the citation read, in part, 'We believe that few writers *in any field of English fiction today* [my italics] use language with more *alertness* and more wit, have greater verbal ingenuity when it comes to describing everyday moods and sensations, or possess a sharper ear for the tones of the human voice.'[5] The case for Alan Garner was put by Neil Philip in his monograph *A Fine Anger*: 'This book is about Alan Garner the writer, not Alan Garner the children's writer ... Garner [is] a very considerable talent, whatever his readership.'[6]

Equally, the 'classic' authors – Carroll, Grahame, Nesbit, Milne, Ransome, and so on – have all received 'scholarly' treatment (including biographies), while there is an *Oxford Companion to Children's Literature*.[7] But for all that, this 'equal status' approach leads rapidly into a quagmire of unproductive status and value arguments.

Similarly, although the list of accepted 'major' authors who have contributed to children's literature is, perhaps, surprising, it is no accident that you can look in vain through many major critical works on these authors for mention of their work for the young. Among these authors are Hardy, Joyce, Woolf, Dickens, Thackeray, Wilde, Huxley, Ruskin, Eliot, Greene, Rossetti, Day Lewis, Twain, Masefield, Graves, and Jefferies. This is an impressive list, but not if their writing for children is dismissed as being necessarily inferior. Several writers have worked with equal distinction in both 'camps' notably Stevenson, Russell Hoban, and, more recently, the 1987 Booker Prize-winner, Penelope Lively, while, as John Rowe Townsend has observed, it is 'a pseudo-Euclidean proposition that any dividing line between children's and adult's fiction will pass through the middle of Kipling'.[8] As we shall see, if 'literary merit' is in the eye of the literary establishment, then no textual evidence is admissible.

Some writers, fighting nobly with this approach, have suggested that children's literature thrives in quality and inventiveness in direct proportion to the quality and inventiveness of adult literature, a view vigorously refuted by Aidan Chambers.[9] On the whole, a more productive answer (as I have suggested in Chapter 1) requires that the very values which distinguish 'literature' from other texts must be rethought.

It is perhaps easier to avoid literary arguments and to consider the use to which the texts are put. In terms of educational value, children's literature has much to contribute to the acquisition of cultural values,[10] and its importance in literary education has been summed up by a distinguished British librarian, Peggy Heeks, who quotes the Bullock Report *A language for life* (1975) thus: 'Literature brings the child into an encounter with language in its most complex and varied forms,' She comments that this rightly emphasizes the engagement with words that is at the heart of the literary experience. It is style which, ultimately, decides the quality of a story.... Style may be enjoyed by children without being identified by them ... but it is essential that we, the adult selectors of books for children, should train ourselves to be sensitive to the words which carry the story.[11]

However, although it is generally agreed by authors and teachers that there is no need to restrict language in texts designed for children or, for that matter, to change the coinage of criticism,[12] the fact that these agreed-upon ideals are not maintained in practice suggests that there is a sub-text to much writing of and about children's books.

Conflicts of Opinion

There are many examples of a deep ambivalence towards children's books among practitioners, as well as 'outsiders', an ambivalence that can be traced back to uncertainty about critical principles. For example, in one notable instance, a major British award-giving committee actually questioned whether 'literary' standards were at all relevant in choosing a 'good' children's book.[13] Similarly, the associations between language and thought, language and education, and language and socialization are recognized. Why, then, in this context, is there a neglect of language itself? To some extent, it seems, the interests of critics lie elsewhere; at root, textual studies are not popular.

With all this in mind, it should scarely be necessary to write a justification for the study of children's literature and its legitimacy as a serious subject of study. But several things have militated against its academic acceptance, as well as against a high standard of study outside academia. As Gillian Avery and Julia Briggs have observed in their introduction to a volume celebrating the work of Iona and Peter Opie:

But though this country has produced the greatest children's literature of any culture, it has valued that tradition so little that many of its earliest treasures have been allowed to slip away across the

Atlantic: until recently Oxford University took no official interest in the subject, unlike the United States where it is recognized as suitable for study at universities and where most recent scholarly research has been carried out.[14]

The first of these is the unexamined assumption that what is written for children must necessarily be simple – as though writing for juveniles were the literary equivalent of juvenilia (and one can gratefully acknowledge Hugh Lofting's comment that he would only permit his novels to appear in his publisher's catalogue as 'juveniles' if the adult novels were listed as 'seniles')[15] or as though a paediatrician were naturally inferior to any other kind of medical specialist.

The assumption that children's literature is necessarily inferior to other kinds – let alone that it is a contradiction in terms – is linguistically, as well as philosophically, untenable. It also assumes a homogeneity of text and authorial approach that is improbable, a view of the relationship of reader and text that is naïve, and a total lack of understanding both of the child-reader's abilities and of the way that texts operate.

The second assumption is that most of the texts are trivial, and perhaps that they are intended for a lesser culture. As we shall see, there is a confusion between text features which are characteristic of children's literature and text features of low-level, or 'bad', adult literature. Obviously, a large proportion of books for children is of negligible worth by almost any 'literary' yardstick; but it is not clear to me whether this proportion is any higher than that for so-called 'adult' literature. The assumption that children's literature is in any way homogeneous is to underestimate its variety and vitality.

It is a sad reflection on academia that the very richness, diversity, and vitality of children's literature has militated against its acceptance. Children's literature (and its study) crosses all established generic, historical, academic, and linguistic boundaries; it requires input from previously discrete disciplines; it is relevant to a wide range of users. It presents unique challenges of interpretation and production. It necessarily involves language acquisition, censorship, and the whole issue of sexuality, which moves the debate into the realm of affect, rather than theory.

The academic outcome of this (which, of course, is also reflected back into the production of children's literature) is that the study of children's literature tends to take place in the practical disciplines of librarianship and education and perhaps psychology, rather than in the more theoretical discipline of 'literature'. The hegemony of the 'English Department' is certainly being challenged, but there is, without doubt, a question of status.

On the other hand, I have some sympathy with the traditional university English Department. However enthusiastic its members may be, time for undergraduate study is limited; if you include children's literature, what will the students *not* read? If you add *Alice in Wonderland* to the Victorian literature paper, does that mean that students do not have time to read, or do not need to read, *Jude the Obscure*?

Educationalists have told me that children's books should not fall into the hands of the English Department; English departments are suspicious of educationalists and librarians dealing with literary matters (or, indeed, of the materials amenable to such use).

But perhaps the most ironical result of this is that children's books are thought to be best studied at postgraduate level. Until very recently, research projects in literature have tended to be on eighteenth- or nineteenth-century writers (age conferring upon them critical respectability) such as Hofland, Edgeworth, Day, and Barbauld – whose books, it may be argued, *were once* children's literature though have now ceased to be so. Of course, many nineteenth-century texts for adults are no longer for any real readers, but are kept alive on academic support-systems.

The result of these prejudices has been, as we have seen, the division of motivation between those with abstract and those with practical interests in these texts. This has led to a certain anti-intellectualism which, sadly, is too often justified. Margaret Meek remarked in her Woodfield Lecture entitled 'Symbolic outlining: the academic study of children's literature' that 'there is a persistent sub-text' of prejudice against the universities.[16] Certainly, children's literature is sometimes seen as a new and promising field for literary studies, a new vein to be mined, when so many academic lodes are becoming rather thin.

Reaction to this has been to adopt a 'user-friendly' approach, which appeals too readily to the immediate reactions of audiences. The strongest attack on such a 'soft-centred' critical approach has probably been by Brian Alderson, in 'The irrelevance of children to the children's book reviewer'. His contrast is between a rather loose appeal to particular children and more rigorous criticism. Unfortunately his attack is rooted in what appears to be an 'adultist' stance.

> But once one assigns to reading the vital role, which I believe that it has, of making children more perceptive and more aware of the possibilities of language, then it becomes necessary to hold fast to qualitative judgements formed upon the basis of adult experience. Naturally a knowledge of and sympathy with children is as vital as a personal response based upon knowledge of the resources of contemporary children's literature.[17]

The reaction to this kind of argument is very often to reject such standards as irrelevant, which is to throw the baby of judgement out with the bathwater of cultural elitism.

The disputes show the need to define literature in such a way that it is not equated (outside as well as inside university literature departments) with the inaccessible, the pretentious, and the difficult, thereby giving rise to the reaction that 'children's literature' is a contradiction in terms. On the one hand, it is understandable that something seen as out of the range of children should not be forced upon them; on the other, there is an anti-intellectualism which leads directly to an implied restriction upon what children should be able to read. As we shall see, publishers are afraid of the influence of librarians and teachers, and so will not be experimental. There is a tendency to ghettoize, which is growing.

This anti-intellectualism is very widespread; it is a suspicion of theory that can be found in the most innocent and worthy areas. For example, take the Federation of Children's Book Groups. These groups are local, involving a town or a village. They raise money to buy books for schools and playgroups and doctor's waiting-rooms; they also put on book events and give prizes – anything to encourage storytelling and reading. The Federation is

unpolitical and highly praiseworthy. Its publicity proclaims both
what it *is*:

- full of enthusiasm for children and their books
- prepared to do anything book-centred, anywhere

and what it is not:

- full of intellectuals
- deadly serious.

One rather depressing result of this stance – at least for a
liberal-humanist observer – is the way in which the word 'literature', which is generally taken to mean the best or most lasting or
most distinguished of a culture's writings, becomes in the children's book world a 'slur' word. For example, in an interview the
successful British popular-novelist Jean Ure (somewhat akin to
Judy Blume in her output) was described thus: 'No-one will ever
say of her, "Well, it's a marvellous book, but is it for children?"
Indeed, she roundly dislikes "pretentious literature at the top of
the age-range" and suspects only critics read it ... [S]he neither
enjoys nor wants to write "Literature" for children, finding most
of it unintelligible.'[18] It seems as though the impulse for revenge
upon that unintelligible thing 'literature', thrust down our unwilling throats at school, is very strong. Is this the old implication
that the standards of 'literature' as defined by adult culture are
not relevant to, or desirable for, a child? Or is it, more subtly, an
ideological statement about 'literature' (and the Book) being a
symbol of power and oppression. 'Literature' is simply not relevant to most adults, and many people are delighted to be in a
position of being able to protect children from what they themselves suffered.

The same attitude to literature can be found among writers.
Kathleen Peyton, who, as K. M. Peyton has written many children's books, including the 1969 Carnegie Medal-winner *The
Edge of the Cloud*, wrote in *The Guardian* in 1970: 'I do feel that
this cult of so deeply analysing children's books for motive,
content, suitability, etc., is getting out of hand. Why the term
children's *literature*? None of the writers I know take themselves

so seriously. We don't use the term for the bulk of adult novels
... I think you take the whole business too seriously.'[19]

Attitudes to the subject therefore remain confused. A respected
teacher of the subject in New Zealand has told me that when she
tells people what she does, they tend to think she is mentally
retarded. In the USA, teachers find that students regard their
courses as potentially 'Mickey Mouse' courses – that is, easy,
comic, trivial – until, perhaps, assessment time.

As the study of children's books becomes more academically
respectable, so it becomes less acceptable to the 'practitioners'.
This has been a constant feature of prize-awarding in Britain for
some years. The British Library Association's choice for the
Carnegie Medal very rarely pleases either the 'book people' or the
'child people', while the latest and the richest prize, the 'Smarties'
prize, seems to be judged at least to some extent by television
'personalities'.

None the less, the world picture of research, teaching, and
resources shows many great strengths. In the USA and Australia,
especially, there are many programmes in children's literature and
major research libraries. Carolyn Field's *Special Collections in
Children's Literature* lists 267 collections; Tessa Chester's *Sources
of Information about Children's Books* lists 157 specialist collections (including the 20,000-volume Opie collection in the
Bodleian).[20] There are specialist journals and societies, including
the International Research Society for Children's Literature, a
major European centre at the Internationale Jugendbibliothek
in Munich, and national children's book centres in Germany,
Sweden, Australia, Wales, and elsewhere. Children's literature is
an accepted division of the activities of the Modern Language
Association of America.

And yet, to some extent, all this is built upon a very wide range
of definitions of the subject. How far the Federation of Children's
Book Groups, which 'promotes an awareness of the importance
of children's literature principally among parents', The Henty Society, The National Committee on Racism in Children's Books,
the Children's Book History Society, and the Followers of Rupert
can be encompassed under a single umbrella definition is not clear.
Too often, people have little idea of what children's books are, or
what they really want from them. This is not simply a question of

censorship. Edward B. Jenkinson called Chapter 6 of his book *Censors in the Classroom: the mind benders* 'Targets of the Censors', and began thus: 'It is tempting to write only the word *everything* and call it chapter 6.'[21] As we will see, censorship and ideology are closely linked; but the difficulty of *seeing* children's books goes deeper.

Typical Confusions

The difficulties in dealing with children's books can be illustrated by four examples. In 1987, after 85 years of 'purity', Beatrix Potter's *Peter Rabbit* appeared in a new edition, with new text and new pictures. Now to some people this is about as logical as, say, writing new words and new music for Cole Porter songs; to others, it may be more like updating the arrangements of the songs. And anyway, why the fuss? Beatrix Potter's books have already appeared in the USA in re-illustrated editions (for example, *The Tale of Peter Rabbit*, illustrated by Allen Atkinson).[22] But in Britain, we are dealing with a national institution – which is why, of course, the new editions by Ladybird Books make commercial sense *and* cause so much trouble. Instead of the small, white editions with their subtle water-colours and short, but highly allusive, texts, we are now given – or rather, sold – meticulous photo-sequences featuring stuffed animals and 'up-dated' texts. This 'up-dating' provides an interesting insight into attitudes. For example, take the famous opening:

> Once upon a time there were four little Rabbits, and their names were –
>
> > Flopsy,
> > Mopsy,
> > Cotton-tail,
> > and Peter.
>
> They lived with their Mother in a sand-bank, underneath the root of a very big fir-tree.
>
> 'Now, my dears,' said Old Mrs Rabbit one morning, 'you may go into the fields or down the lane, but don't go into Mr McGregor's garden: your Father had an accident there; he was put in a pie by Mrs McGregor.'[23]

The new version, 'based on the original and authorized story', reads:

> Once upon a time there were four little rabbits. Their names were Flopsy, Mopsy, Cotton-tail and Peter. They lived in a burrow under the root of a big tree. One day they were allowed to play outside. 'Stay near home,' said their mother. 'Please don't go to Mr McGregor's garden.'
>   'Why not?' asked Peter.
>   'Because he doesn't like rabbits,' answered Mrs Rabbit. 'He will try to catch you.'[24]

Gone are the fir-tree and the sand-bank; Mrs Rabbit, now youthful, is more polite to her children; Peter responds with a question in this more egalitarian world. Gone are the fields and the lane, to be replaced by the urban sub-text that the children are only occasionally allowed to play outside. And, although it may seem predictable enough that the death-joke has been removed (although to those of us who know the original text, it has only been replaced, ironically, by another one), it is perhaps curious that the words of caution, once explicit, have now been replaced by veiled threats.

Certain subtleties have also been lost; what Potter was content to leave the reader to deduce (often in the gap of the turn of the page) has been made explicit. In the original version, Peter

> ... ran straightaway to Mr McGregor's garden, and squeezed under the gate! [Page] First he ate some lettuces and some French beans; and then he ate some radishes. [Page] And then, feeling rather sick, he went to look for some parsley.[25]

Compare the fully 'told' version, in which Peter

> ... ran straightaway to Mr McGregor's garden. [Page] There were lots of vegetables in Mr McGregor's garden. Peter Rabbit loved vegetables. He began to eat them. First he tried the lettuces. Next he tried the beans. Then he ate some radishes. [Page] Peter ate too much, because he was greedy. He began to feel sick. 'I must find some parsley to nibble,' he said to himself. 'That will make me feel better.'[26]

Here we see an interesting revival of one of the central historical discussion points of children's literature. How far are Children's Books didactic? And how far are they *necessarily* didactic?[27]

It is a commonplace to say that nineteenth-century children's books were heavily didactic, and that they were primarily designed to mould children intellectually or politically.[28] Generally, it has been assumed that children's books now represent – and should represent – freedom of thought. Whether this is actually possible might be debated; but what these two versions of Peter Rabbit show is that the concept, as a positive concept, is far from dead. The two books end thus:

> I am sorry to say that Peter was not very well during the evening. [Paragraph] His mother put him to bed, and made some camomile tea; and she gave a dose of it to Peter! 'One table-spoonful to be taken at bed-time.' [Page] But Flopsy, Mopsy, and Cotton-tail had bread and blackberries for supper.[29]

> Then Mrs Rabbit took a closer look at Peter. 'Dear me!' she said to herself. 'His whiskers are drooping! He doesn't look very well!' So Mrs Rabbit decided to give Peter something to make him feel better. She got out her camomile tea and waited for the water to boil. Peter groaned when he saw the tea. He knew that it tasted horrible. Peter was put straight to bed and Mrs Rabbit gave him some tea. 'One tablespoonful to be taken at bedtime,' she said, as she tucked him up. But Flopsy, Mopsy and Cotton-tail had fresh bread, milk and blackberries for supper. *They had Peter's share, too, and they enjoyed every single bit of it.*[30] [my italics]

Now, are these changes shocking, or admirable? There are certainly plenty of arguments *for* the changes. For example:

- The 'old' editions are middle-class, and exclude the majority of modern children because of their ethos.
- Modern children will not understand many of the 80-year-old references.
- The language has changed, and there are many obscure words.
- Some references (such as to death) are not good for, or appropriate for children.

- Children no longer relate to water-colours, but they do relate to photographs.
- The 'old' editions are too expensive; the new ones sell at about one-third of the price of the old ones, which are half the size.
- The new edition will sell in supermarkets and corner shops, and not just in bookshops, which appeal only to a minority. They will reach a mass audience of non-book people, and put thousands of children, who have previously been deprived, in touch with an important part of their culture.

And, perhaps most galling for the purists,

- Without the new editions, the old ones will not survive.

As you might expect, many readers have accused the publishers of straightforward greed. But, worse than that, they feel betrayed; and the story behind their sense of betrayal is significant one.

The rights for Beatrix Potter's books (which expire in Britain in 1993, 50 years after her death) belong to her original publisher, Frederick Warne. A few years ago, Warne became part of the Penguin Books group, and the first reaction of the Potter fans was probably one of relief. Penguin is probably the most respected paperback publisher in the world, with the most extensive and prestigious list, so what better home for Peter Rabbit? The Beatrix Potter Society, an august body, published a letter from Peter Meyer, the chief executive of Penguin Books, in their *Newsletter* in April 1985, which seemed to be both generous and reassuring: 'I do understand the concern of your members and would like to assure them that care is being exercised over the quality of any new project.' But, he went on, 'Our aim is, as always, to broaden the appeal of the Beatrix Potter books.'

There is little doubt that Mr Meyer's policies saved Penguin; by entering more popular markets and publishing 'bestsellers', he was able to maintain Penguin's amazing specialist list. The Beatrix Potter Society might have been alerted by the way the letter continued, 'Whilst some of the development may not appeal to all lovers of the work, surely it is better that this is done with attention to detail under control whilst copyright still exists?'

In many ways, Penguin has more than kept its promise. The Beatrix Potter books have been re-issued in large format, but in impeccable taste; the *Peter Rabbit ABC* (an alphabet book with Potter's illustrations) is a model of its kind; licensing of products such as jig-saw puzzles has been discreet and true to Potter's illustrations; and, best of all, Penguin produced a new edition of all the books, going back to the original paintings. All well and good.

Enter another British institution: Ladybird Books. It is unlikely that any British child of the last thirty years or so has not been influenced by these workmanlike volumes, whose huge range has included reading schemes, simplified fairy tales and rhymes, and information books for the very young. They are entirely admirable, but they are not, it might be said, art.

When *Peter Rabbit* appeared in Ladybird's photographic format, the reaction was fierce. It can be summarized thus:

- *Why* must the language be simplified? Children's book language should be adventurous and mind-expanding; all we have left is a mind-closing parade of clichés.
- To 'simplify' is not to make a text accessible; it is merely to 'ghettoize' the readers. They are not given the *opportunity* to expand their ideas.
- What do you mean by 'not understand'? Children cannot be said to understand any text fully unless they are 'stretched'. And, anyway, has the education system declined?
- It is not surprising that children do not relate to watercolours, if they are deprived of them.
- If you cut out content-items (such as references to death), how do you answer Edward Ardizzone, who wrote: 'we are inclined to shelter ... [the child] too much from the harder facts of life. ... After all, books for children are in a sense an introduction to the life that lies ahead of them. If no hint of the hard world comes into these books, then I am not sure that we are playing fair.'[31] And, especially in the harsh world of the 1990s, is it not unrealistic to suppose that children will be unaware of the violence that surrounds them?
- Why debase the book *vis-à-vis* its greatest rival, television? TV does this sort of simplification better.

- Why not sell the originals in supermarkets? Why make the new books bigger, when Beatrix Potter specifically designed her books for 'little hands'?
- If this kind of product is required, why not write totally new books?

And, worst of all,

- Such alterations are based on ignorance; they ignore the growing body of research evidence which finds children's responses to be subtle and variable, not crude, as all this suggests.

These, then, are the battle-lines; yet behind them lurks a far simpler and cruder set of assumptions which infuse all discussion of children's books. These are that the Beatrix Potter 'original edition supporters' are elitist snobs, who think that old is good, *per se*. They are liberal-humanist fascists – perhaps scarcely a paradox (see Chapter 8) – who appeal to 'absolute' values which are merely a means of appropriating the Book to themselves. On the other side are those who would rather have children read *anything*, however degraded and degrading, than nothing. They do not understand or care for the book-culture at all, and merely wish to appropriate it for their own subversive ends. In doing so, they patronize the child and undermine the book, and give in to lowest common denominators of culture.

However, no one should have been surprised at the publication of the 'altered' *Peter Rabbit*, had they remembered the splendid essay by Rumer Godden in *The Horn Book* in 1963, 'An imaginary correspondence'. Miss Godden there presented an exchange of letters between Beatrix Potter and Mr V. Andal of the de Base Publishing Company, who wished to publish *Peter Rabbit* in plain words, 'simple enough for a child to understand'. Beatrix Potter's imagined riposte might echo around today: 'It would seem to me you are in danger of using "simple" in the sense of mentally deficient. Are children nowadays so much less intelligent than their parents? ... [We should] enrich a child's heritage of words – not diminish it.'[32]

Unfortunately, the Ladybird editors seem to have taken Mr V.

Andal's advice to heart (to cut out words like 'lippety, lippety' because they are not in the dictionary). Rumer Godden cites one page from *Peter Rabbit*, when he is caught in the gooseberry net:

> ... some friendly sparrows ... flew to him in great excitement, and implored him to exert himself.[33]

She then gives Mr V. Andal's advice:

> Not all children will be able to identify sparrows; suggest the more general 'bird-ies'; last five words especially difficult; suggest 'to try again' or 'try harder'.[34]

She nearly got it right. The Ladybird text reads:

> Some sparrows heard Peter sobbing, and they hopped over to see what was the matter. 'Keep trying', they chirped. 'Don't give in.'[35]

This confusion of motive also applies to matters of censorship. In 1988 Collins published a picture book by Felix Pirani, *Abigail at the Beach*.[36] It begins: 'Abigail and her daddy went to the beach. Abigail's daddy took a sun umbrella and a deck chair and a thermos full of orange juice and three cans of ice-cold beer and a box of biscuits and a book. Abigail took a bucket and a spade. Abigail's daddy put up the sun umbrella and put the deck chair under it. He sat down and started to read his book.' Abigail builds a sand-castle, investing it with her imagination. Two boys come and threaten to knock it down: ' "You touch one of my towers," said Abigail, "and I'll get my daddy to hang you both upside down by the heels. He's in the Mafia." ' Three times she fights off stronger and unkind children by threatening that her Secret Service daddy will 'break both your arms and frazzle your bike', and that her 'daddy in the marines' will shoot their dog full of holes. In between, there is a gentle interweaving of the fantasy that Abigail has built around her sand-castle and the fantasy of the book her daddy is reading. He gives her the empty beer-cans to play with.

In December 1988 an article appeared in the London *Times* by the humorist and political commentator Craig Brown. He pointed out that 52 Members of Parliament had signed an early day motion requesting Collins to withdraw the book. 'Meanwhile', Brown says, 'Abigail's daddy is drinking "three cans of beer".... The author does not even have the sense to suggest that it is low-alcohol beer.... "I would think that it would encourage a young child to think drinking beer was a nice thing to do" [the M.P.] commented. Oh, the wicked lies of Abigail's publishers!'[37] Brown, with less than Swiftean subtlety, then considers what would happen if fairy tales were given the same attention: 'Leader of the special commission, Sir Humphrey T. Dumteigh ... claims ... 'I have seen elderly, defenceless ladies shut in cupboards by transvestite wolves, young girls mercilessly tormented by their elder sisters [and] senior citizens thrown into blazing furnaces by children.... Whatever happened to old-fashioned children's entertainment?'[38]

This may have been funny, but it did not stop a great deal of debate in the media. It leaves the division between the ideal of freedom ('all censorship is bad') and the idea of responsibility towards children.

It is hardly a new problem. For every worried reader who would stamp out what he or she sees as irreligion or sex or violence in children's books, there have been writers who have maintained that children's texts should he mind-expanding and developmental; that texts should be 'open', should confront, not confirm. Indeed, as a central problem of the power relationship between adults and children, what should we include and what exclude?

In order to break free from some of these disputes, we need to clearly define our terms. Just what is this category of texts? And what is it *for*? However, the difficulties of definition also have a dimension stemming from the division between literature and practicality.

A classic, and symptomatic, dispute is that over the award of the Library Association's annual Carnegie Medal, which began life in 1936 with Arthur Ransome's *Pigeon Post*.[39] In 1969, the award was given to K. M. Peyton for *The Edge of the Cloud*, the second book in her 'Flambards' trilogy. Dominic Hibberd, in an article entitled 'The Flambards trilogy: objections to a winner' launched a swingeing attack on the critical standards applied by the Carnegie Medal committee. His argument, briefly, was that K. M. Peyton's three books were 'a lively and enjoyable story [which] if judged like any other group of novels, [is] very definitely not of the first rank.... [It] does bear the marks of something written and printed in a tremendous hurry.... But if you're a critic of the Carnegie kind you don't notice ... bad style.... No, you seize upon those dear old chestnuts "frustration and loneliness" and praise the author for "raising issues".'[40] He questions whether it is a children's book at all, maintaining that – 'If it had been serialized anonymously in a woman's magazine we should not have though of it as aimed particularly at teenagers.'[41] Indeed, the three books comprising the trilogy were serialized for television in an 'adult' time slot, and subsequently appeared in a paperback edition that did not acknowledge their origin.

What Hibberd was attacking was the 'dusty mouthful of clichés'[42] applied by the committee in place of what he saw as real criticism: 'outstanding ability in evocation of atmosphere ... conveying a sense of place ... skill in delineating and developing character.'[43] Perhaps because they are clichés, the committee quite patently (as has happened in several notorious cases) seemed to have little analytical sense. Its members were responding at a very simple level to the texts. 'Mr Ray [chairman of the awarding committee] appears to be using standards which in kind are the same as adult ones, but which in degree are lower and less demanding.'[44] In short, his argument rested on the inadequate application of established standards in the face of expectations generated by the label 'children's book' rather than, as might be the case today, questioning the standards themselves.

Colin Ray produced a very spirited defence. But the point he made then has remained central for much discussion of children's books:

> The real trouble, I think, is that we are up against Mr Hibberd's 'critical standards'. These are not defined, but appear to be those of *literary* criticism. If he will refer to the terms of the Carnegie Medal, he will fiind that the award is for an 'outstanding' book. I would personally criticize that adjective as being vague: but one thing it does not explicitly mean is that the Medal is a literary award....

What the committee seeks . . . is a book . . . of the highest quality in its genre. And in considering quality, literary quality is only one aspect: its potential impact on the young reader, its ideas, its chances of being read, its individual aspects which make it stand out from the rest, all are relevant.[45]

This remarkable exchange seems to pivot on a very narrow concept of 'literature' on both sides, and implies an anti-literary and anti-intellectual attitude on the one hand and an appeal to 'establishment' values on the other. Without a clearer examination of the bases of these arguments, it is difficult to proceed.

A similar, and perhaps more damning, view of children's books is the case of Richard Adams's *Watership Down*. It was awarded the Carnegie Medal for 1972, and Alec Ellis wrote: '*Watership Down* is a phenomenon the like of which only appears once or twice in a lifetime, and one could not reasonably ask more of a treasure so scarce.'[46]

The book, apart from being a world bestseller, also had the interesting distinction of the same text being available in both adults' and children's editions simultaneously. When it appeared in the USA, it was reviewed, very shrewdly, in *Newsweek*, and the contrast with the opinion of the Carnegie committee is striking: 'I'll make a deal with you. If you won't say anything dumb like "I'm not interested in a story about rabbits," I won't say anything dumb like "This is a great novel." '[47] The situation predicated there is that there is an unbroken value-scale running from adult classics down to rubbish for children, with acceptably second-rate adult books and the best possible children's books sharing the same rung. Such a suggestion may not bear much scrutiny, but it is one which continues to exist in the minds of academic critics and, indeed, in the minds of children's book practitioners.

As we shall see, because of certain characteristics of plot shape, vocabulary, and narrational control within children's books – demanded partly because of the need to *supply* a balanced view that cannot be provided by the reader – the average children's book *looks like* the low-level adult novel. The book chosen by the adult to read 'below capacity' (what might be called the airport bookstall book) is similar to many children's books; it tends to be a 'closed' text – hence the confusion, and the greater the need for a clear definition.

The writers themselves do not always help, and the system of production (see Chapter 9) also causes problems. All this leads to a certain scepticism among writers themselves. Frank Eyre has noted that 'Writers of children's books still achieve little recognition in any but their highly specialized professional circle, and writers *about* children's books are still regarded, consciously or unconsciously, as a kind of sub-species of critic – doing a secondary task from which the more successful of them may one day hope to be promoted to more responsible work.'[48]

Confronting our Prejudices

One of the most entertaining ways of confronting our own prejudices is to decontextualize our reading: to make apparently simple distinctions from short stretches of text, and to see what this tells us. I would like to make such an experiment here because, whatever the standpoint from which you are approaching this book, it seems likely that you may have certain prejudices yourself. Of course, it can be argued that decontextualized readings trivialize, and are scarcely fair to the texts; that this is an unnatural form of reading, that we do not generally attend closely to minutiae of style, and that we accord each part of a text a different emphasis. On the other hand, what do the contexts actually provide? Most probably, they provide a ready-made decision about the kind of text we are dealing with and the kind of value (and therefore the level of attention) that we should attach to it.

The following extracts are selected from pieces I have used over the years for discussion. Students and others have been asked to read them as extracts from novels, and to decide, if they can, which were the 'cues' that helped them to decide what kind of text it is: good or bad, literature or non-literature, for children or for adults. This is not merely an antidote to the common fallacy that you can tell literature from its linguistic characteristics; it tells people a lot about their perceptions in reading and their unconscious prejudices. It also provides an introduction to 'stylistics' and concepts of 'register' or 'appropriate language'.

You might like to join in the game. Are these extracts from adults' or children's books? Are they good of their kind?

> When Gerard and his friend quitted the convent they proceeded at a brisk pace into the heart of the town. The streets were nearly empty; and, with the exception of some occasional burst of brawl or merriment from a beer-shop, all was still. The chief street of Mowbray, called Castle Street, after the ruins of the old baronial stronghold in its neighbourhood, was as significant of the present civilisation of this community as the haughty keep had been of its ancient dependence.... Pursuing their course along Castle Street for about a quarter of a mile, Gerard and Stephen turned down a street which intersected it, and so on, through a variety of ways and winding lanes, till they arrived at an open portion of the town ...[49]

A selection of past responses will demonstrate the kinds of confusion that such an exercise reveals. Lexical items dominate; 'Gerard and his friend' seems to suggest 'childhood': people are not normally referred to in that way. There is plenty of action; but perhaps it goes on a little too long before there is some gratification. On the other hand, the abstract reflections upon the castle being 'as significant of the present civilization' involves too much stasis or abstraction for the child-reader. Equally, people have asked what two (presumably) male characters are doing in a convent, or object to the mention of a 'beer-shop' or a 'burst of brawl'. Interestingly, the archaic language is not seen as an indicator; it is either a genuinely old text, or, like Leon Garfield's books, an acceptable pastiche.

> There was a mass of rusty metal, two loops with a chain between. Bob stirred it, half-recognising what he had found. One loop came up, flaked with decay. With it came some small white stones that fell lightly down again. They were bones. They were the bones of a hand; and in the other loop lay the separated wrist bones of another hand; and the arms were beyond, and the skull, clean and round and grown to the floor with the settling water, and beyond the skull and backbone, the worn spoons of the pelvis, a broken thigh bone and its whole fellow, and the lower bones of the legs.

In the manacled grasp of the skeleton, Bob saw a small thing that
was gold but not a coin, and hung on a tiny failing fingerbone a
ring; and these he took for [Maggie]; and this was her husband.
And he took the manacles, the handcuffs that had been put on
him.[50]

Rather more people identified this text as a children's book,
rather curiously because of the encounter with the skeleton. The
fact of the style, which carefully mimics the perceptions of the
character and which takes on a positively liturgical tone (*and this
was her husband*) and its many small deviations, was generally
ignored.

Eleanor Cameron points out the importance of Mayne's style:

As Mayne does in the structure of his books, he works the phases
of development of a paragraph towards the final effect by gradual
release with full attention to timing, to pace. Mayne is a master of
the art of exquisite control, of the disciplined paying out of his
line, be it within the structure of his plotting or within the structure of his sentence or paragraph. One feels the mounting tension
of movement conveyed fully as much through sentence structure
as through the heightening of action.'[51]

Peter Hollindale, similarly, observes that, 'The style of a Mayne
novel operates as a form of continuous subdued recoil against the
narrative shape and impetus which his plots demand, and the
effect is a kind of obstructive fastidiousness in the writing which
repeatedly devalues the dramatic and psychological crises in his
stories.'[52]

The prose, then, is ignored. Skeletons are *alright* for children to
read about – or not an adult concern. There is a distinction made
between 'fun' and 'entertaining horror' at this level of initial
response.

The fact that there was a tension between the style and the
content caused some unease, and led people to suggest that this
was 'quality' prose; but then the clear implication was that therefore it could not be for children. The two elements were mutually
exclusive. The sentence structures are simple, but deviant nevertheless. In fact, the average reader was very poor at discriminating
what the analyst might regard as 'quality' or 'deviant' texts. This

is not quite the same as I. A. Richards's conclusions in *Practical Criticism*,[53] which were more a question of recognizing what conformed to the agreed cultural norm. What we are concerned with here is the deviation that signals (as we will see) the 'openness' of the text. (This text was also slightly adapted. The word 'Maggie' was substituted for 'Grandma' in the original. In the context of this task, this seemed to be be too obviously a cue.)

Anything 'out of the ordinary' is difficult to categorize. Chambers has described Mayne as

> a watcher rather than an ally. Even his dramatic technique seems deliberately designed to alienate the reader from the events and from the people described. This attitude to story is so little to be found in children's books that even children who have grown up as frequent and thoughtful readers find Mayne at his densest and best very difficult to negotiate.[54]

As a result Mayne has acquired a reputation as 'a marvellous children's writer for grown-ups'[55] rather than for children – a fact somewhat belied by his prodigious published output for children (around 100 volumes to date) – publishers are not, after all, usually distinguished for their charitable work.

The clearest conclusion from reactions to this text is, then, the unstated assumption that 'If it is literature, it cannot be for children', and the paradox that 'literature' is supposed to be the 'best', but that children cannot have it.

If *Ravensgill* was a problematic text, the next was chosen to see whether a 'neutral' text would be easily identified.

> He swayed across the room to the door, and opened it a chink, with one hand on the door post and the other on the handle. They had no right to keep him here.... He listened. Someone was coming. The steps passed his door. He waited a moment, and tottered out, just as the nurse turned a corner somewhere away to the right. To the right. He turned left, and, with a hand against the wall, hurried weakly along the corridor. At the end of the long corridor there was a landing and steps down into the hall. People were talking down there. A flood of sunshine poured from the open door. He heard a nurse say, 'If you will just wait in here, I'll go and fetch the matron.' Dimly he saw someone go into a door-

way, and then a flurry of white as the nurse came towards the foot of the stairs.[56]

Again, opinion was divided, possibly because we have here an adult character in a children's book 'They had no right' was identified as an adult response. This, with the hospital setting, affected the response ('hospitals are not suitable'). Ransome's prose varies from the clichéd to the original, but generally, it steers a middle course. The childlike progression of perception, mimicking the concussed perceptions of the character (who has been knocked down by a bus), were generally seen as suitable for children. Identification, again, seemed to be almost entirely a function of content-items.

> On one side of the road lay an orchard of ancient olive trees, their gnarled trunks and grey-green leaves standing out in charming contrast to the yellower green of the short grass in which they had been planted a century or more ago. In the hush of midday, with sunlight dappling the grass through leaves unstirred by a breath of wind, it was a truly sylvan spot, having that spell-like quality which made them almost expect a nymph or faun would peep out at them from behind one of the trees at any moment. Instinctively feeling that they could find no more delightful place in which to picnic, they turned into the orchard without exchanging a word, and, sitting down under one of the trees a little way from the road, unpacked their lunch.[57]

This extract could have been from any bestseller, and was selected from an older text to avoid obvious identification.

There are some register-items that might well class this as for children: 'spell-like', 'nymph or faun ... peep', 'a little way'; even the activity of eating (a common substitute for sex in an adult text) and the general air of control and 'telling' rather than 'showing' – 'charming contrast', 'truly sylvan spot'. There is also a phenomenal level of clichéd writing – 'hush of midday ... dappling the grass' – which often produces nonsense ('in which they had been planted') and bathos ('Instinctively feeling ...'). In all, it might have been expected that readers would have at least identified the text as of *poor quality* regardless of which category they placed it in.

It seems, however, that the primary cue for placing it in the 'adult' category was its stasis; the primary reason for placing it in the 'children's' category was the texture of cliché and control. The concept that adults must necessarily control texts for children is very strong.

These, then, are some of the issues that will have to be considered. But, to begin, you will have noticed that I have used the terms 'children's books' and 'children's literature' interchangeably so far. We now need to define 'children's literature' more thoroughly – and; since it is sometimes seen as a contradiction in terms, to define both its parts, as well as the whole.

3

Defining Children's Literature

Though there are no intrinsic norms and constraints that determine how we must read literary texts, as soon as we begin to read the text norms and constraints of some sort will come into operation since the very activity of reading cannot take place without them....

It would be bad faith to conceal the fact, even from young students, that no norms or constraints are integral to literary discourse and therefore privileged. Certain norms will, of course be dominant and there may be justification for stressing their advantage and the dangers of discarding them but there can be no justification for claiming that these norms are intrinsic to the very existence of literary discourse.

K. M. Newton, *Twentieth Century Literary Theory*

I come more and more to the view that there are no children's books. They are a concept invented for commercial reasons, and kept alive by the human instinct for classification and categorization. The honest writer ... writes what is inside him and must out. Sometimes what he writes will chime with the instincts and interests of young people, sometimes it will not ... If you must have a classification it is into books good and bad.

Marcus Crouch, *The Nesbit Tradition*

Aspects of Definition

Just as most questions imply their answers, so definitions are controlled by their purpose. There can be, therefore, no single definition of 'Children's Literature'. What is regarded as a 'good' book might be 'good' in the sense which the currently dominant literary/academic establishment prescribes; 'good' in terms of effectiveness for education, language acquisition, or socialization/acculturization or for entertainment for a specific child or group of children in general or specific circumstances; or 'good' in some moral or religious or political sense; or 'good' in a therapeutic sense. 'Good' as an abstract and 'good for' as a practical application are constantly in conflict in judgements about children's literature.

There is also tension between the way in which people accept plurality of meaning of the word 'literature' intellectually, yet assume a deeply ingrained concept of absolute values. Thus Eeyore and Hamlet are not, in the current system of critical values, comparable figures: not because one is actually, cosmically, any greater than the other, but because the system says so. Hence, the system (although it is crumbling) places Shakespeare as number-one writer, Blyton, Blume, Dahl, and even Mayne a long way down the scale.

But, if we are going to unravel the tangle of judgements, we should consider ways of defining. As we have seen, although there are some characteristics that seem to make it obvious when we are reading a 'children's book', textual features are unreliable. Pronouncements like W. H. Auden's that 'there are good books which are only for adults ... there are no good books that are only for children',[1] or C. S. Lewis's, 'I am almost inclined to set it up as a canon that a children's story which is enjoyed only by children is a bad children's story,'[2] tend to generate more warmth than light.

There is also a wide disagreement as to whether children's literature can be treated in the same way as adult literature. We might contrast Rebecca Lukens's view that 'Literature for children differs from literature for adults in degree, not in kind ... and writing for children should be judged by the same standard as writing for adults.... To fail to apply the same critical standard to children's literature is to say in effect that children's literature is inferior to adult literature'[3] with James Steele Smith's, that 'we can still get involved in the mistaken view that children's literature involves the same criteria of literary excellence as adult literature does'.[4]

One impatient dismissal of the 'academic standard' of distributing worth has been Isobel Jan's:

> Critics, always ready to distribute good and bad marks – are prepared to judge this 'by product' by academic standards, and to declare that one of its productions is or is not 'literature', is or is not 'well written', and that it stands or does not stand a chance of becoming a 'classic'.
>
> Scholastic disputes of this order only disguise the truth which is that such works exist in their own right and not as rungs on a ladder to adult reading. . . .
>
> What is important . . . is not whether or not it is literature, but that it should be for children; its interest and significance depend on this specific characteristic.[5]

There has equally been a certain confusion as to whether children's literature is actually a different creature, as well as to how it should be treated. Egoff, Stubbs, and Ashley, in the introduction to *Only Connect*, 'do not subscribe to the view that the criticism of children's literature calls for the adoption of a special scale of values'.[6]

In a sense, we have stepped backwards; as Lance Salway points out, 'a great deal of critical attention was paid to children's literature during the nineteenth century. . . . In many respects critical discussion . . . was less restricted than it is now; books for the young were considered to be part of the general body of literature and writing about them was not confined to specialised journals.'[7]

Consequently, we can range from Nicholas Tucker's straightforward comparative condemnation:

> In contrast with some others who have written on this question, I do believe there are intrinsic differences between the best books aimed at children and those written for adults, and that no children's literature could ever be a work of art in the same league as say, Tolstoy, George Eliot, or Dickens. If a writer is aiming at a young audience he must of necessity restrict himself in certain areas of experience and vocabulary.[8]

which clearly accepts the standard concept of values, to Marcus Crouch's view that the only difference is the way in which children's books have to be approached: 'One examines books which children will read with the aid of all the criteria applied to books read by adults, and with one additional criterion – accessibility.'[9] If Tucker is right, then Crouch's criteria (whether of value or method) will yield nothing; and if accessibility means simplification of some elements, then this proves Tucker's point.

Jill Paton Walsh's comment on the problems of writing children's books (admirably level-headed among much that is not), suggests that

> The children's book presents a technically more difficult, technically more interesting problem – that of making a fully serious adult statement, as a good novel of any kind does, and making it utterly simple and transparent. . . . The need for comprehensibility imposes an emotional obliqueness, an indirection of approach, which like elision and partial statement in poetry is often a source of aesthetic power.[10]

This positive approach leads on to one thing that is fundamental not only to the argument about status and children's books, but also to the way in which we define the field – that is, to the argument that reading children's literature is, for the adult, a more complex process than reading an adult book.

Ways of Reading Children's Literature

We are dealing with texts designed for a non-peer audience, texts that are created in a complex social environment by adults. In terms of what this means to a sub- or anti-culture, it is tantamount to reading a translation.

Three reading situations need to be distinguished here: the adult reading a book intended for adults, the adult reading a book intended for children, and the child reading a book intended for children. The differences between these situations are fundamental to our discussion. Criticism tends to talk of them as though they were the same – but they are not, except in a rather dangerously illusory way.

The closest of the two are the first and the last, because they share a basic factor of reading. As Patricia Wright puts it:

> Reading begins with processes of perception and attention which may result from the user's past experience (knowing where to look) or from the specification of the reading purpose (knowing what to look for). These will be top-down, conceptually-driven cognitive processes. The user's perception and attention will also be influenced by bottom-up or data-driven processes generated by the text and the task environment.[11]

In other words, our background and purpose are vital. It is clear that adult readers can never share the same background (in terms of reading and life experience) as children; what is less obvious is that they only rarely share the same purpose in reading (just as reviewers are quite untypical as readers). When adults are reading books for adults, they normally read either purely for their own entertainment or edification, taking the book on its own terms and playing the part of, or reacting against, the reader-role implied in the text; or they are reading for an extrinsic purpose – to criticize, comment, or discuss.

When adults find themselves reading children's books, they usually have to read in four different ways, simultaneously. First, despite occasional protestations to the contrary, adults commonly read children's books *as if they were peer-texts*. If we read for anything except pleasure, then we will register the presence of, but 'read against', the implied readership. This certainly accounts for Dorothy Parker's loathing of *The House at Pooh Corner* – as she famously remarked in reviewing it in her column 'The Constant Reader', 'Tonstant Weader Fwowed Up'[12] – and perhaps for the low status of children's books.

Thus a text must 'imply' a reader; that is, the subject-matter, language, allusion levels, and so on clearly 'write' the level of readership. (It is no accident that the Pooh books, or several of Roald Dahl's books, have proved popular with adults as well as children: the audience implied in the books is as much an adult one as a child one.) This is easiest to see where a high level is implied; without certain knowledge or experience, the text will not be – cannot be – 'understood' to a reasonable level. But, equally, very often a limited range of experience is implied; items may be explained to an extent that the experienced reader does not require. This can happen at very elementary levels, and takes us into a consideration of the relationship of the child to the text as text – consider, for example, the levels of experience required to understand Pat Hutchins's *Rosie's Walk*[13] or Rosemary Wells's *Stanley and Rhoda*[14] (and see the discussion of *The Tale of Peter Rabbit*, above).

But we are under no obligation to accept the implied reader's role. In a peer-text, we generally do so; we select a text according to the level it implies (is this a 'hard' or an 'easy' read?) But with children's books, it is easy to read against the implication. This is why the context of reading – the attitude to the text, and the things surrounding the text, the 'peritext' – is so important. In many circumstances, this first way of reading will probably dominate; it may be a more profound and perceptive reading than a child will make, but is it an appropriate reading?

Secondly, and normally for most adult–readings of children's texts, the adult will very often be reading *on behalf of a child*, to recommend or censor for some personal or professional reason. The criteria used here may certainly register the implied reader- ship, and lead to an intellectual judgement as to whether the book in question is appropriate to that readership. The criteria to the fore would then be personal preference (political, sexual, topical), suitability of content (as the adult perceives it) for the use to which the text is going to be put (skills education, social educa- tion, enjoyment), and, perhaps easiest, linguistic complexity. (As we shall see, it is this ideological area that most commonly reveals the blindnesses of readers and publishers.)

More rarely, but increasingly, the adult may be reading the text *with an eye to discussing it with other adults*. The analytic eye may then be dominant, and we may not become engaged with the book, as in the first way of reading. This is, as it were, the super-ego reading, modifying both the first and second types of reading into acceptable communications.

Anyone who has read much in children's books as an adult will probably agree that the most rewarding type of reading – and again, the most unacknowledged by those uncertain of the status of the activity – is that involving acceptance of the implied role; for then the reader will *surrender to the book on its own terms*. This is as close as we can get to *reading as a child*; but this is a very long way from reading as an actual child does.

There are other complicating subtleties here. Do you read as the child you were, or as the child you are ? on your self-image as a child or the memory of the 'feel' of youthful reading? How far can experienced readers forget their adult experience?

Research has shown (for example, that of Michael Benton et al.[15]) that children are far more competent text-handlers than is generally assumed; but even so, it is difficult to replicate their encounters with texts. We cannot rely on, as one critic put it, 'the authority of interpretive communities'[16] – that most readers will understand broadly the same thing from a text. After all, most reception and response theory is based upon peer investigations.[17]

If we wish to define our field of study, then, we must acknowledge that the very perception of the texts within it is problematic. There is a confusion between quality and audience, which has so often bracketed children's books with 'popular culture' and low-level books in general.[18]

Defining 'Literature'

The positive aspect of this is that the concept of 'literature' as it is defined by the cultural establishment – and thus subconsciously accepted – must be seen for what it is, whether or not it is to be challenged. One of the characteristics of the literary establishment has been a reluctance to define. Matthew Arnold, in *The Study of Poetry* [1880], wrote:

> Critics give themselves great labour to draw out what in the abstract constitutes the characters of high quality in poetry. It is much better to have recourse to concrete examples.... They are far better by being felt in the verse of the master, than being perused in the prose of the critic.... But if we are asked to define this mark and accent [of high beauty, worth, and power] in the

abstract, our answer must be: No, for we shall thereby be darkening the question, not clearing it.[19]

This evasion, like the later ones of F. R. Leavis, disguises an arbitrary power-based decision about what constitutes worth and value. His famous rejection of Cleanth Brooks's request for a theoretical statement can be seen as an evasion – a smokescreen put up by the establishment, to avoid stating the plain truth, that something is good because we, the self-elected, say so.[20]

The critical dictum expressed by Leavis, that literature is accessible only to those with 'trained intuition', also automatically excludes all child-readers and all children's books. It is equivalent to Henry James's dictum in 'The future of the novel':

> The literature, as it may be called for convenience, of children is an industry that occupies by itself a very considerable quarter of the scene. Great fortunes, if not great reputations, are made.... The sort of taste that used to be called 'good' has nothing to do with the matter: we are so demonstrably in the presence of millions for whom taste is but an obscure, confused, immediate instinct.[21]

Perhaps the most thorough demolition of the Leavisite position is to be found in Howard Felperin's *Beyond Deconstruction*, in which he describes the Leavisite tradition as a 'curious combination of self-proclaimed democracy and undeclared authoritarianism'.[22] His impression, when he encountered an example of it 'was of a mode of criticism that had stiffened, despite its original impulse to be democratic and plain spoken, into the ritual moves and postures of a priestly elite'.[23] For many people, this is the model, and it is an unacceptable one.

The question of what 'literature' is, has, until fairly recently, seemed scarely worth discussing to those most intimately concerned with it. As Jeremy Tambling puts it:

> [T]he category of 'literature' cannot be held to have any essential meaning: there is no body of writing that 'ought' to be studied as such, as the repository of 'cultural values' or of important traditions ...
> To say, 'we know what literature is', and then to mention some

famous names – Shakespeare, Milton, Wordsworth – means that we work in a circle: we know what literature is because we have these writers, and the writers set up an imaginary standard where literature is defined in relationship to them.[24]

This may seem either a radical or an obvious statement – or, I suspect, both. In my experience, students of literature in higher education carry both a residual resistance to establishment values, together with a shrewd appreciation of what they are expected to say (which is, in its own way, comforting.) This is not merely an educational truism; it is important for children's books, where orality and the sub-culture, or anti-culture, or parallel culture of childhood, are significant factors in the interpretation of texts.

'Literature', then, is a very persuasive term. Let us summarize its meanings. The first distinction is between what literature is generally thought to be and what it logically or conjecturally might be. Literature, as compared to other texts, is thought to be 'higher', 'denser', 'more highly charged', 'special', 'apart', and so on; it is also thought to be the 'best' that a culture can offer. These may seem to be two ways of saying the same thing, but they commonly give rise to a sort of schizophrenia in 'children's book people', as we have seen; for 'literature' is seen as not being 'suitable' for children – not that they are not yet ready for it, but that it does not relate to the normal child.

The complexity of the situation might be illustrated by Elaine Moss's broadside against a new, prose edition of *The Pied Piper of Hamelin* in which there is a 'happy' ending (the mayor and the corporation are drowned, and the children return), and there is no place in the story for the lame boy. Moss's argument is convincing emotionally, but her judgement that 'young people should come across a great deal of literature that, at some point in their lives, they will return to and understand better, even return to for an enlightenment they had recognised as being there but had not been ready fully to absorb'[25] has overtones of a superiority of certain texts, rather than certain *kinds* of texts.

But she provides an important clue. On her definition, literature (as opposed to non-literature) is something to which you can return, something that gives more each time – although there is a residual impression that the classical work is inherently superior, even if I am sure that is not the intention. *Any* work to which you can return has this quality – and, of course, if a text is 'returnable-to' by virtue of its private associations, then, is it not 'literature'? Or is there something more? It is this kind of distinction that we need to explore.

Definitions of literature can be conveniently divided into definitions by features, definition by cultural norms, and definitions according to the uses of text by individuals.

It is not at all obvious to many readers that you cannot tell from simply looking at a text whether it is 'literature' or not. It is not the type of feature, but the value you place upon it which is significant. Certainly the literary text has a tendency to certain linguistic features. These are generally a function of the fact that the message is linguistically 'self-sufficient' and does not need a context of immediate human interaction to be understood. There are certain characteristic 'markers' in the text, such as the fact that whereas in normal discourse the sender and receiver, addresser and addressee, are marked as first and third person, in literature, this is not necessarily so. But that does not make the text 'literature' in its generally accepted sense. It is the cultural context that dominates the categorization.

This is important for children's literature because it is generally assumed that there is an appropriate 'register' of children's books – characteristic words and structures – that identifies the type just as readily as does the 'content'. It is also often assumed that this register is restrictive to the point at which it excludes 'literariness'. Hence, if what constitutes the surface characteristics of literature is a cultural decision, then, whatever image of childhood is current, positive or negative, children's books will inevitably be excluded from the value-system. Cultural norms do not usually apply to a disregarded type.

But if literature cannot usefully be defined by its surface features, can it be defined by use? We read literature in a different way from non-literature; we extract from the text certain feelings or responses. Yet with children's books, we cannot escape the fact that they are written by adults; that there is going to be control, and that it is going to involve moral decisions. Equally, the book is going to be used not to entertain or modify *our* views, but to form the views of the child. Thus the kind of readings that texts for children are given by children involves acquiring both culture and language. This means that the 'non-functional' definition of 'literature' either excludes all children's literature or does not apply.

Here again, because the single thing that distinguishes children's literature is its audience, it is commonly assumed that aesthetic appreciation is not something available to the child, and therefore not something likely to be inherent in its literature. We have seen that narrative is a poor relation of literary studies; but consider this comment by C. S. Lewis, a writer commonly assumed to be on the side of the child. Writing 'Of stories', he notes:

> In talking of books which are 'mere stories' ... nearly everyone makes the assumption that 'excitement' is the only pleasure they ever give or are intended to give. *Excitement*, in this sense, may be defined as the alternate tension and appeasement of imagined anxiety. This is what I think is untrue. In some such books, and for some readers, another factor comes in.... Something which the educated receive from poetry can reach the masses through stories of adventure, and almost no other way.... The re-reader is looking not for actual surprises (which can only come once) but for a certain ideal suprisingness.... It must be understood that ... the plot ... is only really a net whereby to catch something else. The real theme may be, and usually is, something that has no sequence in it, something other than a process and much more like a state or quality.[26]

Lewis's sub-text is worth considering, for his choice of words betrays a basic disrespect for his audience. The child is equated with 'the masses'; narrative is 'a net', and nets catch the unworldly and incapable, and imprison them. We are approaching the idea that children must necessarily have something not only different, but lesser.

The fact that narrative is the dominant mode of children's books has not helped. E. M. Forster, in *Aspects of the Novel*, lamented that 'Yes – oh dear yes – the novel tells a story'.[27] The study of narrative has, of course, burgeoned since 1949, when Wellek and Warren could say that 'Literary theory and criticism concerned with the novel are much inferior in both quantity and quality to theory and criticism of poetry',[28] and with it the possibility of accepting other texts as being amenable to criticism. But, as Lewis's sub-text shows, narrative of itself is not considered to be the highest of modes, as Lewis demonstrated in his own fiction for children, where the narrative, skilled though it is, is merely the carrier.

This may seem like a quagmire, so let us approach the definition from the point of view of logic, language, and culture, and see what the implications are. John M. Ellis points out that the word 'literature' is like the word 'weed'; it organizes, rather than describes, our world.[29] It is not the characteristics of the plant that make it a weed, but rather where it happens to be growing. Similarly, 'Literary texts are not defined as those of a certain shape or structure, but as those pieces of language used in a certain way by the community.'[30] This use is that *the text is not taken as specifically relevant to the immediate context of its origin.* That is, the text is used aesthetically, not practically. Therefore, text may *become* literature, may be used in different ways. Diaries and letters, for example, become literature by virtue of being read by an audience for whom they were not intended and for a different purpose. This, of course, causes problems for children's books, which tend to be used for practical purposes such as education or socialization.

There is also a problem with 'popular' literature: that is, books used (and consumed) specifically for immediate gratification (thrillers, pornography and so on). When used as such, they are *not* (by logic) literature; but when used for something else, they are – and vice versa. Thus, for example, Defoe and Chandler have become 'literature'; whereas *Lady Chatterley's Lover* has sometimes been used as pornography.

Children's literature has this problem, with the added difficulty that we cannot tell how a child reads it – as a 'literary' experience or a functional one. Any text can be given a 'literary' reading – and we must beware of circularity in saying that some reward it more than others – because the values we apply are also part of the cultural system.

As we have seen, a linguistician might characterize 'literary' texts as constituting a small and deviant part of human communication which has become 'fossilized'. Such texts deviate from 'normal' language, and the deviations tend to be organized into patterns. This definition makes no reference to value-judgements, likes, or dislikes; it merely describes, and thus avoids the circularity of definitions such as that given by Raymond Williams in *Keywords*, which makes use of terms such as 'well-written', 'substantial', or 'important'.[32]

None of this satisfies the basic idea that some texts are 'better' than others – not therapeutically, but culturally. We need to take on board the obvious, relative idea that 'literature' is the writing authorized and prioritized by a powerful minority. The concept of a 'canon' or a 'mainstream' is class- and society-based. That 'canon' has been influenced by universities, and if children's literature is to accede to this privileged status, it must either become part of the power structure or that power structure must change.

A very powerful summary of this argument is contained in Terry Eagleton's *Literary Theory*. To select the most trenchant points:

Literary theorists, critics and teachers, then, are not so much purveyors of doctrines as custodians of a discourse.... Certain pieces of writing are selected as being more amenable to this discourse than others, and these are what is known as literature or the 'literary canon'.... Some of those hottest in their defence of the canon have from time to time demonstrated how the discourse can be made to operate on 'non-literary' writing. This, indeed is the embarrassment of literary criticism, that it defines for itself a special object, literature, while existing as a set of discursive techniques which have no reason to stop short of that object at all. If you have nothing better to do at a party you can always try on a literary critical analysis of it.... Such a 'text' can prove quite as rich as one of the canonical works, and critical dissections of it quite as ingenious as those of Shakespeare.... [Literary criticism's] concern is with literature, because literature is more valuable and rewarding than any of the other texts on which critical discourse may operate. The disadvantage of this claim is that it is plainly untrue.... Their exclusion from what is studied is not because they are not 'amenable' to the discourse: it is a question of the arbitrary authority of the literary institution.[33]

There is therefore no reason why children's books should not be included within the respectable canon (as one alternative) or studied with the same rigor (as the other). Equally, there is, no reason why another, different, and parallel discourse should not be created to deal with children's literature. The only real question is one of status, and that is a matter of power.

Many children's literature practitioners have noted the tendency to use 'not just adult literature as a model, but adult tastes as a yardstick'.[34] On the other hand, radical academics who dismiss the canon as a politically motivated anachronism still write books which 're-read' Milton or re-discuss the minutiae of Shakespeare.

The same is true of the idea of 'literary language' as something that defines literature. This is not the same as a linguistic definition: the fact of a certain verse-form does not produce poetry. What is usually meant by the unsympathetic layperson is a deviant and inaccessible language; what is usually meant by cultural insiders is a use of language which most closely approximates the established insider-codes. 'Literary language' *is* different, in the sense that the discourse to which it belongs is exclusive.

This has lead, and leads, to a confusion between generic characteristics of language and value-judgements; and again, children's literature is very prone to these. The most common argument against these definitions is that they lead into a quagmire of personal interpretation, where one judgement is as 'good' as another.

There are several problems with this approach. Sticking to a canon and a 'culture' in effect means prioritizing one group and one discourse, and thereby alienating the rest (in this case, children's literature). The established culture is thus weakened anyway. The second point is that we are, in effect, in such a quagmire now, except that the wild personal interpretations and preferences happen to be those agreed to by a single group.

A sceptic might say that what is going to be lost by such free personal interpretation is, first a lot of money by those with a vested interest in education and the arts and culture, and, second, the privilege of not having to think for ourselves by everyone else.

To invert Dominic Hibberd's argument (in relation to K. M. Peyton's 'Flambards' trilogy), what we need is agreement on the rigour of the method, not a pre-ordained conception of the answers we will find. For children's literature, that will mean a freedom to study it and a clear intellectual approach which will make its study relevant to its users – and a concomitant loss of exclusiveness which will make it acceptable to its users. Far from leading to chaos, such relativity would enable users of children's literature to see clearly whether what they think is admirable commits them to a certain sort of political or social teaching.

There is another dimension to the definition with regard to children's literature. Whereas we might agree that with literature in general the dominant culture decides what is or is not 'good' and that we are – or at least should be – free to agree or not, to join that particular club or not, with children's literature, the non-functionality of art (as Oscar Wilde said, 'All art is quite useless', – and therefore it is art) does not apply. Children's books are defined as much by 'good for' as by 'good'; and, again by definition, that which is useless cannot be good for the child-reader. This problem has been well confronted by Peter Dickinson in an early and influential essay 'In defence of rubbish'. Dickinson defined 'rubbish' as 'all forms of reading matter which contain to the adult eye no visible value, either aesthetic or educational'.[35] After arguing for the social value of non-recognized texts, he concludes: 'It may not be rubbish after all. The adult eye is not necessarily a perfect instrument for discerning certain sorts of values.'[36]

In a sense, then, literature is what we choose to make it, which radically suggests that children's *literature* is an inevitable concept, unrelated to other kinds of literature, although it may overlap with them. That such a 'system', as Shavit calls it, should have a lower status is perhaps inevitable; but that depends a good deal upon how society sees children and childhood.[37]

Literature is a value-term; and it seems that children's literature, in separating itself (for administrative convenience), defines itself in terms (uniquely) of its audience. Hence, when we are admitting to this club, we need to ask what the other half of the term entails. What is a child?

Defining the Child

The answer is culture-bound both synchronically and diachronically. Nicholas Tucker in his *What is a Child?*[38] draws together features of childhood which are transcultural and diachronic. These include spontaneous play, receptivity to the prevailing culture, physiological constraints (children are generally smaller and weaker), and sexual immaturity (which implies that certain concepts are not immediately relevant to them). They have the tendencies to form emotional attachments to mature figures, to be incapable of abstract thought, to have less of a concentration-span than adults, and to be at the mercy of their immediate perceptions. As a result they tend to be more adaptable than the mature person (whose 'schemas' of the world tend to be set), which in turn has many implications for the writer. There is considerable evidence that their cognitive skills develop in a common sequence, although there is a good deal of dispute as to how far the 'stages' can be recognized.

Tucker himself, in *The Child and the Book*, has taken the developmental stages posited by the pioneering child pyschiatrist Jean Piaget, and correlated them to likely texts.[39] That book demonstrates the difficulty of generalization, in that the individual child will differ considerably from the norm. However, it might be useful here to consider the more general implications of these characteristics. (We will consider the specific differences between child-reader and adult-reader in the next chapter.)

Broadly we can say that, at different stages, children will have different attitudes to death, fear, sex, perspectives, egocentricity, causality, and so on. They will be more open to genuinely radical thought and the ways of understanding texts; they will be more flexible in their perceptions of text; and, because play is a natural part of their outlook, they will regard language as another area for playful exploration. They are less bound by fixed schemas, and in this sense see more clearly.

On the negative side – at least as far as the adult is concerned – they have less knowledge about language and book structures; the distinctions they make between fact and fantasy and between the desirable and the actual are unstable; and they are capable of unconscious animism, since the attribution of human characteristics to inanimate objects is less controlled than it is in adults.

It can be argued that they belong, in effect, to a different culture – possibly an anti-culture or counter-culture. Certainly, as Diana Kelly-Byrne points out, there is a considerable complexity in adults' relationships with children.[40] All this is very uncomfortable for the adult dealing with children and texts. Children in some sense belong to an 'oral' culture, which means, as we shall see, that they may well have different modes of thinking, different story-shapes.

Research on children's story telling and the acquisition of story-shapes makes similar claims.[41] Thus, in terms of 'appropriate' types of story, structures will be appreciated differently, even if they are not designed differently. Children may be more susceptible to matters based on folk-memory and not overlaid by schemas, hence the 'relegation', as Tolkien put it, of fairy tales to the nursery.

> Actually, the association of children and fairy-stories is an accident of our domestic history. Fairy-stories have in the modern lettered world been relegated to the 'nursery', as shabby or old-fashioned furniture is relegated to the play-room, primarily because the adults do not want it, and do not mind if it is misused. It is not the choice of the children which decides this. Children as a class – except in common lack of experience they are not one – neither like fairy-stories more, nor understand them better than adults do.[42]

For all these reasons, then, 'misreadings' or mismatchings of both form and content (against the 'adult' norm) are inevitable, and the literature *of* the child may not be the same as that *for* the child. In short, the relationship between the child – that is, a developing reader – and the text is a complex one, and has implications for the way in which we discuss, teach, and select material.

All this leads the adult community to create or allow different kinds of childhood – which, socially, might best be defined as a period of lack of responsibility, as well as one merely of incomplete development. (Adults in their reading may therefore pass into the childish state.)

Diachronically, the concept of childhood is extremely complex, and not well documented. In the past, there have been extreme versions of childhood, from the Romantic noble-savage child who is nearest to God, to the child seen as having been born evil as a result of original sin. When the mortality rate was high, and in strata of society where poverty and subsistence were the norm (that is, until the eighteenth century), the view of childhood as a protected developmental stage was not possible. In medieval times, there was little concept of childhood; in Elizabethan times, little concept of different needs. The rise of the middle classes in the wake of the Industrial Revolution suggests that it is contrasts which define childhood.

In essence, childhood is defined in terms of seriousness – hence the concept of 'childishness'. Consequently, when considering the history of children's books, it may be that the type of childhood for which they were intended – that is, the kind of childhood that they *defined* – varied considerably. Children's books for the working-class child seem to be a good deal more authoritarian and harsh than those for the sheltered middle classes; indeed, they scarcely seem to be children's books at all. And, since the kind of life the young experienced was not childhood as we might know it, this is not surprising.

Hence the definition of childhood shifts, even within a small, apparently homogeneous culture, just as the understanding of past childhoods shifts. Brian Alderson says of Leeson's analysis 'that it is hopelessly crude to try to summarize the sociology of children's reading in an historical survey of a hundred or so pages.'[43] However, some crude generalizations have the virtue of alerting the reader to over-simplifications. For example, if one attempts to describe 'childhood' at any given moment, one is confronted by a series of paradoxes. What is childhood in Britain in the early 1990s? Generally, there is adult-child segregation; that is, children are regarded as, in principle, a different kind of person; they are protected from adult preoccupations, and work in different places. On the other hand, there has been a relaxation of the boundaries of formality. But then, the ubiquity of media input may mean that they are less protected from taboo subjects – or does TV give only the image and not the feeling? Then, children's clothing has become less distinct; fashions for children make them clones of adults. Popular music now caters for children as part of its market. Diet has become homogenized. Yet there is a clear marketing thrust to maintain certain aspects of childhood, even though in Britain it is still legal to sell toy weapons. Childhood is protected by law, and yet the period of 'irresponsibility' lengthens, on average, with increasing technological process.

In short, childhood is not now (if it ever has been) a stable concept. The literature defined by it, therefore, cannot be expected to be a stable entity. Consequently we must be very careful about the mismatch between readings of a book by a given child in a given period as compared with what it might have been at the time of production.

Thus Pierre Machery's opinion in his *A Theory of Literary Production* needs considerable modification, because concepts of childhood will radically alter the text, and are far more unstable than concepts of adulthood. He writes: 'In fact, the conditions of its communication are produced at the same time as the book, at least the more important conditions.... Readers are made by what makes the book ... for otherwise, the book, written from some inscrutable impulse, would be the work of its readers, reduced to the function of an illustration.'[44]

With children's books, of course, this is particularly true. The adaptation of texts or the re-casting of fairy tales or the re-writing and/or re-illustration of Beatrix Potter's books are examples of the ways in which the book culture makes decisions about childhood, and in many ways creates or destroys it.

We thus have two very 'open' and variable definitions to cope with.

Defining 'Children's Literature'

How, then, do we define children's literature? As Paul Heins put it, pragmatically, 'Perhaps we should distinguish in the long run between two different ways of approaching children's books: (1) the criticism of those books as they concern the different kinds of people who use and work with them, and (2) the literary criticism of children's literature.'[45] I would extend this to the books themselves.

There are 'live' books and 'dead' books, books which no longer concern their primary audience (and yet concern no-one else except historians). Paradoxically, although many books 'sink' towards childhood, so many rise towards adulthood. The children's book is, by definition, then, something immediate; and the immediate is prone to be ephemeral, and to interact with the immediate culture. Not many books from such a background subsequently rise to become 'high culture'.

We define children's literature, then, according to our purposes – which, after all, is what all definitions do: they divide the world according to our needs. Children's literature, disturbingly enough, can quite reasonably be defined as books read by, especially suitable for, or especially satisfying for, members of the group currently defined as children. However, such an accommodating definition is not very practical, as it obviously includes every text ever read by a child, so defined.

Most of us, I think, would also be inclined to regard as legitimate children's books only those which are essentially contemporary; there is a limit to which children's books can be said to survive as 'live' books. The ephemeral books have, because of the insensitivity of children and the cupidity of adults, a remarkably long 'shelf-life'; thus, whereas, say, 'Bulldog Drummond' or, to a lesser extent, 'The Saint' survive as period pieces, there is little sense in which Blyton's 'Famous Five' (1942–63) with its marked class and period flavour, is seen by its primary readers as historical. However, with a few obvious exceptions (such as *Treasure Island*), anything else is dispensable. This is not, as might be assumed, because it has no merit in terms of 'old-fashioned' practical literary values. Rather, concepts of childhood change so repidly that there is a sense in which books no longer applicable to childhood must fall into a limbo in which they are the preserve of the bibliographer, since they are of no interest to the current librarian or child.

Consequently, although I can see the arguments, I would exclude from a practical study of children's books Sumerian writings of 2112 BC[46] or Milton's *Comus* ('the leading role and two important supporting roles were actually played by children and written as children's parts'),[47] Comenius's *Orbis sensualium pictus* (1658), or even Chaucer's *Story of the Astrolabe*, which, without question, is a children's book, since it was directed specifically to a specific child; for the childhood to which it was addressed is so different that it is now of antiquarian interest only.

We have to put historical children's books – and by that I mean books which can only be presented to a majority of literate modern children with some 'apparatus' – in a separate category. I have little doubt that a survey of what is taught in contemporary universities would show a massive trend towards the contemporary novel. In the case of children's literature, it happens to be true that historical constraints – social, educational, and moral, all manifestations of the Victorian 'protect and control' syndrome – have meant that it is only in twentieth century that the most notable talents have directed themselves towards children's literature. But in looking at books from the past (in the sense of the inaccessible past) we have to take a modified view: that we are involved in an academic study, in the real sense.

On the whole, then, that a particular text was written expressly for children who are recognizably children, with a childhood recognizable today, must be part of the definition. Hence the fact that little literary distinction was made before the eighteenth century does not admit anything pre-1744 into the reckoning. Even then, the book usually cited as the first modern children's book, *A Little Pretty Pocket-Book* of 1744, published by John Newbery, can be dismissed as 'a sneaky piece of work ... the work of a thoroughly trivial, commercial, and disinherited mind, and its continuing *succés d'estime* is something of a mystery'.[48]

The history of the children's book may be interesting to the adult, but not for the child, and it is this dichotomy which is central. The same applies, by and large, to books adopted by children. I say by and large, because, as we shall see, the distinction between, say, *The Hobbit* and *The Lord of the Rings* may be more theoretical than actual;[49] and so a book like Jefferies' *Bevis* may well have been designed for adults even if it has had much more influence as a children's text.

Which brings us to pragmatics. One of the most clear-thinking of modern critics, John Rowe Townsend, has written:

> Yet children are part of mankind and children's books are part of literature, and any line which is drawn to confine children or their

books to their own special corner is an artifical one.... The only practical definition of a children's book today – absurd as it sounds – is 'a book which appears on the children's list of a publisher'.[50]

Any attempt to define books by their characteristics may be accurate, but in fact describes the least deviant, and hence the least interesting, aspects of the text. Miles McDowell's definition has its merits at this level:

Children's books are generally shorter; they tend to favour an active rather than a passive treatment, with dialogue and incident rather than description and introspection; child protagonists are the rule; conventions are much used; the story develops within a clear-cut moral schematism which much adult fiction ignores; children's books tend to be optimistic rather than depressive; language is child-oriented; plots are of a distinctive order, probability is often discarded; and one could go on endlessly talking of magic, and fantasy, and simplicity, and adventure.[51]

To dismiss the question of classification as totally invidious, as does Isobel Jan in *On Children's Literature*, may be sound in principle, but has little merit in practice.[52] Rather, we might say that children's literature is becoming self-defining. Neil Philip, discussing the relationship of children to the folktale, says:

Writing can be precise [in] ... having a single explicable meaning. ... But writing can also be precise in a more telling sense, by reflecting the complex and ambiguous nature of human thought. It suggests, rather than states. The further a writer progresses along this road, the more nearly his effects approach those of the oral poet or storyteller.... [Such] a writer ... whom teachers and librarians constantly tell me children will not read [is] William Mayne. I say, if children will not read Mayne, it is not Mayne's fault. Children do not read him not because he's unreadable, but because teachers teach them to read in a way which excludes him.[53]

To define children's literature may seem to be marking out a territory. It is, but only in so far as the subject needs some delimitation if it is to be manageable. Yet, despite the flux of childhood, the children's book can be defined in terms of the implied reader. It will be clear, from a careful reading, who a book is designed for: whether the book is on the side of the child totally, whether it is for the developing child, or whether it is aiming somewhere over the child's head. (Shavit suggests that the fact that many do the latter is a function of how children's books are produced.)[54] Whether the text can then be given a value depends upon the circumstance of use.

Finally, we will have to take into account the attitudes of the majority, who remain convinced of the need, culturally, for a distinction in literature that is in some way referable to higher authority – and for the residual need for that in ourselves.

Hence this book will have to deal with a very imperfect situation: with significant books not written for children, either by internal or external evidence, such as *Bevis;* books with very ambivalent status, such as *Winnie-the-Pooh;*[55] books designed for different levels of childhood such as Anthony Browne's *Bear Goes to Town* or *A Walk in the Park;*[56] and books designed for childhood such as Burningham's *Granpa,*[57] Carroll's *Alice in Wonderland*, or Hoban and Blake's *How Tom Beat Captain Najork and His Hired Sportsmen.*[58] The point of *this* book is to make the identification, not to prescribe what can be done with the knowledge.

4

Approaching the Text

We should be less than honest if we did not admit certain perplex-
ities about the way children understand stories.... We know very
little about obvious obstacles – how children understand narrated
time sequences, or the elliptical structure of a ballad or narrative
poem. What clues do they follow to construe a narrative?
Margaret Meek et al. *The Cool Web*

Because comprehension is a state of zero uncertainty, there is, in the
end, only one person who can say whether an individual compre-
hends something or not, and that is that particular individual.
Frank Smith, *Reading*

By now, I hope, I have shown that dealing with complex con-
structs of language is not something one is qualified to do by
virtue of being able to read and talk; anyone who can run and hit
a ball is not necessarily, or usually, any good at squash or tennis
or cricket. Whatever our involvement, technique is useful.

The main problem, however, is that what happens, happens in
microseconds; what meaning is made is never describable, and so
any examination of it must seem endlessly cumbersome. On the
other hand, to me at least, it is endlessly fascinating. We are
looking at features of text, some of which are unarguably *there*,
which are very complex in themselves; we are then looking at a
universe of personal responses. Both are mediated by what Barbara Hardy has called the 'primary act of mind' (making fiction)[1]
and what D. W. Harding has called 'social communication of a
special sort with the author'[2] that is, the rules (perceived, misin-
terpreted, or rejected) of narrative or poetry.

First, meaning is made from the reader and the book. Although it may seem that meaning resides simply in the book, and that the reader takes the meaning by reading, this is neither philosophically probable nor empirically true. As Jonathan Culler puts it:

> while 'meaning' suggests a property of a text (a text 'has' meaning), and thus encourages one to distinguish an intrinsic (though perhaps ungraspable) meaning from the interpretations of readers, 'sense' links the qualities of a text to the operations one performs upon it. A text can make sense and someone can make sense of a text.... 'Making sense' suggests that to investigate literary signification one must analyse interpretive operations.[3]

The idea of words and the idea of meaning are both complex concepts. We have to distinguish between functional and literary uses of language. In good functional writing (instructions, for example, or a book on criticism) ambiguity is cut to a minimum, and, ideally, thought leads to word leads to action. But even in instructions, we have to be careful about tone. As Lewis Carroll wrote of *The Hunting of the Snark* in 1896: 'As to the meaning of the *Snark*? I'm very much afraid I didn't mean anything but nonsense! Still, you know, words mean more than we mean to express when we use them: so a whole book ought to mean a great deal more than the writer meant.'[4]

In 'literary' language, the language of fiction and verse, the reader has to do some of the work to conjure up the image, and so to understand. Laurence Sterne, in that guide-book to how books work, *Tristram Shandy*, summed the matter up thus: 'As no one who knows what he is about in good company would venture to talk all; – so no author ... would presume to think all: The truest respect which you can pay to the reader's understanding is to halve this matter amicably, and leave him something to imagine, in his turn, as well as yourself'.[5] Literary meanings are often emotive or impressionistic, connotative as well as denotative; and so who the readers are, where they are, when and why they read, how much they know, how much they have read, how much they want to read, their capacity for understanding – all these and other factors besides contribute to the meaning.

A More Detailed Strategy

And so we will look first at the reader, and the problem in the case of the developing reader of how much she or he can be said to understand a text not designed for her or him. Next we will look at the book. But before we read it, we will ask, what is it like? What does it tell us about itself? What is its phenomenology, its peritext, its character, its ethos? A considerable amount of the residual 'feel' of a book (which is at least part of, or one of, its meanings), what we remember from childhood reading (and also in adulthood), may reside in the feel, and even the smell for the youngest child. The question 'What was your favourite book as a child?' may well be answered by 'It was blue'. If literature is a whole experience, then we cannot ignore this aspect.

Then there is the situation. When is this book being read? And why? My own impression of Volume 3 of *The Lord of the Rings* is indelibly associated with a very rough flight back from the USA at night – which is so localized as to seem irrelevant. Also, why am I reading the book? It may well be that even the relatively unskilled reader is subconsciously analytic; how conscious the task of analysis becomes has a considerable effect. Reading in the classroom is a considerably different experience from reading under the bedclothes. But beyond the classroom/real life division, this is an area where the variables are so huge and so intangible that little more can be said, except that situation *must* be taken into account, whatever it is. Only then can we get inside the book.

The first instinct of most critics is to tell us what the book is about; but that is merely an account of what it seems to the critic to be about, which may not be a lot of use to me, especially if I belong to a different culture. I would suggest that that should be the last thing that we should think or talk about. Rather, we should see how the text encodes meaning and what tools are available to us to decode it.

The first thing we meet in a text is the texture, the surface. This is sometimes described as the syntagmatic level – that is, the level of the choice made by a writer of *how* to express a meaning, rather than of *what* meaning to express. This may seem to be taking us straight into one of those false alley-ways, that you can have form without content. Nevertheless, you can identify a lot from the surface text: whether a book is fresh or unfresh, the attitude of the writer, and so on. Very many decisions that we make are made merely, or purely, from a response to the language selected; this is the province of 'stylistics', the non-judgemental analysis of what is there in the text.

But, of course, language is the carrier or the revealer or the prison-house, depending on one's taste; it is a 'transform' or a 'generation' of the 'real' meaning, the structure of things, and that itself may only be one form (as C. S. Lewis suggested) of the real deep meaning. This is the difference between saying what the book is about and what the book is *really* about. *Rosie's Walk* is about a hen going for a walk around the farmyard; but is it *really* about security, lack of communication, the superiority of the child to the adult, or life and death? Which of these (or other) options lies 'deeper' than the others is a personal/cultural matter, but it is useful to see language as the uppermost level.

Thus the plot, the narrative, the shape of the story, is the next layer down: the layer identified by narrative theory. That is to say, what is really significant to us is not the actual person or persons 'created', but their relationships and what they do. Actions and reactions, patterns of behaviour, have more potentially universal significance than the particulars. This is easily demonstrated; if you are asked what a book is 'about', it is unlikely that you would repeat it word for word. You might re-tell the story (that is, give your own narrative of a story which the author has narrated), but probably you would shorten it. How you shorten it, what you find significant, indicates the structure of the story. It also links us to folk and fairy tales and similar patterned texts, and takes us both to deeper psychological patterns, and also to politics, and to the position of the person as opposed to the symbol.

Michael Stubbs has an entertaining game in which he suggests asking for a summary of a book in 60 words and then in 25 words.[6] The fewer the words, the more we are forced into abstractions – what a book is really about. Is *The Wind in the Willows* a comedy, a *Bildungsroman* in the first instance, and only on a higher or shallower level a book bout anthropomorphism? Is it at the deepest level about male fears, and only on the surface a rural idyll?

These structural patterns resonate up from even deeper cultural depths which perhaps indicate what we regard as valuable, and perhaps constitute the paradigmatic levels – that is, the alternatives possible of what to express, not merely of how to express them. In identifying what meaning the reader makes, we must also consider intertextuality: that is, what goes on between texts in terms of allusion and genre. What we make of it depends on how we read it; and that in turn depends on what the various genres of children's books allow it to be.

The next stage, then, takes us out to the book and the world, which is bringing us full circle: first, the politics of children's books and, finally, a consideration of how the texts are created, and how we can apply the insights we have gained.

Judgement is a matter for the reader. This taxonomy only supplies the outline.

Having mapped the territory, let us return to the first two elements: the reader as real person and the book as physical object.

The Reader

If we accept that children are different from adults, then we must take up Culler's point:

> Once we see as our task the analysing of literary competence as manifested in the interpretive strategies of readers, then the activities of readers ... present us with a host of facts to explain.... It is ... this notion of what readers can and will do, that enables an author to write, for to intend meanings is to assume a system of conventions and to create signs within the perspective of that system.[7]

As Susan R. Suleiman notes, 'we must take into account *different* horizons of expectation co-existing among different publics in any one society.'[8]

Some very distinguished teachers of children's literature whom

I know begin their classes by asking the (generally mature) students to provide a reading history. What is their attitude to books? By reading, are they acting normally for their cultural background or deviantly? This is a fundamental question in children's books. Do children accept the fact of the book as a normal mode of behaviour? Is reading part of normal life? This will make a considerable difference to what is perceived.

Then, how many books have they read, and of what kind? What associations will be made with certain formats of books? What allusions can they bring?

In short, as a reader, you bring to books

- your attitude to books
- your attitudes to life
- your knowledge and experience of books
- your knowledge and experience of life
- your cultural background and prejudices
- your race, class, age, and sex attitudes

and innumerable other minutiae of personality, background, and upbringing. These will all affect the way in which we make meaning: what we understand and what we take to be important. If you do not believe this, try a few simple games, like getting a group of people to read a page of any novel, then asking them what happened, or showing them a picture of a street scene and asking them to list items in the order in which they think they saw them. They may all arrive at the same composite picture (although that is unlikely), but the way in which they arrive at it will be significantly different. You may argue that the latter is irrelevant if the 'same' meaning underlies their individual perceptions. There is something in that, but only to the extent that saying that the meaning of the parts (or all) of *Stalky and Co*[9] and *Hamlet* and so on is no more than 'revenge', and that how it is expressed does not matter. If you feel that bringing in people makes nonsense of trying to find universals that we can all relate to, then I would ask, what would be the use of such universals once they were found?

But, you might say, surely the meaning resides in the book? There is an agreed code, in which 'dog' to readers of English signifies a certain animal, and no matter what my 'reading history', I cannot make it mean 'cat'. True, but what does 'dog' mean to you? Is it a purr-word or a growl-word? With peer-readers, this is problem enough, especially as the literary text goes out of its way to exploit the ambiguities and possibilities of the language. With children and children's literature, the problem becomes even greater.

How does a child make meaning? Does it differ significantly from the way in which an adult makes meaning?

In her recent short book *How Texts Teach What Readers Learn*, Margaret Meek describes a child-reader as 'possessing' a text.[10] That seems to me to be a good way of explaining something about the act of reading which is usually not approached. Just what do we mean when we say that a child can read and 'understand' a story? What sort of meaning is made by a child from a book? Is it the same as an adult makes? Can we find out?

These may sound like either trivial or obtuse questions, but the answers to them are surely vital to the way we read, write, talk about, and produce children's books. Margaret Meek finds herself unable to answer some of the questions about reading: for example, she says, 'I wish I knew more about how we learn to tolerate uncertainty in our reading and what we are really doing.'[11] Similarly, 'with inexperienced readers I find that their difficulties lie not in the words but in understanding something that lies behind the words, embedded in the sense',[12] and that some of the many questions of how children understand texts can be answered by watching their interactions with texts.[13] Here I would like to consider the matter more theoretically, by investigating how a child-reader makes meaning from a small piece of text in terms of what he or she brings to that text.

Much recent work on reading has been from the child's point of view. Hugh and Maureen Crago, for example, in *Prelude to Literacy: a preschool child's encounter with picture and story*, relate the experiences of their daughter Anna with over 400 books. Among the many tentative conclusions reached, is that the dramatic incident seemed central to storying, and that Anna rejected frames and secondary endings. Her concept of narrative was formed by intensity or vividness or relevance of incident, not by linear plot-shape. Her own stories proceeded in cyclical batches (rather like the *terza rima* form of *aba*, *bcb*, *cdc*, and so on), with the 'crucial factor' in long narratives being a linking character.[14]

Anna had problems with first-person narrators and intrusive authorial/narrational voices, which points up problems of understanding that we are likely to overlook. For example, *The tale of Tom Kitten* ends: 'And I think that some day I shall have to make another, longer book, to tell you more about Tom Kitten' – to which Anna's response was: 'Who said that?'

Other clichés of thinking were challenged. It is commonly supposed that the 'happy ending' cancels out any ill effects of threats and problems within the plot. The Cragos found that on at least three occasions this was not the case. Elsewhere, Hugh Crago says:

> I would also maintain that traditional categories like 'pilot', 'character', [and] 'theme' are often less than useful in discussing the literary experience of young children: the categories that matter, as far as I can discern, are 'chunks' like 'two opposed characters dialoguing', or 'protagonist-acting'.... And finally, 'text-as-mediated' is the crucial variable more often than 'text' itself.[15]

Walter Nash, in his book *The Language of Humour*, notes that 'Allusion in its broadest sense is never absent from our discourse; always there is some fact of shared experience, some circumstance implicit in the common culture to which participants in a conversation may confidently allude.... [These] citations ... are a kind of test, proving the credentials of the initiated, baffling the outsider.'[16] So it is with reading. We enter, by becoming literate, an exclusive society, but its terms can be named quite precisely.

Understanding a text requires two skills: understanding what the language signifies – that is, what it refers to – and understanding the rules of the game – that is, how the text works. All these understandings depend on allusion: allusion to things and allusion to rules.

We make meaning from a text in several ways:

1 Mechanical By this I mean an understanding of grammar, syntax, and punctuation, the primary systems of language coding. A book signals very quickly at what level it is to be read.

2 Denotation that is, what words are agreed by the language community to signify. This is a matter of acquired competence.

3 Connotations At this point, we shift over from allusions to public systems to allusions to private systems. Here we are dealing with what I described earlier as personal and literary meanings. Of course, there are certain cultural associations which may well lie somewhere between these two broad categories.

4 Allusions to other texts or events; literary/cultural allusions
Some of our understanding will come from specific references to other books or to cultural norms. Literary allusion is probably a minority sport, but no writer can truly escape from it, and how well it is *detected* by the reader will be significant. For the adult reader, 'intertextuality', 'the process whereby meaning is produced from text to text rather than, as it were, between text and world',[17] is, unconsciously, a basic element of reading – which is perhaps why professional critics are such untypical readers, and professional readers of children's books even more so. Cultures other than book-cultures also have their unwritten codes. It is not clear, for example, what a child-reader who has no experience of middle-class life would make of the family relationships portrayed in, say, *Swallows and Amazons*,[18] or a southern child of the northern ethos of Janni Howker's *Isaac Campion*.[19] Complete understanding of all the allusions of this kind would be the mark of the fully competent reader, a mythical beast invented by literary theorists. No human, least of all, perhaps, the authors themselves, would be able to give a full account of them.

5 Allusions to how texts work; generic expectations These are the most important and neglected of literary features. They allow us to understand suspense, to recognize 'cohesion' in a text, to assign importance to events, to decide what kind of book we are dealing with, and what kind of attention it is requiring of us. In short, we need to see significances, both to ourselves and to the structure of the text, before we know what we are supposed to be understanding. It is this, more than any purely 'acquired' knowledge, that marks off the developing reader from the 'mature' reader. As Meek et al. note in *The Cool Web*, 'One of the recurrent handicaps of illiterate adults is their inability to anticipate what may happen in a story they are learning to read because they never learned how the rules of the story game are transferred to the print on a page.'[20]

In understanding the elements of structure of texts, character, background, and so on, theory generally deals with distinctions

generated by the analytic methods used (rather than those re-
siding in the texts), and by the ideology of the discriminators.
Normally, within peer-group 'interpretive communities' this does
not matter; but with children's books we can make no simple
assumptions about text or audience. Just as there has been an
inevitable move towards feminist poetics and black poetics, so we
need to reconsider our adult analytic strategies with regard to a
poetics of children's literature.

There is, as Stanley Fish points out, 'always a formal pattern
but it is not always the same one'.[21] Our perceptions of narrative
patterns, and much else, are based on an appeal to a common
culture, and the culture of the primary readers of children's
literature is not necessarily ours; it may be in opposition to it or a
sub-culture of it or in a power relationship with it. In any case,
we have to be aware that 'ordinary' theory, methods, and termi-
nology may not be relevant. The anthropologist and linguist
Shirley Brice Heath has pointed out, for example, that in the two
different USA cultures that she studied, 'they structure their
stories differently; they hold different scales of features on which
stories are recognized as *stories* and judged as good or bad'.[22] In
short, the reader affects text affects analysis; and this means that
the adult has to accept counter-readings, readings which seem
perverse or illogical, as a necessary part of the child interpreting
the text.

Experience (or 'creation') of text is the convergence (or clash)
of two code-sets; those of 'life' (knowledge of the world/pro-
bability/causality, and so on), and of 'text' (knowledge of conventions, generic expectation, intertextual reference, and the rest).
Both are important for theory and for the production of texts
for children, but here I will be primarily concerned with text-
codes.

The implied audience for 'children's literature' is a *developing*
one. Integrating the codes of text and of genre will be an important part of the reading process, while, diachronically, a developing reader may change more radically between re-readings that
a 'skilled' or 'mature' reader. 'Customary' reading allows us, on
our first reading, to 'reach a preliminary hypothesis about genre,
bear it in mind as we glance back over earlier passages, and reread
the whole work in the light of our assumptions about its literary

form'.[23] But we have to have knowledge of the divisions and discriminations implicit in genre in order to form hypotheses or make assumptions. Margaret Meek has written that 'successful early readers discover that story happens like play. They ... feel quite safe ... because they know that a story is a game with rules.'[24] Yet, as E. D. Hirsch notes, 'a genre is less like a game than like a code of social behaviour'.[25]

Hence the developing encounter with text entails reacting against, as well as conforming to and manupulating, narrative conventions. To the developing reader, the ritualized forms of text may seem alien, because they do not have any referential 'truth'; even the simplest structure of beginning, middle, and end is patently artificial. (Some sub-cultures, of course, never appreciate the validity of story. As the mystically inclined Buddy remarks in Salinger's 'Seymour, and Introduction', 'Whatever became of that stalwart bore Fortinbras? Who eventually fixed *his* wagon?'[26]

Perceptions of how texts are 'ordered' (closure, open endings, and so forth) appeal to concepts of psychological satisfaction which, as Piaget and many others have pointed out, are neither universal nor static. Readers may select completely different conceptual sets from the same text (despite – or perhaps because of – authors' attempts to tailor texts to specific audiences).

It is possible to argue that children belong, however briefly, to a primarily oral culture, although one that is in close contact with a written culture. Walter Ong notes in his *Orality and Literacy*:

> Little has thus far been done, however, to understand reader response in terms of what is now known of the evolutions of noetic processes from primary orality through residual orality to high literacy. Readers whose norms and expectations for formal discourse are governed by a residually oral mindset relate to a text quite different[ly] from readers whose sense of style is radically textual.... Even today ... readers in certain sub-cultures [of high-literacy cultures] are still operating in a basically oral framework, performance-oriented rather than information-oriented.[27]

Ong points out that those who are literate necessarily have difficulty in conceiving of an oral universe. The written word is not simply a transcription of the spoken word; contained in the transition between the two is the paradox that orality unites people in finite, interactive groups (especially where narrative is concerned), whereas reading/writing is a solitary activity which gives access to a much wider, if absent, group. It is in this transition that the dislocation of children's literature occurs.

The oral mind-set has a 'spectacular' influence on narrative and plot, 'which in an oral culture is not quite what we take plot typically to be'.[28] It is not simply that formulae are used because they are essential for the preservation of thought in the oral culture (and, of course, for the development of learning and understanding for the child) or that 'heavy' characters are mnemonic and aid noetic economy. Rather, 'you do not find climactic linear plots in people's lives [except by] ruthless elimination of all but a few ... incidents'.[29] In 'performed' narratives, the use of 'strings' rather than patterned groups, disregard for temporal sequence, apparently random analepsis and prolepsis, limited cataphoric reference, opening *in media res*, and so on are not simply devices to aid memory; they are not 'proto-written' strategies.[30] Rather, they relate to a distinctive world-view.

It is interesting that the one example of narrative which Suzanne Romaine gives in her study *The Language of Children and Adolescents* is discontinuous. 'There may be', she concludes, 'crucial differences between adults and children ... in the social significance of performed narratives.... [T]he notion of complexity as far as narrative structure is concerned must take into account both linguistic and social factors.'[31]

If we place these characteristics of performed narrative beside the child's natural tendency towards performance, 'easy access to metaphor', and an ability to handle complex narrative acts, described by Gardner,[32] then it is clear that we are dealing not with lesser ability, but with a different kind of ability, one that seems likely to view narrative (consequently perceive its structures) in a way not accounted for in conventional theory. Further, the text may actually seem to symbolize an alien culture, and as such may be perceived perversely or subversively. In turn, because the reader is assumed not to have code-skills equivalent to those of the writer, texts intended for children tend to be 'overcoded' either by unusually strong narrational control or by frequent summary. The paradox is that such modifications are beside the point, and merely reinforce the illusion that the structures of children's literature are easily accessible.

This, then, is the reader; part of the equation that is certainly dominant, but, as we have seen, impossible to separate from the next element, the book.

The Book

The book-as-object is usually not considered to be significant, except in the case of collector's items, the work of bibliophiles, or picture books (which I shall consider in Chapter 10). 'To a certain extent', says Seymour Chatman, 'the physical condition of the book does not affect the nature of the aesthetic object fixed by it.'[33] The 'to a certain extent' is significant. It means that to some extent we *do* judge books by their covers, and that the style of type or the stiffness of the binding or the quality of the paper or the smell of the ink does influence us. Most people (and not only children) have a sensuous relationship with books; how they feel, how they weigh in the hand, the size, the shape (and, for very young children, the taste) all matter. It may be blasphemous to say so, but could it be that some of the reputation of, say, Dickens for crabby, dusty atmospherics lies partly in the crabbiness and dustiness of those endless uniform editions and the heavily serifed type-faces? Similarly, the difference between the obviously disposable 'bookstall' paperback teenage novel and the hardback version or the laminated school-version will make a difference to the way the book is read, and thus to its ultimate 'meaning'.

There is one more item in the interface between reader and book: that is, the knowledge of books and authors that the reader brings. Skilled readers will have made most of their decisions about what they think of a book, what degree of attention it is going to warrant, and the probable kind of enjoyment they are going to get long before they actually read any of the words. The author's name is obviously important (have you read her before?). The graphics on the cover or the 'blurb' will give clues; even the imprint, for experienced adults, makes a difference. It has been suggested by opponents of reading schemes that the colour-coding and numbering of texts designed to teach reading skills makes them into 'non-books' and can actually limit the flexible response necessary for fluent reading. Advocates would say that the same signals actually help.[34] Our responses are pre-set.

Once past the cover of the book, a large number of 'readability' factors come in: white space, line spacing, margins, layout, type-face, illustrations, amount of dialogue as opposed to blocks of type, and so on. And sampling, as we all do, a random passage from the text, we judge the 'difficulty' of the prose in terms of vocabulary, sentence length, sentence structures, and the rest. The decision we make at that point depends both on us and the motivation we bring to the book, and the satisfaction that the 'peritextual' apparatus has given us.

Reading an Example: *The Eighteenth Emergency*

The text, says the distinguished critic Gerald Prince, 'to a certain extent acts as a guide and constraint to the activity of reading'.[35] When you consider how most of us have been brought up to regard the text as the fixed source of meaning, that 'to a certain extent' (even more than Chatman's) seems absurd. The text says that Toad fell in the river: are you trying to tell me that he didn't? The point is, which is more important, what the text tells you or what you perceive?

But let me, an untypical reader, take a book in hand. (A similar approach was taken by Hugh Crago.[36]) It is a newish copy of a Puffin edition, *The Eighteenth Emergency* by Betsy Byars. Of course, that there is a copy of this book on the bookshelf on the landing outside my daughters' bedroom is no accident. I bought it, along with several other American children's books when I was preparing a lecture for an American conference. The books are on the bookshelf because we're a bookish family, and they're there to be read when the girls learn to read.

So far, so untypical, and I will list my reactions – simultaneous as they are – in a random order. For me, the Puffin logo is more or less a symbol of respectability ('literary canonization', as someone said of being published by Penguin). It means a guaran-tee of quality in some sense, and I am used to the type-face (I do not much like American type-faces; they seem somewhat 'sloppy'). The cover of the book is by Quentin Blake, whose capacity to catch nuances of expression and dress I much admire. (I also met him once.) This cover is not one of his best. There is a boy running, surrounded by crude monsters which seem to be more whimsical than terrifying.

This may seem all rather personal, and I suspect that readers used to criticism as we know it are waiting impatiently until we are done with all these irrelevancies, and I am ready to say something concrete about the book, something that will not be prefaced by 'For me'. Yet, in reality, the atmosphere set up by the book may only be described in very personal terms. We cannot tell people how they should feel (unless we are examiners of English Literature). Critics who write about 'funny' or 'sympathetic' texts are really only dealing in probabilities, however sympathetic or authoritative or authoritarian they may sound. Criticism 'aspires to the universal';[37] it feels that it must generalize to communicate. But if it does, is it really communicating anything worthwhile, except a report on the relationship between this text and sub-sections of the dominant culture?

A reader might react to the greys and pinks of the cover as being weak or dull or effeminate, or to the spindley lettering as suggesting a comic book, or to the suggestion that it is a fantasy. Or it may be that no one would want to read a book by someone called Betsy. However far we choose to pursue this line of thought, it becomes increasingly clear that at this stage of the encounter, non-literary, pre-book items are important enough to override anything the 'contents' of the book can supply. (Elaine Moss describes some of these extra-textual factors in 'The dream and the reality: a children's book critic goes back to school'.[38])

Nor are we finished with the things that happen before we actually read the text. The Puffin edition contains a preliminary commentary and résumé of the book of more than 300 words. Presumably this is intended to be read, and if we take it as the controlling 'adultist' reading of the text, it might prepare us for some of the paradoxes of reading that lie ahead of us.

First comes a version of the situation: 'How could ... Mouse ... stand up and fight Marv Hammerman, the biggest, fiercest boy in the school? ... Inside he was scared.' (This accounts for a considerable portion of the book.) Then the title is explained ('He

and his friend Ezzie had spent a lot of time working out quick
solutions to all sorts of emergencies') and even the import of the
name of the 'villain', 'but there didn't seem to be a solution to an
emergency like a hammering from Hammerman'. Just to demys-
tify the story totally, the answer to Mouse's dilemma is heavily
hinted at: 'the solution to an emergency was to do the hardest
thing'.

What is left? Well, what is left is to prescribe the reaction to the
text, and even to give away the ending: 'Anyone who has ever felt
scared at school (and most of us have at some time) will enjoy
this very funny yet sympathetic history of poor Mouse's terrors,
and feel a relief almost equal to his own when he finally over-
comes them.'[39] This, of course, is aimed at a different audience
from the primary audience of the book: can a child-reader (or
anyone?) be reasonably expected to decode the concept of 'sympathetic'?

The other assumption behind all this, which is common with
children's books, is that the reader will read merely for confirmation, rather than for novelty. It assumes that the reaction is
predictable ('will enjoy ... feel relief'), and that all the reader has
to do is to fill in a few emotional gaps. It assumes that what the
editor felt (that it was 'funny yet sympathetic') is what the readers
will feel. Although this happens as a normal function of publicity
writing, the gap between adult publisher and child-reader is such
that it is difficult to avoid a sub-text of manipulation. Worse, it
leaves us with the illusion that we have said something useful
about the book. It is based on the school exercise of separating
plot, characters, setting, atmosphere, theme, and, finally, reaction,
regardless of the fact that in real life the sequence is exactly the
opposite, and that most of us will probably have silently suspected
that the book *meant what it was*. Old habits die very hard, and
they surface continually on book 'blurbs' or in reviews.

But, once we have made our way to the text, how *do* we talk
about it? That is a question for the next chapter: the difficult
interface between book and reader. Before we can look at the
various elements out of which a text is constructed, we must look
at how the text and the reader come together.

5

The Text and the Reader

The 'realization' of a text, especially a text for children, is closely involved with questions of control, and of the techniques through which power is exercised over, or shared with, the reader. Many of the confusions over the status and quality of children's books and literature stem from the assumption that they must necessarily be what Roland Barthes has called *lisible* rather than *scriptible* (sometimes translated into English as 'readerly' rather than 'writerly').[1] They are 'closed texts' which the skilled reader reads 'below capacity'. In other words, the writer has attempted to do all the work for the reader, to limit the possibilities of interpretation, to heavily guide understanding. The *scriptible*, or 'writerly', text, on the other hand, is 'open' to much more input by the reader.

By attempting to control the text in various ways, writers, by implication, require readers to read only within both implied and defined limits; and texts become, in the theorist Bakhtin's terms, 'monological' rather than 'dialogical' or 'polyphonic'.[2]

Consider the differences between these two encounters with fictional villains:

> The girl stood up, holding the bag, and turned round to face Rebecca. Her brown eyes had narrowed down to frightening slits. Her whole appearance was striking, indeed, overpowering. She had long black wavy hair, bony features and a rather hawk-like nose. She towered above Rebecca for she was almost grown-up and very tall and elegant. She wore her beautifully cut tweed coat open and with graceful flair....
> 'Did you say something to me?'
> Rebecca hung her head, cheeks hot with embarrassment.[3]

Of course, it is not merely the ready-made phrases, but the things that the author chooses to describe that imply a whole structure of preconceptions. Now consider Mouse in *The Eighteenth Emergency* confronting another bully:

> Then he glanced up, squinting at Hammerman, and Hammerman moved his face as if he had chewing gum or a Life Saver in his mouth.
> Mouse said, 'Did you say something?'
> Hammerman shook his head, and with the sun coming in the window behind him, his hair seemed to fan out like feathers. His face didn't change expression, but his eyes were very bright. Mouse thought that this was because he was doing the one thing he was really good at....
> 'I really didn't hear what you said, if you said anything,' Mouse said, stuttering a little.
> 'I'll see you after school.' Hammerman took his finger and touched Mouse on the chest and then passed him and started down the stairs.[4]

Betsy Byars's prose is not over-original: it has its fair share of standard phrases ('glanced up', 'shook his head', 'took his finger'), but it does not hand over experience ready-packaged. It does not simply require the reader to recognize a series of pre-programmed codes ('hawk-like', 'tall and elegant', 'beautifully cut', 'graceful flair'); nor does it tell the reader what the author thinks, rather than what the character thinks ('striking', 'almost grown-up'.) The reader has to make small acts of deduction from the evidence, to listen to Mouse's reactions through Mouse's mind.

We must be careful not to get involved in snobbish arguments about which is the better book, because that depends on what you want to use the book for. Here, all we can say is that the pre-digested style of *First Term at Trebizon* prescribes the level at which it can be read, at which it requires to be read. Because it is very familiar, it is predictable; because it involves little deduction, it can be read easily; because of both these things, the actual transfer of information (that is, new information) is low. It is not so much implying a readership as prescribing the level of reading. (And much the same applies to thousands of books marketed for adults as 'popular literature'.) It neither demands any input from the reader, nor supplies anything other than confirmation of the standard patterns of the fictive world. If this is what you want a book for – to distract, pass the time, provide reading practice rather than development, to reinforce simplistic social stratifications, and rely on the prose of popular journalism – then *First Term at Trebizon* should be praised rather than criticized. It is doing, efficiently, a particular job; it is good value for money.

The Eighteenth Emergency, on the other hand, requires rather more interaction; it is an 'open' text in the sense that the reader is free to fill in the images and the feelings. Of course, there is a fairly firm framework for this; there are limits at which we might say that the reading is no longer 'acceptable' (see below), but, none the less, the book is not doing all the work.

It is quite possible – although we must be extremely careful about assessing probability – that a reader can ignore, or mentally edit out, anything which requires his mental involvement. But the text allows that: it allows reading at several levels of interaction. Developmentally, then, *The Eighteenth Emergency* is a flexible text; it can be used, appreciated, and interacted with at a range of capacities. It may be that the precise, explicit tagging of Mouse's thoughts represents the cut-off point for reading involvement. A very skilled, mature reader may feel that too much work is being done by the author, and thus that involvement is pre-empted.

In short, instead of saying 'better/worse', or 'suitable/unsuitable', criticism would be more profitably employed in saying 'This text has certain potentials for interaction, certain possibilities of meaning.' If nothing else, we would escape from the present confusion of 'good' with 'good for', which leads to lazy writing being praised because to condemn it would be snobbery, and to children being exposed to indifferent texts because adults do not have the means of distinguishing.

Generic expectations are consequently self-fulfilling: children's books are as they are because writers assume, from what they write, that that is how they should be. Hence children's books, as we have seen, are very frequently perceived as being of poor quality by definition, because the mode is primarily defined unconsciously by textures of implication within the text – and these are best seen in stylistic features, as we shall see in the next chapter. Texts which challenge these assumptions commonly find themselves in the no-person's land between writings for adults (so-called) and writings for children (so-called).

In peer-texts, the adult reader (real or otherwise) can adjust to the degree of control which the author appears to be exercising. As an adult reader, my selection of a text may be governed, in part, by the amount of effort I wish to bring to it and by a judgement of how much effort is warranted. With books 'for children', or 'unskilled' readers, because of the status of the audience, the author-reader (or narrator-narratee) relationship is a more than usually unbalanced power relationship. The audience is created by the writer much more directly than with a peer-text, in the sense that the text does more than display its codes, grammar, and contracts; it suggests what the reader must be or become to optimize the reading of the text. Drawing on the power-codes of adult-child, book-child, and written-oral relationships, it *prescribes* what the reader *must* be, and indeed, because there is both an authoritarian and an educational element involved, what the reader *can* be. The exercise of such power is by no means inevitable, although it is so characteristic as to define the children's book for many readers. Very often there seems to be a deliberate attempt to limit the child-reader's interaction with the text. This may seem to be benevolent, if one believes that the 'open' text is fundamental to literary development or, as Jacqueline Rose suggests merely a fact of life for the 'impossible' category of children's fiction.[5]

What Texts Imply

Criticism, especially of children's literature perhaps, is controlled by perception of genre; is children's literature identifiable by lexical items, grammatical structures, higher level narrative units, or an overall tonal strategy? For example, what gives away the 'implied audience' for this quotation?

> 'He woke up with a jerk, shivering with cold. He began to stretch his cramped legs but they hurt. Opening his eyes, he looked around in the darkness. He knew immediately where he was. He

had been locked under the stairs. He peered through the crack at the side of the small door. It was pitch black.'[6]

It could be that the verb 'woke up', rather than 'woke' or 'was awake' and the economical syntax (and lack of punctuation) of the second sentence are intended to link the discourse to the mind of the character. But unfortunately, the stylistic simplicity of the passage – that is, its lack of deviation or variety – merely points up the logical and referential anomalies. (How could he 'peer through' a 'crack' (or is it really a 'gap'?) which he could not see (as it was 'pitch black')? Indeed, how could he know that he was under the stairs if it was so dark; and if he knew by some means other than sight, why are we not informed about it?) The summarizing mode is so pervasive that it constantly shifts towards implicit authorial control, which in turn becomes a marker (or an assumed marker) of the genre of children's literature. And this is quite apart from the grammatical features; five of the seven sentences have the same structure (six if we discount the clause 'Opening his eyes'). Yet Michelle Magorian's *Goodnight Mr Tom* not only won the British Library Association's Carnegie Medal, but also (ironically enough), the International Reading Association's Children's Book Award (1982). Since this extract is characteristic of the novel, we may have here some indication of the relative stress laid by judges upon content and style.

Magorian's text tells rather than shows, explicates rather than demonstrates; and books which retain this dominating narrational presence, the residual or 'transferred' storyteller, are a textual echo of storying as an event which the storyteller essentially controls. In general, it seems that this control is only reluctantly relinquished (which may say something about the adult-child relationship), which can scarcely be for so simple a reason as that the reading audience cannot understand the text without a built-in prompter. In fact, even skilled readers have difficulty with the voice of the storyteller addressing the audience 'directly' in 'two-dimensional' printed texts. As the history of the early novel demonstrates, the act of storying involves a narrative voice or stance, an implied narrator or author or quasi-storyteller (or a device to replace it); and this produces a grammatical and psychological situation of immense complexity.[7]

When, as in texts designed to be read *to* children (or, indeed,

any audience) there is a first-person marker, there can be problems, as we have seen from *The Tale of Tom Kitten.* One of the
most complex instances is the opening of Milne's *Winnie-the-
Pooh.* The narrative begins with a direct address to the implied
reader, marked by second-person form: 'Anyhow, here he is . . .
ready to be introduced to you.' It then moves to a situation
where the first-person narrator describes how she or he tells a
story to Christopher Robin, who now becomes both a character
and an addressee: 'You aimed very carefully at the balloon, and
fired. "Did I miss?" you asked.'[8]

The problems confronting a reader of that text and a listener to
that reader are formidable, not least because the reader implied
(and thus required) by the text is not the actual receiver. Hence
the linguistic needs are different. There is an entertaining paradox
here. The storyteller's summaries, intended to make things easier
for the *listener,* are quite likely when they appear in a text being
read silently to make things more difficult for the *reader.* They
have not sprung from a genuine need (on the part of the reader),
and as a result they require an artificial convergence of text-codes
and reader-codes, rather than, as in the case of the 'given' text,
allowing an exploration of codes which *may not* cohere, *and may
not need to.* (The implications of this can be seen in Robert
Leeson's account of the history of children's literature, which
emphasizes the interplay of oral and written patterns in a socio-
political context.)[9]

An example of both the summary and the quasi-storyteller's
voice can be seen in Ruth Park's novel *Playing Beattie Bow*
(which won the Australian Children's Book of the Year Award in
1981):

> As she stood there, looking up at the askew, rusted pulley, and the
> edge of the roof above it, a small patch of the sky suddenly lost its
> stars.
>   Someone was lying on the warehouse roof looking down at her.
>
> Chapter 7
> When Abigail realised that she was being spied upon . . .[10]

Here we have three renditions, or variations, of the same essential
semantic set, which progressively 'close' the text. 'A small patch

of the sky suddenly lost its stars' requires a considerable interpretive effort by the reader, and it carries several possibilities. 'Someone was lying on the warehouse roof' restricts these possibilities. 'Looking down on her' and 'realised that she was being spied upon' similarly move from 'showing' to 'telling', from 'open' to 'closed'. Of course, it could be argued that this progression reflects the deductions made by Abigail, so that Park holds to the contract of narration through a single consciousness. However, the progression from stylistic deviation (the adverb in an adjectival position in 'askew, rusted pulley') to cliché ('being spied upon') re-assumes control. This is further corroborated by the explanatory work of the first sentence in the new chapter, and of course we need not assume that the presence of a chapter division requires a break in the flow of reading.

The Reader and Meaning

Children are *developing* readers; their approach to life and text stems from a different set of cultural standards from those of adult readers, one that may be in opposition, or perhaps based on orality. Hence they do 'possess' texts, in the sense that their meanings are their own and private, even more than adults. Adult readers know the rules of the game, even if they don't know that they know; and their understanding, as we have seen, may rest on belonging to 'interpretive communities' which not only know the rules of the game but share their knowledge and attitudes. I would like to lay bare some of these rules, and suggest that child-readers cannot possibly have access to all of them. So, regardless of what the text prompts, they are not necessarily in a position to make use of it.

But surely we can have *some* idea of what children understand, otherwise the whole edifice of communication, publishing, and language teaching for children comes tumbling down. For example, what about comprehension texts, still so much alive in public examinations?

It seems obvious that all we are doing if we ask questions about the 'content' or 'meaning' of a text is testing a child's social competence (which is, perhaps, all we should do, or should hope to do). That is, children who are successful in comprehension tests demonstrate no more than that they can find the answer implicit in the question. The 'real' meaning of the text to the individual remains hidden; children (perhaps for ever afterwards) develop the skill to say what they are supposed to say, and may well assume that their private understandings are in some way 'wrong' – just as those who set the examination questions must assume that their own reading of the text is in some way 'right'.

In his excellent book *Developing Response to Fiction*, Robert Protherough suggests that there is a spectrum between what is 'objectively' correct – that is, something which all speakers of the language will agree on as being 'there' in the text – and things which are subjective and purely personal. His spectrum (which could, I think, bear some modification) runs, in outline, thus:

1 Matters of fact
2 Clear implications
3 Manifest literary effects [e.g. symbols, motifs, shifts of viewpoint]
4 Shared associations
5 Significance to the reader based on 'a particular stance' [that is, a doctrine or ideology]
6 Private associations[11]

Some of these – perhaps the first four – might seem to be the common property of all readers. We read within a reading community, and therefore can share meanings and understanding. But is this really so?

To look at it another way, are there degrees of understanding, which, when we are writing or prescribing fiction, we will accept? Is there another spectrum between total understanding of what the writer intended and a free-form, totally personal reading, which, say, takes *After the First Death*[12] as a drawing-room comedy or *The Lion, The Witch, and the Wardrobe*[13] as a pagan text? (The latter example is not as grotesque as it may appear. The book has been banned in certain areas of the USA on just those grounds.) Is there such a thing as 'total' comprehension? And are there degrees of comprehension which we might accept as adequate, or normal, or worth giving a good mark to?

It is obvious that there are limits to the shared making of

meaning. What the author meant is, strictly speaking, unknowable, even to the author. But we have to assume a certain congruence between what you see and what I see and what a child-reader sees; otherwise the whole business of making books (and, especially, talking about them) becomes a nonsense. There must be a middle ground of common-sense agreement about what meaning is.

This may not seem to have got us very far; but it may at least have made us cautious about assuming any similarity of understanding between readers. What we need to do now is to investigate the way in which texts work – what the shared rules are – so that we can see where individual readers are likely to go their own ways.

Equally, the way texts are organized and our understanding of that organization have a profound effect on the way we see the world. As Roger Fowler puts it: 'Linguistic codes do not reflect reality neutrally; they interpret, organize, and classify the subjects of discourse. They embody theories of how the world is arranged: world-views or ideologies. For the individual, these theories are useful and reassuring, making his relationship with the world simple and manageable.'[14] That is, *if we comprehend them*. For, as Fowler says, 'in continuous text, sentences are linked together by an intricate system of cohesive ties';[15] and unless we understand these, we will be in some danger of not understanding the text. Or, as Frank Smith observes: 'The more unconventional the reader finds the text, the less the reader is likely to have any relevant expectations about it and the less understandable it is likely to be.'[16]

Reading is a matter of expectations; and the question is, how do your expectations and my expectations differ from those of a developing reader?

Decoding the Text

Thus, texts do not, in themselves, teach anything.[17] They contain potential meanings structured in complex linguistic and semantic code-systems. Our access to those meanings depends on our decoding skills. If we are to understand what children tell us about texts, it is important that we know just what the codes are, and what skills we actually need to unravel them. But, at the root of this, we need to establish the difference between the way a skilled reader decodes and understands and the way a developing reader does so.

So, I would like look not at what readers bring to the text and how they react, but at what codes texts actually contain. Then, I would like to work out the difference between the way a child reads and the way an adult reads – but not by trying to find out what children can do, but rather, what they *can't* do. If we examine the way in which a 'skilled' reader reads – how *we* as adults make meaning – we may be able to see what a developing reader lacks. What do *we* need to know about texts before we can 'understand' them? What do texts offer us by way of clues and cues to understanding?

It might be worth pausing for a moment to ask just what we mean by 'understanding'. Philosophically, there is probably no such thing as complete understanding of a text, because what an author meant is inaccessible even to the author. Therefore there can only be, as it were, degrees of understanding. Some of these might be testable, but, as Frank Smith points out, meanings are always personal. This is particularly the case with 'literary' understanding, where it might be said that 'zero uncertainty' perhaps *should not* be achieved.[18]

The best way to approach this is by a practical example. Let us see, first of all, what meanings there are, potentially, in a text (staying within that middle ground of 'common sense' – although a child-reader may not have the same concept of common sense as a mature reader), and then try to work out what skills and knowledge are needed to understand them.

Let us take the opening of Isaac Campion's narrative in Janni Howker's celebrated short novel.

Now then, I was twelve, rising thirteen, when our Daniel got killed. Aye ... [sic] it was a long time ago. I'm talking about a time of day eighty-three years back. Eighty-three years. It's a time of day that's past your imagining. I'm talking about a different world. You may as well say it was a different planet, the world I was born in.

No radios. No televisions. No World Wars. They'd not even built the *Titanic*, let alone sunk her.[19]

What does the text tell us? And how do we know what it is telling us?

This can be an entertaining party game. I have played it with several groups of undergraduate students, in whose skills as developing readers I have great faith – even though I strongly believe that they are all still 'resisting' readers, playing a game of 'right answers' against what they really believe. What their readings showed me was a revelation. Nor did we get very far before fierce debate broke out.

'Now then' This is an oral marker, and implies that someone is speaking. It implies older to younger; and to some it implied a male speaker rather than a female. In any case, it implies someone in control of narrative rather than conversation. It suggests regional dialect ('quite normal' to the Lancastrians among the readers, but deviant to the South Welsh, who might have begun, 'Arright'). It might also imply someone with not much education (at least to southerners, perhaps). It sets the 'mode' of the text as being the illusion of the present, and implies a story that must be set in the past.

As you can see, an analysis like this could go on for some time, but let me just pick out the most significant things that emerged from that first paragraph.

How important is the dialect? Regional linguistic markers do more than simply characterize the speaker. 'Rising thirteen' identifies for the reader the potential interest of the text; 'our Daniel' marks a closeness of relationship which indicates family, and probably the intimacy of the narration. (Incidentally, only one reader did not assume automatically that Daniel was a person rather than, say, the family dog. That may be simply that dogs usually have contracted names, or, more probably, because it would be unusual to have such a marker in a 'pole' position so early in the text); 'Aye ... talking about a time of day ... past your imagining' again reinforces the speaker's character, but also indicates that the text is going to contain material not immediately relevant to the action. Readers are therefore given the choice of editing out reflective passages, thereby turning the book into, perhaps, a thriller, or of adjusting their expectations.

We may well assume by now that the killing of Daniel is not going to be either over-dramatic or trivial. In other words, we have been given a lot of clues about the way we are being invited to read – that is, not simply what kind of reader is implied, but the kinds of levels and techniques and expectations that the reader is expected to bring to the text.

What is the story going to be about?   In the first line, after the throat-clearing, there is the 'hook': 'when our Daniel got killed'. To the skilled reader, this represents a clear indication of the first, and perhaps the central, incident of the narrative. But it is important to see that this 'hook' is only such if we understand generic rules and, indeed, if we have identified the genre correctly. At this stage, we might simply react to the 'got killed'. This is interesting (positively or negatively) to most readers because it is outside their normal experience; it deviates from ordinary life, and therefore produces a reaction (of some kind). How significant the killing is, or how we are supposed to take it, remains to be seen. (I am reminded of a cartoon in the American 'Bloom County' newspaper cartoon feature, where child TV-watchers cannot distinguish between fictional and factual killings, and there comes the plaintive cry, 'Will someone please tell me whether I should be enjoying this or not?'[20]).

The early position of the 'hook' suggests that the killing is going to be important. It would, after all, be very surprising (to the skilled reader) if the narrator, five pages later, said, 'Oh yes, our Dan was killed, but that wasn't very interesting; after all, he was only a wood-louse, so I'll tell you about the flower arrangements I saw yesterday.' But if that is banal and obvious to the skilled reader, is it so to the apprentice reader? And if it is not, what sort of book is the apprentice reader going to make it out to be?

What is important for us to remember when we read a story?
In any text, not all the information is of the same importance. The eighty-three years mentioned in *Isaac Campion* might well be important; the reference is, after all, repeated. But does the

killing take precedence? As adults, we tend to prioritize anything to do with death, and also to give weight to anything in a written text. But do other readers? Frank Smith, in *Writing and the Writer*, distinguishes between the author's *global* intentions (the general kind of book he or she wants to write) and *focal* intentions (what each word, sentence, paragraph, and chapter is intended to do). When the reader starts to decode the text, these intentions are replaced by expectations.[21] The problem is that, unless we know what we are supposed to take notice of, we cannot organize our expectations; and, as a result, we cannot *predict* what will happen.

When is our curiosity going to be satisfied? By the end of the first paragraph, and probably before, the apparent ramblings of the narrator will be perceived as establishing his character, rather than advancing the story. Thus the skilled reader will make a judgement about the *kind of attention* that the text is seeking from him or her. It is clear, even now, that the book is of a certain kind. There is reflection as well as action – although we might be wondering whether this is just temporary. But again, we only understand this from experience of storytelling and texts.

What facts do we need to know? The second paragraph requires special knowledge. Presumably we all know what radios are (things in cars, perhaps, in 1991),˙ and all but a very few will regard television as a natural part of their lives. But what of World Wars? Is this a concept we can define? We 'know what it means' by definition. But 'knowing' about a war might be taken from what the media present, which is quite another matter. And if you happen to have lived through one, your concept will be quite different. (I have always been faintly amazed to discover from my parents that people actually went on holiday during the Second World War. For somebody not acquainted with wars at first hand, the assumption is that war is all over the place all the time.) So there is going to be a considerable gap of understanding between the narrator, the readers, and different types of readers of different ages and at different times and in different cultures.

And take the next sentence. Should you happen not to know anything about the *Titanic*, you would deduce from the italics and the context that she was a ship (because you 'know' that proper names attached to certain inanimate objects are printed in italics, and that ships are given a female pronoun). But what happened to her? 'They'd not even built the *Titanic* let alone sunk her.' Why should 'they' want to sink her? This is the first example where external acquired knowledge is required simply to decode the next.

In a moment, I will draw together some of the points from this analysis to see if we can categorize the kinds of knowledge and skills we need to have to decode a text, and how far children – that is, developing readers – can be said to possess them. But first, I will answer three possible objections. One is that the whole exercise is invalid because people don't read in that way. True; but only if we laboriously sketch out some of the possible processes in the experience of texts can we move on to the much more important stage of deciding which of those processes are probable for any given reader. The second objection is that such an analysis is grossly over-simplified (despite its apparent complexity). One of my own objections to much reader-response theory, liberating as it has been, is that it posits a cretinous reader who has to lumber along each line of text, constantly surprised by the next lexical or grammatical development. I doubt if this is true even of the most fumbling beginner.

It is true that writing and reading are at least to some extent linear, and that we gather information sequentially. But, as we have seen, each level of each sentence predicts something to a greater or lesser degree (or cues the reader to make predictions). At the simplest level, we can predict grammatical completion; we can also predict lexical selection. In a sentence like 'You may as well say it was a different _____', the structure and the context predict a noun, probably of place, possibly of time; less probably, a qualifier of some kind. Any incongruity of word selection would be deviant, in ways ranging from the incomprehensible ('a different typewriter') to the humorous ('sausage') or the suggestive ('ethos'). The actual selection by Janni Howker is just deviant enough to demand some thought, as it plays upon the expectation of the cliché 'a different world' and expands it.

The third objection is simply 'Why don't you ask the children?' The answer is not just that what answers you get depend on what questions you ask, or that children tend to say what you want them to say. In fact, skilled work with children is richly informative. Rather, most adults do not realize what is happening when they read, so we need to make a map of what happens, so that when children say where they are, adults will be able to recognize what they are saying.

The first four of the categories of how we make meaning deal with semantics, or 'meanings', rather than, directly, with the codes which make them accessible. And because it is meanings that most of us are interested in, I would like to start by asking what would happen if we took away those things that we know because we are skilled readers. Obviously, of all the things suggested by all readers, only a small proportion are knowable by a single reader. Where adult skilled readers have the advantage over child-readers is in their ability to see through the codes to an area of *choice*.

Let us look at the text again:

> Now then, I was twelve, rising thirteen, when our Daniel got killed. Aye ... [sic] it was a long time ago. I'm talking about a time of day eighty-three years back. Eighty-three years. It's a time of day that's past your imagining. I'm talking about a different world. You may as well say it was a different planet, the world I was born in.
>
> No radios. No televisions. No World Wars. They'd not even built the *Titanic*, let alone sunk her.[22]

If we start with 'mechanical' skill, then we might say that the text is relatively easy, because it is 'oral'. A few dialect expressions and phrasings ('rising thirteen', 'a time of day') could cause trouble; some teachers of my acquaintance may query the verbless 'sentences'. But in 'ease of reading' terms – that is, patching together the grammatical associations – the text is straightforward enough.

But what happens if we move on to things in the sphere of 'acquired knowledge' and question the 'denotation' of some of the words? If we don't know what some of the things mean, then do we end up with something like this (the square brackets indicate uncertainties)?

> I was twelve ... when [our] Daniel got killed. It was eighty-three
> years ago. Things were different, then. No ... televisions ... no
> ship which was sunk by somebody.

Or, if we take away a consciousness of 'connotation', we might
end up with:

> I was twelve ... when [somebody – possibly in my family –
> called] Daniel got killed. I was born on a different planet, without
> radios or televisions and something hadn't been sunk.

Or, if we take away a knowledge of the conventions of texts
(both in a short space and in narrative), there will be little left but
questions:

> [Is somebody speaking? Is this a letter, or what?] Eighty-three
> years ago [from when?] Daniel was killed [got himself killed?]
> [Who is Daniel?] [Where is this different world?] [Is this a sea
> story?]

These are not (as far as I can make them) whimsical or personal
alternative readings; they are 'best possible' readings by people
deprived of some of the codes of reading which make meaning.

The original question was, how are meanings made? This is
part of the answer. They are made by building up interlinked
kinds of meaning, from denotation, connotation, and inter- and
intra-textual meaning. Without these last two, especially, we are
in a poor state, and may be forced to create a very different kind
of text, if we keep reading at all.

We should, therefore, bear this in mind when interpreting what
a reader tells us about a book. The more complex the layers of
meaning (and we commonly praise such complexity in a book),
the more difficult it will be for the reader to make a meaning
close to either what the writer meant, or what a majority of us
make of it. And that is nothing to do with how difficult the book
is mechanically.

There is, then, a considerable difference between what a child
might perceive a text to be and what an adult decides that it
must be. Allusion is central to perception. It controls the

making of meaning in sophisticated ways. Satire cannot work until we recognize the hidden opposing idea; irony cannot work unless we can deduce the implied opposite moral point of view. To read 'competently' – that is, in a way which smooths out the differences between individual readers – is not merely a matter of acquiring knowledge, but of acquiring schemata. As the psychologist Richard Anderson observes: 'Whether people possess the schemata for assimilating a text should be an important source of individual differences in reading comprehension.'[23]

Other Aspects of Reading

The connections to be made between this way of considering a text and the ways in which children learn to read are, of course, well worth exploring. Clearly, we are puzzled as to what sense children who are 'developing' readers make of a text, as compared with adults or skilled readers. As I have already suggested, they cannot make the same meanings for reasons of

- counter- or anti-culture
- psychology
- life experience (denotation)
- text experience (genre)
- the whole structure of allusions being different

Are children, then, true 'deconstructors' of texts, ready to read 'against' texts, to use them as a basis for extravagant readings, free of tiresome constraints of understanding, and hence free to misread? 'Deconstruction', of late a fashionable mode of criticism, has been described thus:

> [In deconstruction] the object of the critic, then, is to seek not the unity of the work, but the multiplicity and diversity of its possible meanings, its incompleteness, the omissions which it displays but cannot describe, and above all its contradictions.... [This can be compared with] Anglo-American critical practice, where the quest is for the unity of the work, its coherence ... In thus smoothing

out the contradiction, closing the text, criticism becomes the
accomplice of ideology. Having created a canon of acceptable
texts, criticism then provides them with acceptable interpretations,
thus effectively censoring any elements in them that come into
collision with the dominant ideology.[24]

Rather more sceptically, Howard Felperin has suggested that
'deconstruction' is, in effect, a mode of play:

> Once criticism realizes ... the inadequacy of its own law-making
> ... it turns into deconstruction, which is nothing other than
> language scepticism in the mode of play, an exacting and rigorous
> form of play, but play all the same.... After all, if literature is the
> foreknowledge of criticism, if the literary text – and deconstruc-
> tion must maintain that category; *its* question is not whether
> 'literature' exists, but how inclusive the category should be –
> always already knows in advance what the critic seeks to discover,
> then the legislative labours of the latter can never be completed.[25]

In a sense, then, from the child-reader's point of view, every act
of reading which reinterprets a text in terms of a universe of
discourse (or anti-discourse) which the child knows, will be an
act of deconstruction, a play with the words. Children are soon
taught that words are not to be played with, but as long as they
do play, they are deconstructors *par excellence*.

For all readers, and for developing readers especially, the encounter with the text, although rule-governed to some extent, is
very volatile. The question of whether children are capable of a
'literary' reading, in any of the types of definition suggested, is
thus very complex. As Frank Hatt notes:

> One reader will read different texts in different ways; one text will
> be read in different ways by different readers. One reader will read
> the same text differently on different occasions; indeed, he will
> read different parts of the same text in different ways during the
> course of one reading act, as his mood, his purpose and his knowl-
> edge change.[26]

This raises the question of whether there can ever be such a
thing as a 'merely' functional or denotative meaning. In a sense,

all readings partake of the reading self, and are thus 'literary'. As far as the observer of the reading process is concerned, whether writer, publisher, teacher, or psychologist, the unfathomable internal responses can only be intelligently guessed at. For assessment purposes, we are dealing only with the 'acceptable'. As Michael Benton suggests, 'Literary reading demands nothing less than the concentration of the whole self,'[27] and that is not something readily accessible to grading.

In short, the interaction between reader and text resides as much in the volatile person as in the text itself.

> If what the reader gets from the text depends on the questions he addresses to it, then these questions derive initially from expectations which are aroused before he encounters the text.... [A]s soon as he is able to read silently, his perceptual activity is bound up with speculations about the meaning of text: he receives the graphic information from the page, not into a vacuum but into a set of expectations, which he must modify if the information does not fit.[28]

Thus far, we are working with tangibles, but there is, of course, another element, as Harold Rosen has pointed out: 'Let the story grammarians beware. Sentences end with full stops. Stories do not.'[29]

6

Style and Stylistics

Introducing Stylistics

As we have seen, it is artificial to make any distinction between the things that we perceive and the things that we respond to in a text. We do not distinguish the medium from the message, any more than we distinguish our own input from the text's. However, it makes a great deal of sense to consider separately the elements of the 'surface' of the text and the organization that this might be said to display.

What part do style and stylistics play in the overall communication process? To begin with, we cannot isolate the perception of style – and thus its study, stylistics – from the act of reading. Reading is an interaction, and we make sense of texts in terms both of their codes and of the codes we bring to them. The reader fills in the 'gaps' in the text, thus reducing its 'indeterminacies' (although there is also the paradox that the more information the text provides, the more indeterminate it can become; for, far from clarifying, each additional word may widen the possible range of connotation). This contribution by the reader means, for Wolfgang Iser, that 'the most effective literary work is one which forces the reader into a new critical awareness of his or her customary codes and expectations',[1] and this process of coming to a new awareness will begin with a perception of stylistic deviation. However, Eagleton observes that this rationale implies a liberal-humanist ideal of reading (that the mind should be open to influence by the text), but also masks a power structure, in that the reader becomes no more than a mechanic, 'recouping the "meaning" of the text according to a kind of "do-it-yourself kit" of cues provided by the author'.[2] (Some of the implications of this are discussed below, in Chapter 8.)

The relevance of this to children's literature is striking. For example, can Eagleton's criticism of liberal-humanist readers be applied to the implied readers of a text 'for children' when they are exploring and discovering text modes and when the indeterminacies are part of a much more fundamental learning process? And if Iser (despite what Eagleton detects) is at pains to support the 'open' text, what can we make of a situation in which, when it comes to children, limitation and restriction are seen as virtues by some critics? It may be correct to assume that child-readers will not bring to the text a complete or sophisticated system of codes, but is this any reason to deny them access to texts with a potential of rich codes? Equally, the argument that the child-reader does not understand complex indeterminacy would be more convincing if what is commonly substituted for it could be 'simple'; but 'simplicity' is often equated with unoriginal phrasing and a tendency to summarize thought or action.[3]

While this may derive from a residual attempt to build the oral storytelling situation into the written text, the summary and the allusion which provides the semantic content of the unoriginal phrase are both quite sophisticated devices in terms of the decoding they call for. Paradoxically, although they require considerable input by the reader, they remain reductive, rather than interactive.

Here is an example from a characteristic text:

> By good fortune they encountered Uncle John himself cutting up a
> felled tree as an offering of gratitude to the good brothers who had
> given him hospitality. He stuck his axe into the wood when he saw
> them and invited them to sit down on the trunk.[4]

The summarizing clauses 'they encountered' and 'when he saw them' are so placed as to impose the narrator's authority from the point of view of information transfer. The qualifier 'as an offering ... hospitality' cannot be related to the 'they/them' characters, while any dialogue is only implied ('and invited them') by a formal choice of lexis. Similarly, the preliminary clause 'By good fortune' is not only a precise judgement, restricting interpretive alternatives, but its relationship to the characters who are the 'consciousness-focus' of the text is – in part because of its structural place in the sentence – ambiguous; significantly, it is also a cliché requiring a complex decoding through generic sets of various kinds.

As we have seen, textual limitations are in direct opposition to both the theory and the practice of teaching and producing children's texts. The association between language and thought, language and education, and language and socialization are recognized. Why, then, in this context, a neglect of language itself? To some extent, it seems, the interests of critics lie elsewhere; at root, textual studies are not popular.

This may seem surprising in view of the legacy of 'Practical Criticism' which has dominated literary education in the USA and the UK for the last 50 years, but three influences have been at work.

The first is the emphasis placed on the *use* of children's literature. This has led to concentration on affect, which has led in turn to some very simplistic models of the reading process, and concentration on thematic analysis. Secondly, the point of stylistic analysis has rarely been made clear. Early 'formalist' stylistics shared with 'practical criticism' the danger that, as Ian Watt put it, 'its air of objectivity confers a spurious authority on a process that is often only a rationalization of unexamined judgements,'[5] and its relation to affect has been challenged frequently. Consequently, it has come to be seen as an arid exercise by comparison with the thrust and interest of narrative itself. Thirdly, the main drive of critical thought over the last 20 years has been towards contextual studies, reader response, plurality of readings (in itself a misleading term for multiplicity of readings), and the philosophy of the text (perhaps, a sceptic might say, more portable concepts for students).

However, if we agree on the relevance of the study of style, what methodology is available to us? Stylistics, or linguistic criticism, has had a chequered history. Its early claim to be the area where linguistic and critical exegesis overlapped[6] and the claim that it provides 'a basis of aesthetic appreciation by bringing to the level of conscious awareness features of the text accessible only to trained intuition'[7] have been questioned. Since style cannot be related directly to response,[8] the study of stylistics was seen for some time as only a 'pre-critical' activity, a mechanical act, endorsing, as Fowler puts it, 'a complacent and unprogressive ideology of literature'.[9] However, as Cluysenaar and others have noted, the selection of both text and analytic method is in itself a critical act: to describe form is to make a critical statement.[10] Stanley Fish's argument that, because the analytic method dictates what is perceived, stylistics is a 'closed' system, is only a stumbling block if stylistics pretends to be definitive rather then suggestive. The recent work of Fowler and the revival of interest in Bakhtin and others who provide ideological correlatives for stylistics, place it once more in the mainstream of critical techniques.[11]

Methods of stylistic analysis, like the analysis of narrative acts, are open to the objection that if they are seen 'as merely technical operations, leaving the construction of meaning to other studies, they leave us empty-handed if not empty-headed.'[12] Nevertheless, the 'technical operations' are vital, and useful taxonomies have been developed, usually working back from the particular to the general.[13] Typical is the scheme of Cummings and Simmons, who progress from phonology and phonetics to graphology (clause, group, unit-complexes, and rank-shift), lexis (collocations and sets), context, and varieties of language. In themselves, of course, these operations have scant critical meaning, but as Cummings and Simmons observe, 'stylistic analysis is ultimately a study of context and situation.... Items in literary texts ... mutually define their meanings'.[14] Similarly Fowler notes: 'Linguistic structure is not arbitrary but is determined by, or motivated by, the function it performs ... Within a given community, particular ranges of significance tend to be conventionally attached to specific types of construction.[15]

The interrelationship between the style and the discourse of children's books is clearly complex, and in the remainder of this chapter I will deal with two central aspects of it, the concept of 'register' – that is, language supposedly appropriate to the children's book – and the implications and realization of authorial stance and the power structures and controls implied by the style of dialogue presentation.

The Importance of Language

To begin with, we commonly identify children's books by the kinds of words used. There seems to be a 'register', a set of words thought to be appropriate in writing for children. This is despite noble declarations of many writers and critics, such as the following:

> A writer ... should feel himself [sic] no more under the necessity to restrict the complexity of his plotting because of differences in child understanding ... than he feels the necessity of restricting his vocabulary. – Eleanor Cameron.[16]

> Another factor which I think is of tremendous importance is ... language that is going to stretch the readers' mind and vocabulary. Words, in themselves, are such a pleasure to children – and even the most deprived childhood can be well supplied with THEM. – Joan Aiken[17]

> Anyone who writes down to children is simply wasting his time.... Some writers deliberately avoid using words they think the child doesn't know. This emasculates the prose, and, I suspect, bores the reader. Children are game for anything. They love words that give them a hard time, provided they are in a context that absorbs their attention. – E. B. White[18]

In fact, children's books are rapidly recognizable by just this kind of distinctive language; and E. B. White's view that 'some writers deliberately avoid using words they think a child doesn't know' is nearer the truth.

In educational terms there remains the paradox that it is the 'context that absorbs attention'; the language is merely the carrier, and foregrounding gives way to 'automatization', but automatization within a restricted register. As Janice Dohm observes of the work of Enid Blyton: 'There is no denying that it makes easy reading: the reader need use no intelligence or vocabulary, can even skip whole sentences and passages without losing his way, and simply sits back and watches the film unroll.'[19]

This feeling that limitation of language is not only unnecessary but stultifying to the child has been supported by educationalists, who nevertheless accord storytelling rather small importance in language acquisition. Developmental psycholinguists contribute valuable evidence as to the process of language acquisition, such as the fact that syntax acquisition comes much earlier than is commonly supposed.[20] Educationalists generally concur. David Holbrook has lamented the use of outdated texts and concepts in schools, as well as the fact that literary appreciation (and hence, to some extent, linguistic sensitivity) is restricted by the examination system.[21] John Holt, in his *How Children Learn*, suggests that children are voracious random collectors of data, and that educational systems tend to train them out of this.[22] James Britton, in *Language and Learning*, asserts that children need a wide range of language contacts, and he gives evidence that in their own writing they 'try others' voices'.[23] And Connie and Harold Rosen's *Language of Primary School Children* posits that while children accept limitations, these are not necessarily good for them.[24]

In storytelling, then, there is little logic in restricting any element. None the less, the element of conditioning makes for circularity. Geoffrey Summerfield notes that:

In animating the imagination, literature is vital and indispensable. ... It is potentially the most educative aspect of our work... It is a notorious but ill-acknowledged fact that, as we grow older, our language tends to become tired and jaded, more approximate and generalised, less intimately responsive to experience, less individual, less vivid. The signs we wish to make conform more and more to a set pattern, become rational and mechanical; so our idioms become more conventional and stereotyped.... Too often we impose our wearied neutralised language on our pupils; if we are not careful, we begin to expunge from our pupils' usage anything that is vivid, startling, incisive, edgy, adventurous, or vulgar.[25]

Style and 'Register'

The most obvious result of presuppositions about language is the presence of oral discourse markers such as 'Once upon a time', 'Now, this story is all about', 'Are you sitting comfortably? Then I'll begin', 'lived happily ever after', 'well', 'and then', 'of course', 'naturally', 'right', 'after that', and so on. Obviously there is nothing deleterious *per se* in such usages: the danger is that the author/narrator is so clearly in control of the storytelling, so obviously present and dominant and more knowledgeable than the implied audience, that the interaction cannot seem to be between peers; for simplification and familiarity slip into patronizing, and not only in language.

Surface language takes over and controls thought. Hence restricted language, if it leads to cliché and register-formation, too often, and possibly inevitably, leads to the expression of simple and simplistic ideas. An extreme example will make the point, and also suggest that critics may be led to look at results rather than causes. In a typical Enid Blyton short story, a child saves a neighbour's Christmas tree from disaster and receives the appropriate reward:

> Well, think of that! Janey could hardly believe her ears! She took the mother's hand and they ran across the road. In a few minutes Janey's mother had heard all about how Janey had saved the Christmas tree from falling onto the tea-table, and Janey was putting on her pink party frock and brushing her hair in the greatest excitement!
>
> Robin stood and watched. How he wished he had been as kind as Janey! If only he had run across with her and saved the tree, perhaps he would have been asked too. But he had been jealous and sulky – and that never brings treats and surprises, as kindness does!
>
> Janey went to the party, and oh, what a fine one it was! All the children were told how Janey had saved the party and they thought she was wonderful.
>
> And what do you think Janey had off the Christmas tree? Guess! She had the beautiful fairy doll off the very top, because everyone said she ought to have the nicest present of all. Wasn't she lucky? But she did deserve that doll, didn't she?'[26]

The difficulty here rests in the immediate response to the materialistic morality, complete with sly instructions on safety that read slightly oddly ('she took the mother's hand') and the uncomfortable relationship of the parable to reality. This distracts attention from the poverty of the language. The strong period/class tone is more obvious than the high cliché level which expresses it. The rather excessive and simplistic reward/retribution pattern disguises the almost unrelieved register lexis and the transferred storyteller mode which is used for preaching, rather than to establish a peer-contract. Whereas the sub-oral approach *can* find strength in simplicity, here there is little more than 'negative' predictability. The patterns of language do not allow for any ambiguities within the author-reader contract. The text may become an 'ironic object' to the skilled reader, but it is at least probable that at early developmental stages a child will take the text to be characteristic of the capabilities and potentialities of text *per se*, regardless of the validity of the social views expressed.

Janice Dohm has identified the major features of this type of text:

> The adult reader becomes increasingly conscious (and the child reader presumably increasingly aware) of the repetition, inconsistencies, tricks and triviality. The listener is perpetually asked questions, exclamation marks pepper the pages, and the tone is too often that of a superior adult exaggerating horror at some nursery vices, or an arch adult pretending to believe in fairies.... Fairyland, that country of infinite possibilities, is usually reduced to a mere miniature surburbia.[27]

Hence the 'critical' response tends to be to the material and its implications, rather than to the lexis – although this must be partly due to the lack of agreement on, or evidence for, the role of literature and written language in language acquisition. This situation is gradually changing, however, as the processes of reading are absorbed into, and contribute to, a coherent theory of literary transmission of the book to the child.

The blend of cliché, spoken idiom, and simplification have typified writing for children since the early nineteenth century, and writers unconsciously follow these patterns. What is not so obvious is that this occurs in books with good reputations. One might expect to find it in re-tellings of stories, where there is a strong influence of traditions and Victorian translations. For example:

> A soldier came marching along the high road – left, right! left, right! He had his knapsack on his back and a sword by his side,

for he had been to the wars and was now returning home. On the
road he met an old witch and a horrid-looking creature she was.

'Good evening, soldier,' she said. 'What a bright sword and
what a large knapsack you have, my fine fellow! You're a proper
soldier. So I'll tell you how you could have as much money as you
want.'

'Thanks, old witch,' cried the soldier.[28]

This kind of re-telling does not have to have this kind of language, as Fiona French's version of Snow White, *Snow White in
New York*[29] or the work of Alan Garner in collecting and re-
casting English folktales shows.[30]

What is also often overlooked is that books which have acquired a high reputation because of their subject-matter may still
be selling their audiences short. Language is a remarkably accurate betrayer of less-than-thoughtful writing.

Take, for example, C. S. Lewis's *The Lion, the Witch, and the
Wardrobe*. This book, a strong seller (and occasionally a bestseller) for over 40 years, has a high reputation as a moral tale. But
consider this passage. How many phrases are 'recycled' – that is
belong to the thoughts of others? I have italicized those that give
me pause.

> *And so* Lucy *found herself walking through the wood arm in arm*
> with this *strange creature* as if *they had known one another all
> their lives. They had not gone far before they came to a place*
> where *the ground became rough* and *there were rocks all about* and
> *little* hills up and *little* hills down. *At the bottom of* one small
> valley, Mr Tumnus turned suddenly aside *as if he were going to
> walk straight into* an unusually large rock, but *at the last moment
> Lucy found* he was leading her into the entrance of a cave. *As soon
> as they were inside she found herself blinking in the light of a wood
> fire.*[31]

Of course, some of my decisions may be – and indeed are –
arbitrary. But to analyse a text in this way provides a fairly
objective yardstick, one that does not involve literary snobbery.
An author who lets his heroine 'find' herself three times in a
hundred words or whose adjectival imagination goes no further
than 'strange' or 'little', whose fires are 'wood', whose ground is

'rough', and whose heroine can only 'blink' is hardly stretching himself or his readers. This all sits rather uncomfortably with some of the high allegory that many critics have detected in the book. Lewis has a very high reputation; but this sort of examination should give us pause. What we are seeing is also an example of the covert 'control' of the audience so common in children's books.

Stylistics and Control

It is commonly assumed that control (or attempted control) by an author of the reader through the text is efficiently exercised by modifying (that is, restricting) content, vocabulary, plot-type, and so on. I would like to suggest that, simply because such modifications *are* obvious, they are not as significant in their potential effect as the stylistic features that convey them. Furthermore, stylistic features may well reveal convert attitudes in the author, in that the syntagmatic structures of language can be a remarkably accurate reflection of the paradigms they express – that is, style can reflect not only 'conscious' choices, but also unconscious prejudices.

As we have seen, the fact that readers 'know' when they are reading a children's book rests on both lexis and a characteristic stance or mode of narration. Together, these constitute a 'register' which may expose a sub-text that is actually anti-child. As Eagleton has pointed out,

> All literary works contain ... sub-texts, and there is a sense in which they may be spoken of as the 'unconscious' of the work itself. The work's insights, as with all writings, are deeply related to its blindnesses: what it does not say, and *how* it does not say it, may be as important as what it articulates; what seems absent, marginal or ambivalent about it may provide a central clue to its meaning.[32]

Indifferent writing, working on the assumption that children cannot distinguish one kind of writing from another (and that they should not), demonstrates a patronizing attitude, and suggests that, too often, adult readers of children's books are themselves unable or unwilling to make fundamental distinctions. As a result, the primary audience is not given the opportunity to compare what is original with what is unoriginal, what is unfamiliar with what is familiar, what is challenging with what is merely confirming, or, perhaps, what is 'fresh' with what is 'stale'. (If this seems to be unjustifiably judgemental, let me point out that the first item in each of these pairs is the declared preference of most writers of and about children's books; it also represents the most efficient means of information transfer, and perhaps another working definition of 'literature'). The residual storyteller tends to direct responses, telling rather than showing,[33] and in the absence of a narrator we have seen that various stylistic devices may be substituted.

In the case of the narration of 'speech' and 'thought', a reasonably sophisticated stylistic apparatus has been developed for distinguishing the strength of the narrational intervention. Thought and speech presentation has been described in a variety of terminologies, of varying degrees of subtlety.[34] Very broadly, a distinction is made between 'tagged', 'free', 'direct', and 'indirect' representation. 'Tagged' refers to speech or thought presented in inverted commas, usually with a 'tag' (or reporting clause, or inquit) – for example, 'she said'. 'Free' representation does not have a tag. The distinction between 'direct' and 'indirect' is the traditional one between 'showing' and 'telling'; Chatman's example is 'I have to go', as opposed to 'She said she had to go.' Of course, there are may instances where tagging is by implication or where the narrational summary is so abstract that it effectively puts itself into another category, what Leech and Short call the 'narrative report of speech acts',[35] or it becomes 'free indirect discourse'. This mode 'gives the impression of combining direct discourse with indirect discourse', and includes 'not only the copresence of two voices but also that of the narrator's voice and a character's preverbal perception or feeling'.[36] Fowler calls this 'mind-style', 'any distinctive linguistic presentation of an individual mental self'.[37] The more sophisticated the readership is assumed to be, the more easily the transition can be made away from control and towards free direct or free indirect thought.

There are further interesting gradations within these broad

categories of 'speech' and 'thought', when the boundaries between perception and feeling and between thought and expression
are blurred.[38] Leech and Short posit a cline from the mode in
which the narrator seems, instrusively, to be in total control,
termed 'narrative report of speech acts', through stages of progressively decreasing control designated 'indirect tagged speech',
'indirect free speech', and 'direct tagged speech', to the point at
which which control seems to have been relinquished, with
'direct free speech'.[39] They also suggest that 'the norm, or baseline for the presentation of thought is indirect tagged, whereas the
norm for speech is direct tagged'.[40] Both these norms represent
acceptable illusions. Whereas we are used to perceiving speech
verbatim, 'a direct perception of someone else's thought is not
possible'.[41] Thus 'indirect free thought' occupies the middle
ground between showing and telling, while 'direct tagged thought'
is the most artificial form, that most governed by the reductive
narrative voice.

Let us take two examples, from different ends of what is conventionally regarded as the 'quality' spectrum. The first is from a
mass-market, syndicate-produced, formula novel for adolescents
called *The Invisible Intruder*.

'By the way, an octopus is pretty lucky – it has three hearts.'
'O-oh,' said Bess. 'What does it do with them all?'
    Mr Prizer chuckled. 'I suppose they provide a better circulatory
system to get the blood to all the eight legs.'
    As the man paused, Bab remarked that an octopus exudes an
inky smoke-screen when it is confronted by an enemy.
    'The moray eel is the natural enemy of the octopus.'
    Bab asked Mr Prizer if she might see the rest of his collection of
shells.
    'It's not unpacked yet. But I've got some beauties.'
    The elderly man did not sit down again and the visitors took
this as an indication that the interview was at an end. They all
thanked him for his interesting talk, but Nancy and Ned noticed
that he did not invite them to return. They mentioned this to the
others as the group trudged up the hill to the road.[42]

The fact that this is the most elementary kind of formula writing
is marked by the lexis ('chuckled', 'trudged') and by the obvious

insertion of 'improving information' with its appropriate forms. More important, they implied audience is 'marked' by the strong control of dialogue presentation. Of the nine speech-acts, only two are presented directly (both, interestingly enough, spoken by the adult); of the rest, one is tagged ('said Bess'), while the following two are tagged by implication. The remaining four are either reported indirectly ('Bab asked'; 'Bab remarked') or absorbed into the narrative as summary ('They all thanked him'; 'They mentioned this'). This mode of reporting seems to imply that the audience will *need* to have things explained and will need to have deductions made on its behalf. This may seem to be helpful for developing readers, but, in fact, it defines them reductively, and limits their involvement. This may be convenient for an author who has nothing to say, but many educationalists would see this as deleterious from an educational point of view, and probably from a literary point of view as well.

At the other extreme is dialogue in which the authorial voice is absent, or appears to have relinquished control. (There is a paradox here, too, in the relationship between writer and oral storyteller. The written 'tag' has to substitute for the change in voice-tone or colour which may distinguish speakers. These tags draw attention to the artificiality of the written medium; but to dispense with them may increase our awareness of that artificiality through the effort required to assign roles.) While it is not possible to make any correlation between open versus closed texts and the amount of tagging, because texts which imitate other media (such as those deriving from television scripts or using the ready-made characterization of television and film) have similar characteristics to 'open', 'text-contained' pieces, texts with a predominance of 'free' elements generally make more demands on the reader.

The potential effect of judicious control of dialogue can be seen in the next example. In a key scene from Alan Garner's *Red Shift*, Jan is sunbathing in her bikini, and her boyfriend Tom is finding the situation very frustrating (especially as he has recently discovered that Jan has been sleeping with someone else):

'Listen to me,' said Jan. 'Being together: OK? That's what I mean. That's what's new, important. The silences. OK? The bikini was a mistake: but only because I didn't understand. Don't cane ignorance. Please. I love you.'

'Understand what?'

'Please Tom.'

'Understand that intelligence isn't the same as finesse? ... You're tearing me. You're tearing me. Bikini!'

'I'm trying to be honest! I don't understand! It's my fault. I love you. I love you like nothing else.'

'Bikini!'

'I love you.'

'Bikini!'

'It's hurting you too much,' said Jan. 'I'll get rid of it.'

'Have you caught up?' said Jan.

'Don't.'

'I only want to know.'[43]

Red Shift is only arbitrarily on the 'juvenile' lists (which in itself says something about the rhetoric which controls the production of children's literature), and it demonstrates the dependence upon 'open' reading and reader-deduction which is a mark of the *scriptible* text. These two facts may not be unconnected. Neil Philip has pointed out the subtlety of Garner's technique, and part of this may well be due to the restricted tagging. 'What is interesting about this technique is how much it enables Garner to communicate without ever expressing it in words. The whole of Tom and Jan's sexual relationship, for instance, is contained in pauses between sentences. It is quite clear, but it is neither described nor mentioned.'[44] In fact, Garner brackets the implied sexual act with the two tagged speech items ('said Jan'), a positive use of the device, as compared with the arbitrary (although perhaps unconsciously revealing) use of a far wider range of devices by the author(s) of *The Invisible Intruder*.

The choice of mode, then, can make a considerable difference (at least in theory) to the perceived status of the narrative. As Chatman observes, the use of 'indirect forms in the narratives implies a shade more intervention by a narrator, since we cannot be sure that the words in his report clauses are precisely those spoken by the quoted speaker.'[45] Conversely, 'free' dialogue entails 'more inference than other kinds of narrative. To a greater degree than normal, the reader is required to interpret the illocu-

tionary force of the sentences that are spoken by the characters
... to infer what they "mean" in context ... to supply, meta-
textually, the correct verb tag.'[46]

Of course, we are dealing only in possibilities, and there is no
statistical method for proving that one form is more common
than another in any particular kind of text, or of judging affect.
None the less, Leech and Short's ideas are highly suggestive. Are
children's novels more prone to tagging? Can the process be revers-
ed? If we perceive control of speech and thought presentation,
do we deduce that we are reading a children's book? Our experiment in Chapter 1 suggests that this is so.

An example from the 'second golden age' of British children's
books (conventionally taken as the period 1950–1970) may make
the point. It seems to me that this aspect of style clearly identifies
both the period and the implied audience for *When Marnie Was
There*.

> Anna smiled. 'Yes, you were painting on the marsh.' She would
> have liked to add that she had remembered her ever since as if they
> had been friends, but felt this would be too extravagant.
>   The Lindsays were delighted and amazed, wanting to know how
> and when the two could possibly have met. And why hadn't they
> been there, they demanded. Miss Gill told them. It was the last
> time she had come down to Barnham for a few day's sketching.[47]

Even the projected thought is heavily tagged ('She would have
liked to add') and placed within authorial control by the omission
of 'she' in 'but felt this would be too extravagant'. The point here
is that once an author employs indirect reporting, summary
words ('delighted', 'amazed') and graphic tags ('demanded') replace in the first instance a deduction by the reader and in the
second the purely functional (and hence more or less invisible)
tag. For this reason, the text may seem to peer-readers to be
simplistic and, possibly, patronizing.

In children's literature we might expect to find a relatively high
proportion of dialogue ('"And what is the use of a book",
thought Alice, "without pictures or conversation?"') and of highly organized dialogue at that; and where 'thought' items occur,
we might expect to find tagging and indirect presentation (and,

possibly, direct tagged thought, as this is clearly the simplest mode). In addition, authors whose status is ambiguous – in terms of whether they are writing for children or adults – may show significant differences in these stylistic patterns. (Of course, individual style may run counter to these overall generalizations, as in the case of Garner. Malcolm Bradbury's 'middle' style, for example in *The History Man* (1977) and *Rates of Exchange* (1984) is much given to relentless tagging which deliberately emphasizes – or over-emphasizes – the overbearing narrative voice.)[48]

Impressionistic sampling suggests that children's books are likely to have twice as many indirect tagged thought items as adult texts. Both direct tagged thought and (to a lesser degree) direct free thought items are also far more common in children's texts. Unfortunately for those who would claim that similar evaluative standards can be applied to both children's and adult's texts, tagging tends to be more common in 'popular' than 'serious' adult novels (with, of course, individual variations).

There may well be a correlation between the perceived status of a writer and the extent to which these generic tendencies are resisted. For example, we have seen that the impression that may have been gained from *When Marnie Was There* was one of strong control by a residual storyteller. In Alan Garner's *The Stone Book* (1976) the reported perceptions tend to paraphrase the consciousness of the central character, and the status of many of the sentences is somewhere between direct free thought, narrative report of speech, and free indirect discourse. Consider the opening:

> A bottle of cold tea; bread and half onion. That was Father's baggin. Mary emptied her apron of stones from the field and wrapped the baggin in a cloth.
> The hottest part of the day was on. Mother lay in bed under the rafters and the thatch, where the sun could only send blue light. She had picked stones in the field until she was too tired and had to rest.[49]

The revealing words are the unqualified 'Father's' and 'Mother', as opposed to 'her father's' or 'Mary's mother'. Hence 'Mary' in the third sentence retrospectively qualifies 'Father', and, in effect, implies a tag to the first sentence, which is then seen as a thought emanating from Mary, rather than an observation by the narrator. The same applies in the second paragraph, although the comparative remoteness from the controlling noun 'Mary' may suggest a certain ambivalence of status of some of the sentences. The success of *The Stone Book Quartet*, both critical and popular, points up the fallacy of prescription in this area.

Stylistics tends to prove what it sets out to prove, because it follows its 'hunches' with analytic equipment designed for, or adapted to, each hunch. As Stanley Fish points out, 'Formal patterns are themselves the products of interpretation and therefore there is no such thing as a formal pattern, at least in the sense necessary for the practice of stylistics (as an absolute science), that is, no pattern that one can observe before interpretation is hazarded and which therefore can be used to prefer one interpretation to another.[50]

Consequently, the most rewarding applications of stylistic analysis will be those that confirm or refute a perception which itself has a socio-political origin. In the case of children's literature, a field without a canon, such perceptions, confirmations, and refutations have a much more direct influence on the development of the discourse than in most discoursal areas.

A controlled narrative decreases the possibilities of interaction, and, ultimately, proscribes thought. By reducing the distance between teller and tale, it makes the narrative contract more specific; when this is placed in tension with the authoritarian mode of the implied narrator, then that contract becomes a very fragile one. This is especially the case when the implied emotional capacity of the audience (signalled by the content–items and the structure of the text) is perceived to be at variance with that of the controlling mode. What may then be perceived is an inappropriate simplification, an intrusive violation of the narrative contract. (This may account for why so many 'teenage', 'problem' novels appear to be unsatisfactory to the adult reader – and, conversely, why so many 'children's books' seem to be unsatisfactory to children.)

The cliché, the 'standard phrase', may well be an automatic identifier of children's literature because it tends to occur where summaries are demanded; and summaries are demanded by the choice of level of control, which in turn is based upon assumptions about what the readership is and what it should be allowed to be. The guiding voice of the storyteller has itself become an ominous cliché in a narrative relationship, a device which overtly encourages freedom while covertly suppressing it. Didacticism (in the sense of deliberate indoctrination or specific pedantry) is far from dead in modern children's literature, and it may be that because it is ineffective when it is obvious, it tends to disguise itself in modes of telling and controlling.

The wide acceptance of restrictive texts not only limits what readers think about, but also their ability to think at all. Neglect of this problem is part of a general neglect of children's literature by socio- and psycholinguistics, and it reflects the immense influence that unsophisticated practitioners have on the production of children's literature. Most readers can feel superior to material written for children, and therefore they feel more free to prescribe.

Thus the stylistic demonstration of how certain modes of thought and writing may operate in relation to children's literature suggests links between hidden and/or unconscious rhetorical strategies and the way in which they surface in language use. But this is linked to ideology: children's books are commonly seen as 'innocent'; yet, because of the part they play in education, their linguistic characteristics have direct significance.

Stylistics, then, can expose a rather troublesome area in the relationship between children and adults in children's books. It can also be used, very fruitfully, as a quick check on the *originality* of any given text. I would claim no more than that originality, or freshness, is something which potentially opens the mind, and that it can be detected in single sentences. As an experiment, open any text at random and select sentences. That is, rather than judge a book by its cover, judge it by its chromosomes!

But style is only, in a sense, the surface of the book. The second element is the structure, the narrative.

7

Narrative

Yes – oh dear yes – the novel tells a story. That is the highest factor common to all novels, and I wish that it were not so, that it could be something different – melody, or perception of truth, not this low atavistic form. For the more we look at the story ... the less we shall find to admire.

E. M. Forster, *Aspects of the Novel*

Narrative and the Reader

Children's books centre on narrative; in a sense they are *about* narrative. But, until very recently, narrative was the poor relation of criticism. Children's literature has suffered from this association, being seen as inferior, merely a thing of 'sheer narrative lust', as C. S. Lewis put it.[1]

Yet, equally, one major trunk of critical theory has its roots in Propp's work on the folktale.[2] Theories of developmental stages of literary response are strikingly similar to the way in which we come to understand criticism,[3] and even the history of the novel itself, which moves away from the 'embedded' storyteller to the classic realist text of the nineteenth century and from 'chained' narratives to complex interwoven narratives, parallels the developing relationship of the child-reader with texts.

Similarly, most experimental fiction tends to replace the narrative of *resolution* with the plot of *revelation*. As Chatman puts it, the 'strong sense of temporal order is more significant in *resolved* plots rather than *revealed* plots'.[4] As we have seen, children's books tend to favour the plot of resolution.

This has a political axis, of course. As Rose points out, any scheme which tries to equate development levels with appropriate texts carries with it an ideological freight:

> Increasingly, the terms of 'capacity', 'competence' and 'behavioural repertory' are used to refer to the way the child acquires the ability to identify with narrative. The acquisition of fictional competence is laid out according to stages which echo, in their idea of an assured progression (leaps, sequences, primitive narrative, unfocussed and focussed chains, narrative proper [from Applebee, after Vygotsky]) that march into rationality which dominates one particular conception of the development of the child.[5]

However, the last twenty years have shown that Wellek and Warren (see p. 52 above) need not have worried about the criticism of narrative, at least in point of quantity. The mushrooming of narrative theory reflects, rather belatedly, the primacy of narrative fiction in the lives of 'real' readers. Narrative has both ancient roots and deep psychological and cultural wellsprings; at the same time, it is the most commonly read literary form. Unfortunately, much narrative theory has tended to descriptive, classifying processes which are not always enlightening. Virtuoso performances such as Wayne Booth's pioneering *The Rhetoric of Fiction*[6] are the exception; leaden 'naming of parts' exercises such as Shlomith Rimmon-Kenan's *Narrative Fiction: contemporary poetics*[7] are more the norm. At its worst, narrative theory only rehearses the obvious, and leads to spectacularly pretentious non-statements such as this one by the narratologist Mieke Bal, quoted (unfortunately with approbation) by Jonathan Culler: 'The events [of a novel] have temporal relationships with each other. Each one is either anterior to, simultaneous with, or posterior to every other event.'[8]

That narrative theory should come to this seems to me to be a pity, because it is an obvious area for the child-centred and book-centred critics of children's literature to meet (and we are still in need of such meeting-places). Why narrative appeals, how the storyteller tells her or his story, what keeps us turning the page, how we recognize what is important for the narrative (what we *need* to know as opposed to what is *nice* to know), must be the concern of theoretician and practitioner alike.

Seymour Chatman suggests that narrative theory is an enabling, descriptive discipline, rather like a larger-scale stylistics: 'Narrative theory has no critical axe to grind. Its objective is the establishment of minimal narrative constitutive features.'[9] Recently 'Discourse Stylistics' has become an established branch of the discipline.[10]

Yet, as I have suggested, narrative theory is really rather disappointing from a practical point of view. Propp's identification of elements of the folktale may have very specialist applications for comprehension of the tales and a very broad set of implications for our understanding of new texts. But to analyse the use of the thirty-one functions in a text does not provide us with a similar level of edification. Genette's distinction between *histoire*, *narration*, and *text*, which highlights the fact that a story is an abstraction which we narrate and then crystallize in text, seems to me far more useful than his detailed classifications of textual features.

In children's literature, much of this elegant and detailed analysis founders on the 'cultural dislocation' between a child's reading of a text and an adult's. Narrative theory cannot escape the problem of audience. Perception/reception controls what the test is seen to be and, consequently, how it is described. As Rimmon-Kenan puts it, 'The reader ... is both an image of a certain competence brought to the text and a structuring of such a competence within the text'; or, a little less pretentiously, 'Users cannot produce or decipher stories without some implicit competence in respect of narrative structure.... This competence is acquired by extensive practice in reading and telling stories.'[11] If this is true, and most of us would feel that it is, it only serves to emphasize the gap between the 'skilled' and the 'unskilled' reader – as well as disguising the fact that such a distinction makes a nonsense of any theory which implies an homogeneous audience.

Adult theoretical concepts of the purpose of plot – indeed, of the novel – run counter to the customary expectations of the children's book. Robert L. Caserio, for example, feels that plot is a 'defamiliarising agent'.[12] We tell stories in order to change, and so the erosion of the ending in the modern novel is in fact a 'retrieval of humanity'.[13] But with children, are we not usually asking them to conform to the text, to make the conventions of fiction *familiar*, rather than placing the book in the world? Does our concept of an 'appropriate' ending derive from what we wish to see, rather than what the child sees?

Similarly, Michael Zeraffa, expressing a view which contrasts with Frank Kermode's that the work of a novelist is 'making sense of our lives', suggests that since Balzac and Dickens, 'the novelist seeks to reveal the essential *dis*order within the individual; he tries, in fact, not to make sense but to make nonsense of our lives'.[14] Thus the best of contemporary fiction aims to break those schemas and conventions of text which children's fiction is committed to teaching: which leaves us with a very interesting conundrum. What is the relationship of learned narrative patterns to normal critical readings?

Most narrative theory automatically assumes peer-reader discriminations – 'literary competence' – and perceptive skills that are nuclear rather than linear, synchronic rather than diachronic. If we take narrative theory to be concerned primarily with 'higher level' units than those of concern to stylistics, then we are immediately confronted with problems of validating any analysis; for, as Jane Tompkins puts it, 'An individual's perceptions and judgements are a function of the assumptions shared by the groups he belongs to.'[15]

Reading Narrative: an Example

To clarify the possible range of alternative readings, or 'misreadings', and to demonstrate what modifications to conventional theory might be appropriate, let us take an example from a 'classic' text, Kenneth Grahame's *The Wind in the Willows*.[16] Although it originated in oral stories for Grahame's son,[17] few oral mannerisms survive in the text, and its 'classic' status tends to be challenged only in terms of large narrative elements such as its divided structure, 'adult' characterizations, and social and sexual implications.

To perceive and codify such elements – indeed, to perceive narrative at all – we have to discriminate discrete *events* which make up the text, and theorists have spent much time considering how these might be distinguished. Such elements (or narrative units, or 'plotemes') can be seen, in Culler's words, as 'culturally marked significant actions. . . . What the reader is looking for in a plot is a passage from one state to another – passage to which he can assign thematic value. . . . The analyst's task is not simply to develop a metalanguage for the description of plots, but to bring to the surface and make explicit the metalanguage within the reader himself.'[18]

The problem, of course, is *whose* culture? And will the meta-languages be mutually comprehensible? Consider the opening of Chapter 12 of *The Wind in the Willows*, 'The Return of Ulysses', in terms of how its 'events', or narrative units, might be described.

When it began to grow dark, the Rat, with an air of excitement and mystery, summoned them back into the parlour, stood each of them up alongside of his little heap, and proceeded to dress them up for the coming expedition. He was very earnest and thorough-going about it, and the affair took quite a long time. First, there was a belt to go round each animal, and then a sword to be stuck into each belt, and then a cutlass on the other side to balance it. Then a pair of pistols, a policeman's truncheon, several sets of handcuffs, some bandages and sticking-plaster, and a flask and a sandwich-case. The Badger laughed good-humouredly and said, 'All right, Ratty! It amuses you and it doesn't hurt me. I'm going to do all I've got with this here stick.' But the Rat only said, '*Please*, Badger! You know I shouldn't like you to blame me afterwards and say I had forgotten *anything*!'

When all was quite ready, the Badger took a dark lantern in one paw, grasped his great stick with the other, and said, 'Now then, follow me! Mole first, 'cos I'm very pleased with him; Rat next; Toad last. And look here Toady! Don't you chatter so much as usual, or you'll be sent back, as sure as fate!'

The Toad was so anxious not to be left out that he took up the inferior position assigned to him without a murmur, and the animals set off. The Badger led them along by the river for a little way, and then suddenly swung himself over the edge into a hole in the river bank, a little above the water. The Mole and the Rat followed silently, swinging themselves successfully into the hole as they had seen the Badger do; but when it came to Toad's turn, of course he managed to slip and fall into the water with a loud splash and a squeal of alarm. He was hauled out by his friends, rubbed and wrung out hastily, comforted, and set on his legs; but the Badger was seriously angry, and told him that the very next time he made a fool of himself he would most certainly be left behind.

So at last they were in the secret passage, and the cutting-out expedition had really begun![19]

The simplest view is that units are marked grammatica.y: 'When it began to grow dark ...', 'When all was quite ready ...', 'when it came to Toad's turn ...', or are indicated by summary: 'Rat ... proceeded to dress them up', 'the animals set off', 'So at last they were in the secret passage'. But, as Michael Stubbs has demonstrated, summary and paraphrase (which are evidence of the mode of comprehension, as well as of comprehension itself) are essentially a matter of semantic concepts.[20] It is not simply a question of grammar; and although grammar may indicate authorial judgements, what is perceived as significant could be categorized in various other ways. For example, units could be discriminated by settings – in Rat's parlour, on the river bank, at the tunnel entrance, in the tunnel – or by actions – dressing up, walking, swinging, Toad falling, drying, talking – or by the successive foci on characters – Rat, all the characters, Badger, Toad, Badger, Mole and Rat, Toad, all the characters, Badger. At one extreme there might be a close paraphrase – summoning, dressing, Badger talking to Rat, and so on – and at the other, the whole extract might be seen as a macro-unit of the complete novel – 'The cutting-out expedition began'. In terms of the progress of the story, we might classify the elements as preparation, advance of action, delay, summary. Thematically, they might be aggression, assertion, travel, success, failure, reunification. In terms of character, they might be, successively, Rat's reliability, Badger's bluffness, Mole's quiet efficiency, and Toad's incompetence.

Any of these, and many others, are possible; but, I would argue, not all are equally *likely*. (This can be a revealing game for adults. What I have found is that if they are asked to read such an extract and, ten minutes later, to say what happened, the differences can be remarkable. For example, many do not mention Toad's fall at all; some concentrate on Badger's leadership; some mention only the weapons, others only the sandwich-boxes.) If this section of the text is taken as (or presented as) part of an unreflective 'action' plot, then the broadest divisions, centring upon nodes of particularly 'striking' action might be made. Thus, Toad's slip might be seen as the central significant event, because, first, it is the most violent action; second, it reinforces an apparently dominant character; third, it fulfils a prediction about Toad's character; and fourth, it is deviant, and thus threatening, in the story context. As we shall see, psychological evidence suggests that this may be an appropriate form of narrative unit; certainly it should not be assumed that the child's reading will be, *ipso facto*, the crudest. If *The Wind in the Willows* is read as a series of moves to and from the security of home, then the shape and nature of the units would shift. Equally, if the stratification of relationships is seen as the important element, regardless of just how the characters are seen (for example, Badger as father-figure, Rat as brother-figure, Toad as child rebel, Mole as conformist child), then the organizational nodes might be small segments of speech-acts.

If narrative theory is to concern itself with matters of discrimination or to subscribe to the basic concepts of 'histoire-récit-narration' or Culler's 'autonomous level of plot structure', we must become aware of the multiplicity of ways of describing the story's realization – not merely the *level* of abstraction, but the *type* of abstraction involved. To do this may mean escaping from systems which are adult readings of children's behaviour, those which speak so confidently of 'appropriate' story-shapes.[21]

This kind of reading may also give us some insight into individual texts, and help us to speculate on what child- and adult-readers are reacting *to*.

The Wind in the Willows has been seen by many critics to be divided between, if not fractured by, action and reflection; between Toad's adolescent (or childish or manic or socially irresponsible) adventures and the more lyrical, static experiences of 'Dulce Domum', 'The Piper at the Gates of Dawn', and 'Wayfarers All'. The division has been confirmed, perhaps, by A. A. Milne's skilful stage adaptation, which brings Toad to the centre and virtually eliminates Grahame's *fin-de-siécle* mysticism on the grounds that it is untheatrical.[22]

Certainly, the 'reflective' chapters can be read as having considerable structural similarity: few characters, few scenes, few 'incidents' (although this last is, as we shall see, more arguable), and firm 'closures', in that they all end in sleep or stasis – peace at Mole End, peace on the river, Rat writing poetry. These chapters punctuate the much more varied, densely packed chapters devoted to Toad's adventures ('Mr Toad', 'Toad's Adventures', and 'The Further Adventures of Toad'), not at points of closure, but at nadirs – Toad in the dungeon, Toad lost and asleep in a hollow tree. Such a reading seems to support the view that two distinct audiences are implied by the book.[23]

However, the remaining chapters featuring Toad, 'The Open Road' and the two final chapters, 'Like Summer Tempests Came his Tears' and 'The Return of Ulysses', are hybrids. They have few scenes, but many 'incidents', and such unity as exists is provided by the characters of Mole and Rat. After all, Toad is only an incidental character, seen through the eyes of Mole, at first; in the first chapter he appears only in passing, and by the end of the book Mole has a central role and Badger the last word.

In a sense, then, at least part of the book may be seen as Mole's *Bildungsroman*, as he moves from his suburban villa to acceptance as a hardened campaigner, and/or from outsider to insider, from child to adult, from lower class to middle class. (Badger, clearly of the old squirearchy, is symbolically, and romantically, drawn to Mole by their mutual work-ethic, symbolized by the similarities between these animals). These potent elements, which form a very fluid book-long series of interrelationships, are crystallized in the inversions of Chapter 5 ('Dulce Domum'), when Rat is benevolently in charge of Mole, and Chapter 9 ('Wayfarers All'), when Mole takes charge of Rat; of Chapter 2 ('The Open Road'), in which Toad dominates Mole, and Chapter 12 ('The Return of Ulysses'), where Mole quietly patronizes Toad.

Structurally or operatively, then, the first five chapters of *The Wind in the Willows* might be read as a unit, pivoting, classically, on Mole's lonely nadir in the Wild Wood in the middle of Chapter 3 and beginning and ending at Mole's home. Mole, of course, has grown, but home remains for him a reference point. Indeed, his final speculations in 'Dulce Domum' could almost be taken from a textbook on the psychology of children's literature:

'the upper world was all too strong, it called to him still, even down there, and he knew he must return to the larger stage. But it was good to think that he had this to come back to, this place which was all his own, these things which were so glad to see him again, and which could always be counted upon for the same simple welcome.'[24] If there are two texts in *The Wind in the Willows*, they are sequential, rather than interleaved: Mole's serious study once resolved, we can move on to Toad's more farcical one.

To explain the lasting appeal of *The Wind in the Willows*, a sceptic might be inclined to suggest that it has become, like, say *Robinson Crusoe* or the protean *Peter Pan*, a cultural myth in its own right: it is simply passed down the family/cultural establishment. On the other hand, the theme of outsider/insider, which seems to emanate poignantly from Grahame's own circumstances, is very strong in children's books generally; Kipling, for example, uses it extensively in *Puck of Pook's Hill*.[25] Equally, the theme of a hierarchy of childhood is used by Milne in the 'Pooh' books, where there is also animism as well as farce. But underlying all these is the shape of the narrative.

Looking at patterns of closure in psychological terms, we might note the progression in Mole's story from chapters which have a strong, secure ending (the first, which ends with Mole in bed at Rat's house; the second, ending with Mole among the society on the river bank) to those with less resolution, such as the third, in which, although they reach the safety of Badger's house, Mole and Rat are still away from home, and the fourth, where Mole is on his way home from the Wild Wood 'eagerly anticipating the moment when he would be at home again'.[26] These endings might be said to symbolize Mole's growing maturity; the circles, within the larger circles of the five-chapter unit, do not need to be completed.

The assumption that circularity is an appropriate narrative pattern for a given audience and that texts can usefully be described in these terms suggests that a book like *The Wind in the Willows*, for all that it apparently requires a skilled readership, might appeal and satisfy in ways not necessarily accounted for by conventional readings. The obvious difficulty is that I have based all these descriptions on my own, 'adult', British, middle-class, white, male perception of a story grammar, assuming that an 'event' (for example, 'Mole and Rat Go To Mole End') is an unarguable fact of the text, with boundaries that can be more or less agreed. How can we escape this solecism? Perhaps by considering associative semantic fields as providing the cohesive feature of children's literature, each field activated by significant single stimuli.[27] The danger – or perhaps the excitement of this – is its very variability.

The Shape of the Story

What may be more significant than what the story is about may be the way in which it is shaped. It is a truism that in early developmental stages, children prefer stories with an element of 'closure' – that is, where there is a 'sense of an ending'. More than this, they prefer that something is resolved, that normality is restored, that security is emphasized.

Classic children's books conform to this pattern; both the 'Alice' books end where they began, with a restoration of normality; Peter Rabbit ends, as he began, at the burrow, with the same characters around him; *Swallows and Amazons* begins and ends at the field outside the lakeland farm called Holly Howe, with the same character; *Rosie's Walk* is completely circular, from the title-page illustration, which maps the book, onwards. Rosie is untouched by her experience.[28] This strong resolution is clearly very important to certain kinds of texts, for it provides comfort. It can also be found in 'low level' adult texts, where reassurance is required. However disturbing the content of the book, resolution will at least temper the effects – although the Cragos' studies (as well as common memory) suggest that this may be simplistic.[29] Tolkien's *The Hobbit* has the subtitle 'or, there and back again'.[30] Interestingly, Tolkien's language becomes less that of the transferred storyteller the further Bilbo goes from home. In many books, notably in the late Victorian period, the whole book is about the restoration of normality; Nesbit's *The Wouldbegoods* and especially *The Railway Children* are examples.[31] In fact, *The Railway Children* is frequently seen as the lesser book because the closure is so strong, the return of the father being stressed to the point of oversentimentality.

The novel suitable for older children may have the form of the *bildungsroman*, the growth-novel. In this, the characters, while they may return home, do not satisfy all the elements of closure. They have changed; and the book is in some way ambivalent. Nor is the form of the book any indicator. Take, for example, the notorious example of David McKee's *Not Now, Bernard*.[32] One summary of this apparently innocuous text might be as follows: Bernard, a small boy, tries to tell his parents that there is a monster in the garden; he is ignored, and duly eaten ('every bit') by the monster in the garden. The monster takes over Bernard's place in the household, eats Bernard's supper, and is sent to bed ('"But I'm a monster," said the Monster'). The bedroom light is switched off, and the book ends. One set of readers may see this as a variation on the classic *The Shrinking of Treehorn*,[33] the superior child versus insensitive adults. Another may see it as a simple equation from an adult point of view – Bernard = Monster. I have heard it said that some children are worried about the lack of resolution (although not about Bernard being eaten); but it could be that visual elements which extend between successive 'openings' (or 'spreads') of the physical text may provide 'units' quite at odds with grammatically or 'significantly' marked units. Indeed, my summary of the text, which only communicates something to my reader because, as Stanley Fish has it, 'a way of thinking, a form of life, shares us'[34] is almost certainly, as far as the primary audience is concerned, a 'misreading', which makes the 'wrong' units, and traces less than central events.

Another classic, Russell Hoban and Quentin Blake's *How Tom Beat Captain Najork and his Hired Sportsmen*,[35] may seem to appeal simply because of Tom's triumph over his iron-hatted Aunt Fidget Wonkham-Strong and the fairly fearsome Captain Najork. Yet the shape of the narrative reinforces this triumph from a different perspective. Instead of resolving the plot within the context of home, Tom escapes.

> Tom took his boat and pedalled to the next town down the river. There he advertised in the newspaper for a new aunt. When he found one that he liked, he told her, 'No greasy bloaters, no

mutton and no cabbage-and-potato sog.... Those are my conditions.'

The new aunt's name was Bundlejoy Cosysweet. She had a floppy hat with flowers on it. She had long, long hair.

'That sounds fine to me,' she said. 'We'll have a go.'

The contrast in aunts, Hoban's neat parallels (the flowers drooped where Aunt Fidget walked), and Tom's complete triumph imply an ending – but then there is a coda. On the last page, we look back at the happily married aunt and captain and the unfortunate hired sportsmen (who have taken over Tom's tasks). Tom has not simply escaped; he has, in a sense, left the central scene, left the book. And the triumph is as much as anything a visual one; for throughout, the pictures stress the innate superiority of the child's world, and, significantly, circumvent the adult, literate mechanism, the verbal text.

It is sometimes complained that at the end of *The Secret Garden* Mary does not appear, her position being usurped by the Colin.[36] Yet I think it can be persuasively argued that we have here an ambivalent text. Mary has grown sufficiently that she does not need to be there; Colin's story produces the closure, while hers is the *Bildungsroman*.

Some texts are marginal in this regard. *The Shrinking of Treehorn* has Treehorn restored to his proper size, but ends with Treehorn turning green. The ambiguity of this ending is defused, of course, by the experience we already have of how the Treehorn household works.

This difference in shape is the difference between *Tom Sawyer* and *Huckleberry Finn*, for example. One of the many reasons why it can be argued that the latter is not really for children at all is that Huck Finn himself is never truly associated with security; the coda, which involves Tom Sawyer's cruel game with Jim, is false to the shape as well as the tone of the book.

And this is the third shape of the novel, one that might for convenience be called the 'adult', or mature, mode. In such books, endings are ambiguous; we see part of the texture of life. An adult book tends to resolve some part of a problem, but to leave much else open: take the ending, for example, of *Sons and Lovers* or *The French Lieutenant's Woman*. (This last provides an

interesting contrast to the highly 'resolved' endings of the 'great'
Victorian novels, generally considered the lesser the more resolved they are.)

The classic example of an ambiguous text is Tolkien's *The Lord
of the Rings*, a book with ambiguous subject-matter, fantasy but
with links to the great legends, a subject-matter which, as many
critics have implied, is worthy of attention only by children, since
adults can supposedly deal with less symbolic transformations of
truths. Equally, Tolkien's language, by turns (especially at the
outset) that of the pseudo-storyteller, the high-flown archaic
romance, and the fast-paced thriller, seems to be unstable.

I would argue that the plot-shape underlies all this, just as there
is an underlying thematic structure beneath the plot. There is,
first of all, the closed, childlike, comforting structure of the story
of Sam Gamgee, the most childlike of the child-shaped Hobbits.
He is untouched by his experiences. He doesn't understand all of
what is going on; he has certainly developed in a simple way; and
the last lines of the book, provide total closure: 'And he went on,
and there was yellow light, and fire within; and the evening meal
was ready, and he was expected. And Rose drew him in, and set
him in his chair, and put little Elanor upon his lap.

'He drew a deep breath. "Well, I'm back," he said.'[37]

The second thread is a *Bildungsroman*: this is Frodo's story.
Tolkien might write in his preface, that 'As for any inner meaning
or "message", it has in the intention of the author none. It is
neither allegorical nor topical' But he shrewdly goes on, 'I cor-
dially dislike allegory ... I much prefer history ... with its
varied applicability to the thought and experience of readers. I
think that many confuse "applicability" with "allegory"; but the
one resides in the freedom of the reader, and the other in the
purposed domination of the author.'[38] Nevertheless, Frodo is
stabbed literally (and perhaps symbolically) by experience, with
something which injures his innocence. He returns, a changed
person, to Hobbiton, to the point of the circle at which he began;
but then, before the book ends, he leaves for the Grey Havens,
the world of the unknown, the grown-ups, outside the book.

The third strand is, of course, the adult one. The characters
move, as it were, on a straight line through the book; they enter
with a history, and leave to die. These characters are represented

by the elves and the men. It is hardly surprising that these three strands give rise to some conflict in the book.

This multiplicity of forms can also occur in the course of a sequence of books. The series book, so characteristic of writing for children, often portrays a compounding of events: there is, commonly, little back-reference; the characters are established, in so far as they *are* established, by immediate action. In Arthur Ransome's *Swallows and Amazons* sequence, the shapes of the books reflect the development of the characters. As we have seen, *Swallows and Amazons* is circular. Its immediate sequel, *Swallowdale*, moves on a little way; it begins with the children already sailing on the lake, and ends with Susan raking the sticks of the fire together on the island and saying, ' "Isn't it a blessing to get home?" '[39] From then on, displacement is a common feature of the series (with the exception of the early romance *Peter Duck*, which is circular).[40] *Winter Holiday* ends away from home, although there are adults around to provide the security;[41] *Pigeon Post* ends with a climax, high on the fells.[42] The most striking example of closure is *We Didn't Mean to Go to Sea*,[43] while the sequence ends in *Great Northern*, with the children (now adult, although not portrayed as such) left in the Minches, without even a verbal coda.[44]

The ambiguity of many modern teenage 'problem' novels lies in just this clash between form and content. The situations are serious, but the resolutions trivial. ·

The ideal proving ground for these ideas is the one area of children's literature which has developed away from the 'classic realist' text towards the genuinely discontinuous and interactive. This is the picture book, a text in which the verbal and the visual components both carry the narrative rather than merely illustrating or clarifying each other. (This will be debated at greater length in Chapter 10.) Far from being merely the province of the beginner reader, it has become so complex as to require a new metalanguage to describe it. Despite the problem of visual conventions, the encounter with the experimental picture book seems, for the child, to be akin to an oral encounter, and the book is likely to be read far more fluidly and flexibly than the purely verbal text. And so, as satisfying and seductive as the perception of circularity may be, the picture book may under-

mine its validity. The basic narrative 'shape' of a picture book
may well remain recognizably of the three types we have looked
at; but the reading is even less controllable, since there are more
elements. In a sense, these texts can be read in three dimensions:
linear, temporal, and spatial.

Cohesion and Genre: How do we Understand Narrative?

If the individual perception of story-shapes and narrative units is
problematic, the 'technical' cues that narratives provide as to how
they work – intra-textual codes, allusions, and generic constraints
– depend more clearly on the 'text-skills' of the reader. These
cues are the most important, as well as the most neglected of
literary features. They allow us to

- understand suspense
- recognize 'cohesion' in a text
- assign importance to events
- decide what kind of book we are dealing with
- decide what kind of attention it requires of us

We need to see what is significant, both to ourselves and to the
structure of the text, before we know what we are supposed to be
understanding. It is this ability, more than any purely 'acquired'
knowledge, that marks off the developing reader from the 'mature' reader. How soon do we realize what is important for us to
remember when we read a story? As Frank Smith has noted,

> When the reader starts to decode the text, authorial intentions are
> replaced by expectations. . . . The problem is, unless we know
> what we are supposed to take notice of, we cannot organize our
> expectations – and, as a result, we cannot *predict*. . . . The more
> unconventional the reader finds the text, the less the reader is
> likely to have any relevant expectations about it and the less
> understandable it is likely to be.[45]

Unskilled readers must find *all* texts 'unconventional'. Similarly,
Roger Fowler has noted that in continuous text, 'sentences are

linked together by an intricate system of cohesive ties',[46] and hence, unless we understand these, we will be in some danger of not understanding the text.

Likewise, even the re-reader of a text knows 'what to expect' in a much more subtle way than merely knowing 'who did it'; and the pleasure of re-reading may well come from the perception of things in a text which we could not attend to the first time because we were feeling our way along. In some sense, then, experienced readers are *always* re-reading; they are reading variations on themes and structures they have absorbed before, something that cannot be true of the child-reader.

Halliday and Hasan list 157 types of cohesion in 4 categories, but the key categories are references that are anaphoric – that is, backward-looking, whether they be immediate, mediated, or remote, and those that are cataphoric – that is, forward-looking.[47] Basically, prediction and fulfilment occur at all levels of books, from *Rosie's Walk* to *Northanger Abbey*. We 'know' from experience that in certain books the hero is never killed, or that he wins the heroine, or unmasks the murderer. We know too, before we even begin to read, that the heroine is unlikely to be eaten by a fox. But even if we are sure of the generic category of the book, there can still be doubts. As Eric Rabkin says: 'Reading can be seen as a continuous process of forming hypotheses, reinforcing them, developing them, modifying them, and sometimes replacing them by others or dropping them altogether.... [R]ejected hypotheses may continue exercising some influence....'[48] Let us see how this works in practice, by taking a longer extract from a book we have already considered, *Isaac Campion*:

1 Now then, I was twelve, rising thirteen, when our Daniel got killed. Aye ... it was a long time ago. I'm talking about a time of day eighty-three years back. Eighty-three years. It's a time of day that's past your imagining. I'm talking about a
5 different world. You might as well say it was a different planet, the world I was born in.
No radios. No televisions. No World Wars. They'd not even built the *Titanic*, let alone sunk her. This is it, you see. This is what I'm trying to tell you. When you look back over
10 all those years, you think that what happened was bound to happen. You can't imagine that it could happen any different.

They've got this notion about the past, about history – they
forget that folks lived in it – well, we didn't know what was
going to happen. It's the same for the young ones, they think
15 they're going to live for ever. And good luck to them, I say!
Good luck to the young ones, let them live to ninety-six! Let
them live to a hundred!

Eighty-three years back ... It's me that should be dead and
buried in my grave, but I'm telling you, I can remember the
20 day Dan died just as clear as *that*!

There's me and Joe Flitch, the clogger's son, crouched in
this muddy little drainage ditch behind the schoolhouse on
Chapel Street. Stinker Beck, we called it. Crouched in the
smelly yellow mud, we were, where no one could see us.

25 'Go on,' I says to Joe. 'Go on. I dare thee! Eat one!' I was
egging him on, you see.

We'd been let out of the school-room after a day of chant-
ing times-tables and 'Twelve inches make a foot. Three feet
make a yard ...' with tall Miss Whitehead glaring down at us
30 like the eye of God! She was a terror was that schoolmistress.
We were all scared of her.

But she couldn't see us in the ditch. 'Go on!' I says to Joe.
Just to see if he would. Poor Mazey Joe starts sniggling and
snorting. He wasn't right in the head. He wasn't the full
35 shilling. We were always daring him to do daft things. The
pleasure wasn't in teasing him. Teasing Joe Flitch was too
easy. No. I'd say the pleasure was in thinking up something
crackers enough for him to do so's you could tell tales about
it afterwards.

40 'Ah can, Isaac! Ah can eat 'em!' he kept spluttering. 'Ah
swallered a clog nail once.'

I can just see him – crouched in the mud like a fledgling
that's fallen out of a nest, with his tuft of hair bristling on his
head, and his thin elbows and knees poking out of his clothes.
45 Spitting and giggling.

I was watching the water dripping between his fingers, and
these two tadpoles were wriggling and stranded in his hand.
Well, I didn't really believe that even Mazey Joe Flitch was
daft enough to eat a tadpole.
50 I should have known better.

'Oh, put 'em back,' I says. It was giving me knee-ache,
squatting there, and anyway I wanted to go and meet our

Daniel outside *The Bear and Staff*. So I was just going to
reach out and knock the tadpoles off his hand and back into
55 the ditch, when Joe suddenly stops giggling, claps his hand to
his mouth and sucks![49]

As we proceed through the text, let us ask ourselves: How
many questions are unanswered? What do we know is significant? How long does it take to get satisfaction? And does the
length of time indicate the kind of attention we are expected to
pay to any fact?

By the end of the first paragraph, probably before, the apparent
ramblings of the narrator will be perceived as establishing his
character, rather than advancing the story. Thus the skilled reader
will make a judgement about the *kind of attention* the text is
seeking. It is clear, even now, that the book is of a certain kind.
There is reflection as well as action, although we might be wondering whether this is just temporary. But again, we understand
this only from experience of storytelling and texts.

The major 'hook' is clearly 'got killed' (lines 1–2). This is the
most deviant information, and it will be merely a matter of time
before our curiosity is, presumably, satisfied. But we have to wait
until line 20 (where the reference changes to the more passive 'died')
for a reinforcement, and then until line 53 before Dan is next
mentioned. The main narrative is continually interrupted. (A
good way of seeing this is to draw circles around the linking
references, with connecting lines. This demonstrates the 'embed-
ding' and the possible hierarchy of importance. Once that is
done, we can make local inferences about possible responses by
individuals.)

The intervening material is not merely setting up the philo-
sophic basis of the story; it is announcing the way in which the
book requires to be read. Thus the second and third paragraphs
not only tell us something about the character of Isaac Campion,
but also tell us that there are not going to be any quick thrills.
This reflects not the kind of reader intended (as the level of
reference does) but the way the reader is to read.

The third paragraph establishes further the kind of narrative,
but there is also an anaphoric reference to the age. This is actually

non-functional, unlike the next paragraph, which looks back to the first paragraph, bringing us back on track, as it were, with both the years and the reference to the murder, and moving us on to the very day that it happened, judging from the shift into the present tense in the next line.

The reader might well assume at this point that we are going to get to the business in hand, but there are other mysteries. What has Joe Flitch got to do with it? And, more pressingly, what are they doing in the ditch (to ram this home, there is 'where no one could see us')?

The next two lines (25–6) raise the question, several times, of what he is being egged on to do. To eat, but what? We are now into a sub-routine, as it were. Joe is going to eat something. How important is it? Moreover, its importance will probably be signalled by how long we have to wait for the answer. As we might expect by now, there is another digression, which the author would seem to be asking us to take as either intrinsically interesting (non-metric counting, establishing the age of the characters, more scenery) or perhaps as vital. But because it is embedded in a 'sub-routine', experienced readers will not expect it to turn out to be significant. Miss Whitehead, we know, is not important. (It is interesting that any doubt about who Miss Whitehead is, is instantly dispelled (line 30). But enough of that: we are brought abruptly back to what they are doing in the ditch (line 32). But it takes three more paragraphs of teasing cataphoria before we reach the tadpoles. This seems to me to be coming perilously close to bathos, especially as the narrator seems to tire of this mountain of anticipation, and confirms the tadpole thesis seven lines before the event.

It may seem that it has taken too long to return to Daniel and the inn and, presumably, the rest of the plot. But that is only half the story. Understanding how a text is constructed and balancing the expected against the unexpected are important parts of the reading process. Knowing what or what is not permissible in a certain *genre* controls our reactions to a text; perceiving what we should remember depends on the conventions built into any type of text. How much patience we have with unanswered questions, hints, and implications in a story or, alternatively, how soon we become bored has as much to do with our understanding of how texts work as with what is said in them.

In his book *Narrative Suspense*, Eric S. Rabkin points out how pervasive allusion is, and incidentally shows how its exclusion necessarily changes the nature of the reading experience for the developing reader:

> [L]egitimate allusion is clearly a potent force for creating the reality of fiction. Unlike words themselves, however, associations with proper names are useful only to an audience whose education includes those proper names. The idea of audience education holds not only for the common association with names, but to the less common allusion present in quotations, stylistic parody, and so forth. Since so much of what has been called allusion does *not* contribute to our reading it is fortunate that we read an allusion into our experience of a work *only when something else in the work* indicates that is a proper procedure.[50]

So the assigning of importance to items in the text depends upon recognizing signals elsewhere in the text, and these in turn depend upon experience.

Rabkin's point is that the skilled reader skips past irrelevant associations with a word, thereby limiting the range of possible interpretations. He goes on: 'These associations do not creat ambiguity because, *excluded by the context*, they do not enter our reading.'[51]

As Frank Kermode put it in his remarkable book *The Genesis of Secrecy*: 'What is the interpreter to make of secrecy considered as a property of all narratve, provided it is suitably attended to? Outsiders see but do not perceive. Insiders read and perceive, but always in a different sense. We glimpse secrecy through the meshes of a text.'[52] Children are outsiders to the adult secrets of text; and to understand why they are outsiders, we must attend not only to what they know, but also to just how the meshes of a text are made.

8

Politics, Ideology, and Children's Literature

[The king] said, he knew no reason, why those who entertain opinions prejudicial to the public should be obliged to change, or should not be obliged to conceal them. And as it was tyranny in any government to require the first, so it was weakness not to enforce the second: for, a man may be allowed to keep poisons in his closet, but not to vend them about as cordials.

Jonathan Swift, *Gulliver's Travels*

Literature itself isn't elitist. People make it so by a deliberate act of deprivation.

Aidan Chambers, *Booktalk*

Literary theories are not to be upbraided for being political, but for being on the whole covertly or unconsciously so − for the blindness with which they offer as a supposedly 'technical', 'self-evident', 'scientific', or 'universal' truth doctrines which ... relate to and reinforce the particular interests of particular groups of people at particular times.

Terry Eagleton, *Literary Theory*

A few years ago, in a very important interview, Alan Garner, who has some claim to be *the* major twentieth-century English author for children, discussed censorship with another major author, Aidan Chambers. In his book *Tom Fobble's Day*, part of *The Stone Book Quartet*, Garner has a child character sledging at night. Garner said: 'I was told that it was dangerous. I said that I was relating an activity, not promoting it. The argument got nowhere.'

Garner saw in this not a movement to protect the child, but 'a
movement to turn books for children into tracts for authority.
It's producing a literature, or an industry, that has little to do
with life, but offers instead an inorganic, cosmetic cleanliness that
one sees in totalitarian cultural enterprise.... Such dead-end
mediocrity will attract the conformist and the derivative.'[1] This
sets up a simple opposition between the writer who feels free to
write anything he or she likes and a society which feels that
children need to be protected from such authors, an opposition
which has been with us since the beginning of children's books.
As the redoubtable Mrs Trimmer wrote in 1802: 'books ... have
... been written, expressly designed to sow the seeds of infide-
lity, and of every bad principle, in the minds of the rising
generation.'[2]

But the problem is far more complex than that, of course. To
begin with, we might well accuse Garner of being at best naïve,
and at worst disingenuous. The description of sledging was not
simply *told* to his audience: it was *in a book*, and to many readers
a book has such authority that the simple fact of something being
included in one gives it the stamp of respectability. There is a
mystique about *the book* that is increasing as competition from
other media increases. So we are not absolved from facing the
questions: just who is, or should be, responsible for what goes
into children's books? What part should writers, or parents, or,
indeed, society as a whole play?

In the USA, the 'private' censorship of books read by children
is far wider than in Britain. The idea of parents burning books of
which they disapprove (barring the recent Salman Rushdie case)
or of taking a publisher to court because a book includes a man
washing up in an apron has not really caught on here; nor, I
think, is it likely to do so. Possibly it is because of the way in
which book-purchasing for schools and libraries is organized
here; there are few centres of power to which moral pressure can
be applied, unlike the situation in the USA, where centralized
book-buying for schools in some states (a declining practice)
means that self-appointed censors can influence state policy, and
thus dictate editorial policy of major publishers. Possibly it is the
attitude of the law; the British Obscene Publications Act, since its
baptism by fire with the *Lady Chatterley* case in 1959, has made

the British judiciary as keenly aware of the problem of plur ity
of meaning as any deconstructionist critic could wish. We are a
comparatively small and increasingly culturally mixed society,
and censorship is as likely to work in terms of positive as negative
discrimination, to promote anti-sexism or anti-ageism, as well as
anti-racism.

But we are left with questions such as whether the depravity
and horror in the world have anything to do with childhood. But
that depends on what you mean by these things. One view is that
of Patrick Shannon in his article 'Unconscious censorship of
social and political ideas in children's books' (one of a long-
running series in *Children's Literature Association Quarterly*).
Shannon notes that 'the consensus sets the the "natural" boundaries for appropriate social thought and action',[3] which means
that we all unconsciously accept some kind of societal norms for
behaviour. This means that overt and specific censorship is a good
deal more complex than it may seem at first sight. As Shannon
continues, 'If we do not teach our children to question our basic
beliefs ... we become locked in an ahistorical illusion that the
past, present, and future was, is, and will remain just as we
understand our current existence.'[4] But that, of course, is not a
truth, only an opinion.

One should not under-estimate the complexity of the influences on the author, from foreign-rights buyer to specific
child. The writer begins with a freight of societal restraints, and
tends to accept other implicit and explicit restraints as well.

Robert Leeson, in his impassioned account of politics and
children's books, *Reading and Righting*, feels that the two 'com-
peting' elements, writer and society, are reconcilable:

> This *is* a special literature. Its writers have special status in home
> and school, free to influence without direct responsibility for
> upbringing and care. This should not engender irresponsibility –
> on the contrary. It is very much a matter of respect, on the one
> hand for the fears and concerns of those who bring up and educate
> children, and on the other for the creative freedom of those whose
> lives are spent writing for them. I have generally found, in discus-
> sion with parents or teachers, including those critical of or hostile
> to my work, that these respects are mutual. [5]

But it is a complex and personal matter, for it is clear that the *important* meanings of texts – that is, emotive, associative, and connotative meanings – are personal, and override the mundane, functional, and denotative meanings. What this means, I am afraid, is that the liberal's point of view is not merely justified, it becomes the rationalist point of view. You can, to paraphrase an old saying, take a child to a book, but you can't make him or her think the same way as you do. All the psychological and educational evidence points to children having a different culture from adults and to them understanding and making associations in different ways. Of course, this is one of those obvious things that nobody ever admits. We like to think – because it is easier that way – that books have a direct, linear effect on others. No doubt they have an effect – but quite what it is, is unknowable. This is why 'bibliotherapy' has always been such a dubious exercise: who can say what a book does to him or herself, let alone to children. Even those who, like Nicholas Tucker, take a Piagetian view of developmental psychology, readily admit that 'literary responses are always going to be impossible to describe in anything like their essential variety'.[6] So not only are the 'visible' targets of sex, race, and class quite likely to be invisible to the child-reader – unless we *want* them to be visible – but the apparently innocent, desirable text may carry corrupting meanings which we cannot see.

The main problem, however, is one of attitude: is children's literature an innocent profession?

Identifying the Illusions

When I was invited to speak recently at a Conference on Ideology and Children's Literature, the responses of my friends and colleagues were predictable enough. The non-experts lamented that it was a pity that politics had to find its way into the innocent world of children's books; the academics congratulated me (somewhat ironically, perhaps) that children's book criticism had at last caught up with the rest of the critical establishment; and some children's book people said that it was sad that children's books had succumbed to the intellectually 'trendy'.

Such opinions underlie – and undermine – a lot of what is said about children's books, and stem from two related attitudes, which I would like to explore in this chapter. The first is that anyone can be a children's book expert; the second, that we are all on the side of the angels.

They are both aspects of a very dangerous cast of mind. The first leads to the anti-intellectualism noted in Chapters 1 and 2: the idea – or non-idea – that thought is not really appropriate to children's books. This then paves the way for the second idea: the idea that children's books, like children, are innocent, and that the motives of writers and critics and parents and the rest of us are ideologically neutral. As a result, we fail to see not only that we cannot be apolitical, but also that much of the ideology in and around children's books is hidden – and indeed often masquerades as the opposite of what it really is.

Both attitudes were certainly present at the conference I attended. Despite the fact that the subject of the conference was 'ideology', few people seemed to be concerned with abstract ideological issues, and few would have been interested in, say, the Marxist critic Terry Eagleton's view that 'the history of modern literary theory is part of the political and ideological history of our epoch'[7] – that you *cannot* abstract politics from talking about books. They were certainly aware, as Bob Dixon noted in his controversial *Catching Them Young* in 1977, that 'Anyone interested in how ideas – political ideas in the broadest and most important sense – are fostered and grow up in a society cannot afford to neglect what children read', even though they may not have agreed with his corollary, that 'Much of the material in children's books is anti-social, if not anti-human, and is more likely to stunt and warp young people than help them grow.'[8]

The conference discussed sexism and racism in children's books, as well as whether certain books were left-wing or right-wing, middle class or working class, or belonged to the developed world or the Third World. It took the norm of the conferees as a base. Two things became clear as the conference progressed. The first was that many people just assumed that children's books are *easy*. This is what I would call the 'literalist fallacy'. It rests on a faith in the power of the surface of the text and a belief in the similarity of children's and adults' perceptions which goes against basic common sense. What was lacking was any suspicion that what may appear to us as to be an obvious feature of the text may not be at all obvious to the child; or that what truly communicates in a text is the hidden attitude, the underlying philosophy and stance, the status accorded to books generally. It is not the specific act of violence that corrupts, but the acceptance of violence as a norm. It is not 'bad' language *per se* which is potent – in any case, few of us dare to print the language of the playground – but its appearance *in print*, which gives it a different force. As Jill Paton Walsh has said, 'what is in print still has a special quality in many people's eyes. What is in a book is somehow official, sanctified'.[9]

The second was the problem of the 'norm'. If we are all on the same side, what has happened to all the huge differences in sex, race, culture, age, class, ideology, and politics which so obviously separate us when we're not talking children's books? Are children's books a magic talisman which purifies and unifies all those who talk about them?

Wherever children's book people get together, it seems to me that these attitudes are usually there, vitiating the discussion. And so it is most interesting to look at these unconscious attitudes as they exist in the *critics* rather than the books. If this seems perverse, I would argue that it is the *critics* who ultimately *make* the books, not children. Children do not have freedom of choice; they may have freedom to choose *from what is there to be chosen*, but that is not the same thing. Critics create the intellectual climate which produces the text.

And I would go further: when a child comes to choose, her or his capacity to choose will have been moulded already by the ideologies of her or his mentors.

To identify major ideologies is a huge task. What I would like to attempt here is the more modest task of seeing if we can reveal some of the processes of double-think which surround writing on children's literature.

'Anyone can be an Expert'

What, then, do criticism and writing *about* children's books tell us about the attitudes and 'blindnesses' of those who control the production and transmission of books for children?

I would like to begin with the 'anyone can be an expert' phenomenon – which of course, is highly irritating to those of us who consider ourselves experts. In *Suitable for Children?* Nicholas Tucker observed that 'children's literature ... is fortunate: it can usually depend upon an initially interested response', but that this response is based on nostalgia, and 'this sort of popular expertise has its limitations'.[10] (It is obviously difficult to make such a judgement without being accused of protecting one's own turf.)

My own view is that for most adults who are not 'readers' (and most aren't), children's books are open territory because there is nothing to be afraid of. Adults who would feel unqualified to express even an opinion about a peer-text feel free to talk about children's books because they do not have the shadow of the schoolteacher's 'right answer' hanging over their heads. Not only can children's books be legitimately read 'below capacity'; they are also things that can be prescribed and censored. They are not part of the mystic Leavisite priesthood's province; they are part of the real world, and can be challenged. They are truly 'popular culture'; and I suspect that for many (perhaps, at an extreme, the local school-board book-burners) they are an opportunity to revenge themselves upon what is essentially an alien, elitist, and *excluding* cultural symbol, the Book. Of course, all this involvement with books is very healthy. Robert Leeson, the radical British writer and storyteller, looks forward to a time when 'do-it-yourself' criticism 'will become the universal practice'[11] and to a thorough democratization of the literary transmission process. But can it be done? Does it lead to anti-intellectualism?

At any conference or gathering of children's book people, the most popular sessions will always be those at which writers or illustrators talk about their work (the personality syndrome), closely followed by those on classroom practice, storytelling, and fairy tales (how to survive as a teacher). The more sparsely populated sessions will be those devoted to analyses of texts, and the most sparsely of all, those featuring critical theory. As I am often one of the lecturers conducting the last of these, I can quite legitimately be accused of bias if I observe that all this looks suspiciously like people reading *around* books rather than *through* them.

However, that objection would also be ideologically based: it would imply allegiance to the twin pillars of criticism, the exclusiveness and decontextualization that I mentioned in the Introduction. Why should readers not 'read around' the text? If there is a good deal of suspicion of the 'academic' among those at the 'sharp end' of teaching and librarianship, there is no doubt that some of it is justified. The mines of canonical literature are becoming exhausted – or, at least, rather unsafe – and children's literature is a rich new vein from which to hew an academic reputation. Consequently, when Leeson observes, 'I see little future for the academic critic making an exhaustive study of *angst* in the writings of William Mayne',[12] he is, however strong his point ideologically, simply wrong. There is a great deal of academic security and status to be made out of Mayne's *angst* or its equivalent.

But we should remember that academia is no guarantee of serious thought, and the fact that some criticism is pretentious or lazy or self-serving should not be used as an excuse for refusing to think. Such a refusal may masquerade, as we have seen, as pragmatism and practicality, as a no-nonsense refusal to countenance interference in the jolly, practical, unproblematic, *innocent* world of children and books.

When Leeson goes on, 'I see an ever expanding future for the librarian, the teacher, the parent, above all, the child as critic,'[13] this may seem to be either common sense or anarchy. Either way, our response – and this is vital – will be an expression of our ideology. There is no such thing here as 'self-evident' truth, just as there is, once we are out of the cradle, no such thing as innocence.

'All on the Side of the Angels'

The novelist Jean Ure was cited in Chapter 2 as an example of a writer suspicious of both academic criticism and 'pretentious literature' for children. As a perpetrator of both, I might well be accused of bias. But I would enter the same plea as everyone else: I am on the side of the angels. Like everyone else, I want the best for the children; and, like everyone else, what that best is, is self-evident.

Aidan Chambers has lucidly described how in the 1970s the pendulum of thought about publishing and teaching children's books in Britain 'swung from an elitist to an equally narrow, populist extreme'.

> The litmus test was no longer the judgement of a particular group of adults from a literary background ... and was quickly shifting to the judgement of groups of adults with other special interests.... These caretakers often made a near-fetish of selecting books according to two criteria: first, whether the book met the demands of their own specialist point of view ... and second, whether on an untutored reading children instantly liked the book.... [S]hould the teacher ever intervene between children and their reading was a seriously asked question?[14]

Chambers does not stress the point, but both of these attitudes have ideological roots; they are not merely matters of conflicting practical interests and methods.

The essence of the problem was summed up by Terry Eagleton in an article entitled 'The subject of English' in *The English Magazine* of Spring 1985. Broadly, his argument was as follows: Humans do not 'produce themselves'. They are produced by society, and in the process are given certain 'modes of subjectivity'; and the mode of subjectivity in our (western) society is one which deceives us into believing that we *do* 'produce ourselves'. 'Literature', which becomes 'a question of the signifier and not the signified' – that is, how we talk about something is more important than what we talk about – and liberal-humanist thought *about* literature (which, of course, creates the literature) are both 'state-certified' casts of mind. The key terms of liberal-humanist criticism – 'sensitivity, responsiveness, sympathy' – and its expected benefit to the reader – of having his or her experience 'enriched, heightened, intensified' – are self-serving. They are an end in themselves; they are not focused (or transitive), nor do they lead anywhere.

Worse than that. These conventional values *seem* to be liberal and unpolitical; they *seem* to see all sides of a question and contribute to human growth and happiness. But in fact, to be unpolitical actually means to uphold the status quo, that is, 'liberal capitalism'. (You may *like* liberal capitalism, but you cannot at the same time claim neutrality.) To borrow Eagleton's example, liberal-humanist criticism encourages us to read, say, *King Lear* as a document concerned with oppression, and to feel strongly about the play, thereby absolving ourselves of the need to *do* anything about *actual* oppression. Abstract empathy is an end in itself.

'The space of modern subjectivity', Eagleton goes on, 'is a prison camp which offers itself as an endlessly open horizon,' and the myopic liberal-humanists patrol this camp, supporting the very oppression that their 'literature' purports to despise. In short, 'any liberal humanist who desires peace, justice, and love is in utter self-contradiction,' because the achievement of those goals would require struggle, identification, action and change, all of which are precluded in liberal-humanist discourse. Hence a new discourse is necessary.

How the group of teachers to whom Eagleton addressed these remarks reacted is, regrettably, not recorded. His is not an attractive argument, for two reasons. First, it suggests that all loving and caring teachers, doing their best to educate and to pass on the best and purest of values, are in fact a bunch of jackbooted fascists; and, second, its very formulation suggests that if you have the temerity to disagree, you prove yourself to be myopic or fascist or both.

We say one thing, then, and actually do its opposite. Many disagreements in the field of children's literature are based on this paradox, but let me take the example of two opposing ideological stances, as expressed by two writers: one an overtly political exponent of storytelling, Robert Leeson,[15] the other a journalist/scholar who is sometimes concerned with children's books,

Humphrey Carpenter.[16] Leeson in his *Reading and Righting*, sets
out to rewrite the history of children's books from a leftist viewpoint and to put forward the political proposition that 'The
future of literature for the young, with fiction at its heart, forms
an important part of our striving for a better life for all.'[17]
Carpenter's book, *Secret Gardens* is more 'academic', and
wonders 'why so many children's classics ... of a particular kind,
should have appeared in England in the space of about sixty
years'.[18]

Are these two books merely occupying different parts of the
landscape of children's book criticism? Or can we detect profound ideological differences between what the two authors say,
as well as in what they don't say? What they are on the surface is
very clear. Carpenter's urbane tone makes him sound as though
he has spent his life in the calm of the Bodleian Library in
Oxford; whereas Leeson's book is rough, passionate to the point
of incoherence at times, and deeply concerned with children in
the schools and on the streets.

But it is what the two writers *don't* say that betrays their
ideologies; and it may come as a surprise to find that, under the
skin, they are in some ways brothers. Their preoccupations are
obviously different. While Carpenter writes that George Mac-
Donald in *The Princess and Curdie* used 'the stuff of folklore to
construct a parable about the Christain universe ... creating an
alternative religious landscape which the child's mind could
explore',[19] Leeson chooses to see that 'In the 1890s and early
1900s, while the "free" child is wrecking the nursery and roaming
the woods, half a million anonymous children went hungry to
school.'[20] Carpenter's book might seem to be 'innocent'; it is not
concerned with politics or ideology; it is just a book about
children's books written by a good British scholar who together
with his wife, also edited the *Oxford Companion to Children's
Literature*. But he is not neutral. For example, in an interesting
moment of 'blindness', he unwittingly supports Leeson's sardonic
view of the 'culturally invisible' majority, those servants and
inferiors who are ignored by middle-class children and authors
alike. Thus, when discussing Richard Jefferies's *Bevis*, Carpenter
notes that 'Bevis finds John the farm-hand, and tries to bribe him
to help drag the raft, but the Bailiff is keeping an eye on John, so

this is no good. At last he persuades the carter's boy to help, with his horse. The raft is brought to the water's edge, and is launched'.[21] He thus silently edits out what happens to the (working-class) carter's boy: '[I]nstantly the carter's lad left a grip on the back of his neck. It was the Bailiff who marched him up the meadow ... Bevis and Mark were too full of the raft even to notice that their assistant had been haled off.'[22]

Even more disturbing is Carpenter's critical – rather than political – sub-text, which makes one wonder about his attitude to his subject-matter. Speaking of Alan Garner's work, which he sees as the end of children's literature, he observes that *The Stone Book* is 'scarcely a work of literature for children', and that it shows that Garner wants to 'write about what matters, to create fiction of integrity and maturity'.[23] Are the two mutually exclusive? Again, the old argument, but not an argument one expects to find embedded in such a book. The apparently 'liberal-humanist', book-centred, respectable writer is revealed, if we 'deconstruct' the text, to betray not only suspiciously right-wing undercurrents, but undercurrents which question his whole respect for his material.

On the surface, Leeson is absolutely against this kind of attitude. Declaiming against what Elaine Moss called the 'adulteration' of children's books, he says: 'the literature which came into existence to give children a more abundant life cannot now decide that it has no more lessons to teach and that when it says children it doesn't mean children'.[24] But when it comes to the ideological status of the children's book, things are different. Moreover, the position in which Leeson finds himself is instructive for all of us, because it reveals a very deep ideological assumption of which we are very often unaware.

Claiming the Book

As an account of the history of children's books, *Reading and Righting* is refreshingly partial and polemical. Leeson is not 'dragging politics into children's books'; he is merely being frank about what he is doing, rather than doing what most critics do – namely, claiming neutrality while policing the liberal-humanist or some other, political camp. Leeson's aim is to widen the book market and to change the book to meet the challenge of other media. Writing must be available to all, so that 'we may now begin more easily to realise the full potential of our minds. . . . The ability not only to read stories but to write them, the essence of the discovery of life's patterns, an active rather than a passive involvement, should be encouraged in every child.'[25] Clearly, this is also on the side of the angels, although it destabilizes the hierarchy of literature by demystifying authorship. Surely we can't *all* be writers – what on earth would people do at conferences?

It is beyond question that a majority of children are excluded from the familiar use of books; but in supporting the book *as book*, Leeson reveals himself to be of the 'old' left, rather than with Eagleton on the 'new' left (and not only because on the cover of his book his name appears as 'Robert' rather than 'Bob'). For Leeson, the answer is not a new discourse, but rather that the masses must appropriate the Book. The Book, so long the preserve of the middle classes, must widen its appeal. '[The] audience may be bookish or unbookish, but it loves a story and will take it from wherever it comes most pleasurably. Why not from the book? To abandon the quest for true universality, which was once held to be the great merit of the book, just when the goal is in sight, is to abandon the future of the book . . . [W]ithout the "unbookish", the book will die.'[26]

This sounds like good sense, and may stem from Leeson's own encounters with the middle classes. His books on working-class life have been attacked frequently for the 'bad language' and 'bad' social attitudes they are supposed to portray. But, as he says, the attacks come only from adults; children tend to complain that his books are unrealistic because they *lack* these elements. His attempt to democratize the novel has been seen by many indignant correspondents (who usually do not prejudice their judgements by actually reading his books) as subversive. It is hard to escape the conclusion that the middle classes see the book as a function of power in society, and wish to preserve it for themselves.

But there is an ideological blindness in Leeson's text also, which, it seems to me, resides in the answer to the question 'Why not from the book?' in the quotation above. For the majority, it is too late for the book. Since its invention, it has always been the prerogative of the few. To write is to have power; to read is to have only the illusion of power. One of the fundamental problems of 'reluctant readers' is not simply that they do not have books or do not know about books, but rather that, to them, the book is of another, alien, powerful culture. And it may well be that the book as book cannot become part of the mass culture. For Leeson to treat the book with the respect he does is to subscribe implicitly to the liberal-humanist argument which he claims to reject. It could be Carpenter speaking, for such faith in the book is very exclusive. As Charles Sarland has pointed out, the status of the Book is something which has been created and fostered by a very elitist group:

> Leavis claimed that literature in general, and the novel in particular, is the central repository and interpreter of value in our society. Now this argument, I have to say, is junk. A huge minority if not a majority of the population reads no fiction, or very little fiction, and yet they seem to have no difficulty in establishing their value systems.[27]

Leeson's overall thesis that the real rupture in our culture has been the loss of the oral tradition, the true interactive involvement of storyteller, story, and audience is interesting, because any debate about it must have ideological roots. Oral storytelling is not merely 'of the people'; it is *different in kind*. As Ong has shown, habits and structures of thought are different in oral cultures;[28] therefore, if we abandon the book, we are in some danger of ghettoizing working-class culture. If, on the other hand, we feel, with Leeson, that the Book should be mobilized in the cause of democracy, then we must be aware that it does different things from the oral story, and may be inimical to oral forms altogether. (To test our own stance, we might consider our reaction to the suggestion that the book has been a blind alley in the development of storying.) Thus it is curious how rarely 'folk tales' are successful when they are written down, as compared (in the same terms) with the story generated for text-forms. They are, anyway, pre-categorized as 'folk' tales, and who are the 'folk'? Always, I suspect, somebody else, and somebody lesser.

In short, Leeson draws our attention to a central ideological dilemma: the status of text itself. However we may purify our political approaches, can we escape the ideological implications of the decision that we *must* make on this issue?

Positive Moves

Of course, it is too easy merely to point out how self-aware we should be or, like many post-structuralists, simply to leave us in a vacuum, deconstructed, with nowhere to go. Fortunately, the positive side of children's literary-critical pragmatism encourages me to pursue the implications of some of the ideological knots we have found, Perhaps the most important of these, as well as the one which provokes a defensive 'blindness', is the question of the text. What status does it have? To whom does it belong? Where does it go from here?

Back in 1974, Susan Dickinson challenged Leeson's position, which was much the same then as now: 'Why does he expect 100 percent of children to be readers of books? A high percentage of adults never open a book. Many people would rather kick a football around ... and these people may be from any class. I think he is in danger of over-emphasising the literary needs of working-class children.'[29]

Now, that last statement can be read in several ways, depending on where you stand socially or politically. Is it merely a neutral truth, that books do not speak to the non-bookish? Or is it a libel on the working class, implying that their needs are inferior and, necessarily, because of the definition of literature, lesser? Or should the working classes be rather pleased that their culture lies elsewhere? To take meaning from that last sentence is itself to make an ideological decision.

Thus, we can see the book either as a great subjugator of the masses or as a great liberator of the human mind. If we take the first view, we can either try to take the book over and use it for ourselves or reject it as being too tainted with middle-class values and attitudes. If we do the first of these, we may play into the ideological hands of the middle classes; for then, it may be said, we are only able to *see* in one way, regardless of any veneer of non-sexist or non-racist content we may apply to the shape of the text. In many ways, then, the answer would seem, logically, to be to reject the book and to claim that a non-book culture is dominant, and must find its own ways of storying and its own ways of articulation. Should there then be an acknowledged cultural apartheid, of book and non-book cultures? Can storying shake off the patterns imposed by print and find itself again? Are the 'new' media the way forward?

On the other hand, many of us will want to hold on to the book as a liberating influence, the repository of freedom and correct thinking – in which case we shall have to reassess just what we are doing with books. Books are now conspicuously a minority pursuit. Other media give our children access to very sophisticated forms of perception and to a very complex range of storytelling techniques. If the words of writers like Jean Ure are anything to go by, the book is deliberately turning its back on this challenge *for ideological reasons*. It is trying to compete on the least important level, that of content, because content *seems* to be the area where, as I said at the outset, we can make clear decisions.

So, if the book is to survive its friends, as well as its enemies, something more than the subject-matter must change, and it is significant that the whole thrust of those who might be called the true frontierspeople of children's *literature* is for innovative *form*. To break the ideological deadlock which either openly tries to use the book as a social weapon (as Jacqueline Rose pointed out, the more absorbing the text, the more potent its potential for indoctrination[30]) or strives to keep the book the same, we must experiment. To change the content, as we have seen, makes no difference ideologically.

But if we want experimental books, where do we find them? Aidan Chambers *Breaktime* and *Now I Know*[31], Ellen Raskin's *The Westing Game*[32], and William Mayne's Australian *Salt River Times*[33] are rarities. In the picture book, there is more freedom, not only because the word is displaced, thereby freeing the text to some extent, both in cultural and in class terms, but also because, as William Moebius puts it, 'the graphic codes ... are interactive, simultaneous, though not always congruous with the codes of the verbal text or of the presented world'.[34] And so much of the most 'liberating' work may well lie in the books of John Burningham (for example, *Granpa*[35]), Janet and Allan Ahlberg (*The Jolly Postman*[36]), Raymond Briggs (*Fungus the Bogeyman*[37]), and David McKee (*I Hate my Teddy Bear*[38]). (Some of the implications of picture books will be discussed in Chapter 10.)

However, it is clear that the shortage of texts which extend the range of the book or its *genuine* (rather than superficial) availability is an ideological, rather than (as might be claimed by publishers) a pragmatic matter.

To write about politics and ideology in children's books may seem to be creating a new hegemony to fill the vacuum left by the demise of the certainties of traditional literary criticism. But if children's books are going to be, as they should be in all but the most repressive ideologies, genuinely mind-expanding (and here, of course, I am revealing something of my own ideology), they must be seen in terms of the world which creates them and the world which surrounds them. The child may be innocent, if innocence and amorality may be equated; but if we, the adults, are to talk usefully about children's literature, we cannot afford the pretence that we are similarly innocent.

We have to accept, then, that, rather like A. A. Milne's Christopher Robin saying his prayers, children's books may look sweet and innocent, but they cannot be – and nor can their critics.

A recent, influential contribution to this debate has been Peter Hollindale's 'Ideology and the children's book', in which he argues that 'in the very period when developments in literary theory have made us newly aware of the omnipresence of ideology in all literature, and the impossibility of confining its occurrence to visible surface features of a text, the study of ideology in children's literature has been increasingly restricted to such surface features by the polarities of the critical debate'.[39] It is also restricted by a lack of consciousness of attitudes to text, politics, and children.

9

Producing Children's Literature

The uniqueness of the production of books for children is very closely linked to ideology and to the market-place, to tradition and genre. Plotting all the societal and literary influences is like describing the shadows on a wall beside a log fire; the outline of the process of burning wood is relatively straightforward in principle, but no two moments of burning are the same. As Machery put it as long ago as 1970:

> In fact, the conditions of its communication are produced at the same time as the book ... so that these conditions are not absolutely given and they have no temporal priority. Readers are made by what makes the book – although it is a question of two different processes – for otherwise, the book, written from some inscrutable impulse, would be the work of its readers, reduced to the function of an illustration.[1]

Because non-peer-readers are involved, we have to take into account not merely the didactic, but many reactions to the didactic. But, as in other literatures, the process is circular: the author makes the text makes the readers makes the response makes the author ad *infinitum*.

In this chapter, I will look at the position of author, publisher, and child in today's publishing climate and whether any specific synchronic analysis is inevitably irrelevant in the context of larger, controlling concepts such as politics, economics, or social psychology. To illustrate this, I will take the case of my fourth novel for older children, *Going Up*,[2] which was considerably re-written on the advice of the publisher, with regard to both technique (narrative mode, structure) and in content. It may be instructive to look at the reasons for the changes and the kinds of changes.

The vast amount of writing by authors of children's books on authorship for children tends to deal with inspiration, technique, and the writer's relationship with the child or with art, but not with the circumstances surrounding the production of the text, which, ultimately, have a decisive effect on the 'poetics', the critical grammar, of children's literature. For example, the recent compilation of material from the Simmons College Center for the Study of Children's Literature, Harrison and Maguire's *Innocence and Experience*, devotes over 300 pages to authorial reflection, and 5 to material on editing and publishing.[3] Much the same balance can be found in other collections.[4]

Consequently, writers tend to produce pious exhortations on what should be, rather than what *is*. An example is Joan Aiken, who writes: 'Words, in themselves, are such a pleasure to children – and even the most deprived childhood can be well supplied with *them*.'[5] There are, of course, many pragmatists such as Geoffrey Trease and Aidan Chambers, and author Wallace Hildick has produced a shrewd guide to the problems and ethics of writing for children (including changes that are thought necessary in going from British to American publishers). Nevertheless, such analyses are necessarily simplistic.[6]

It may seem that there are three elements in bringing a book to a child: the author, the publisher, and the child. The publishers are generally credited (especially by publishers) with having the key role; for it is they who identify the market and often commission, modify, or, more rarely, select texts to satisfy this market. This is not a precise science, of course; the very distinguished publisher of children's books, Julia MacRae, has described the 'pattern of publishing' as 'ever changing, ever fascinating, and always unpredictable'.[7] The author is at one end of the system, the child at the other. Occasionally there is a short-circuit as when an author writes for a specific child; but even then there is generally a great difference between the text produced for the single child and that produced for the general public, *The Wind in the Willows* being a classic example. There is only a superficial resemblance between Grahame's original letters and 'Bertie's Escapade' and the final text.[8]

As we have seen, the overall process of transmission is generally regarded as benevolent, but it can be seen as an exercise in power, which surfaces in textual characteristics, or as an exercise in class-bound pressures.[9] While there is some truth in all these views, the actual process of production and transmission of the children's book is far more complex. There are many elements, of which Figure 1 shows a simplified grouping of the most important and easily identifiable, together with their interrelationships. But, like childhood itself, all these elements continually change.

We can, however, base an outline model of the circular process of transmission and reaction on the three major elements of author, publisher, and child, each with its own group of influences. Authors will be influenced by their own childhood, by the books they have read, by observation of their own families; and they will experience pressures from peer-groups, general cultural codes, and generic controls. Basically, they will start with some idea of the kind of book they wish to write, but not the book itself.

To return to the example of Jean Ure, cited earlier. Her writing is pragmatic; she says: 'I had to cut out two of the girls [in *You Win Some, You Lose Some*] and change the end, because they said it was anti-gay and would bring in hate mail.... I do have a terribly jaundiced view of the world now, but you can't put that into a book for kids.'[10]

To unpack that statement is to see the influence from below of the pressure group upon the publisher impinging on a personal concept of what books should and can be. Of such confluences and conflicts are the poetics of children's literature made.

Before authors begin to write, they make adjustments within the genre in which they are working. Dubrow quotes E. D. Hirsch that 'A genre is less like a game than like a code of behaviour,'[11] and the code of behaviour relating to children's books has structural and stylistic axes based on a far more personally nostalgic and publicly didactic sense of text than that of any other type of book. Just as we read children's books in several ways simultaneously, so the writer, consciously or unconsciously, has to consider the generic, socio-cultural, and didactic implications of writing children's books. We might also add, or distinguish, the influence of landscape and place,[12] both on the personal and on the cultural level.

Before we come to the publisher, there may be an agent (in-

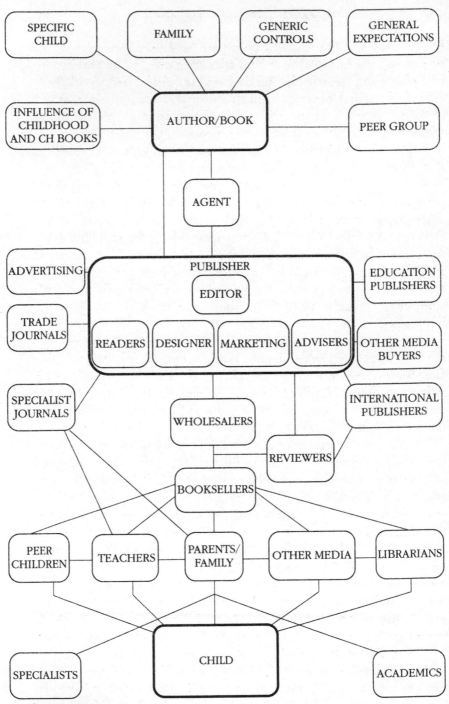

Figure 1   *Links in the transmission process*

dicated on Figure 1 as an optional feature) acting and reacting, lobbying, selling, and influencing the situation. The publisher is not monolithic – especially as, in Britain at least, there has been a rapidly accelerating change from small to big firms. There is no longer (usually) a single autocrat controlling everything; rather, within the publishing house is a team, with internal and external referees. Around them are direct financial, social, and literary influences in the form of buyers for different cultures, who will all have their own demands. (I have not included a separate calegory of 'censors' in Figure 1, because every external referee will in some sense act as a censor.)

Then, between the publisher and the child is another grouping, consisting of wholesalers, booksellers, and all those who must buy books if they are ever to reach the child: parents, teachers, librarians, and so on. What the book is presented as being at this stage also involves reviewers, publicity agents, other media, specialist educators, and bibliotherapists. Tony Bradman observes in his *I Need A Book! The parent's guide to children's books for special situations* that, 'Given the right context, the books which I recommend can be enormously useful in helping both you and your child begin to understand problems and work out ways of dealing with them.'[13] This approach, which is increasingly common, suggests that the reading of books – the generation of meaning – in today's multi-media context is essentially interactional and situational, rather than solitary and inward-looking.

In general, the lines of influence and transmission between the various elements are downward and inwards, although many of the influences go both ways. Thus there are six influences upon the author writing; from there on, the book reaches and influences other groups on its path to the child. (It is not possible to show every possible interaction – such as the simplest, in which the author gives a book directly to a child – which is merely to say that the line between author and publisher is two-way.) Several groups are interactive in a highly complex way, such as those immediately 'above' the child; a book may move from librarian to teacher to parent to peer in any order.

The next stage is to add the reaction, the feedback, which generally proceeds not only upwards, but inwards and outwards. The complexity of Figure 2, which does not show all the possible

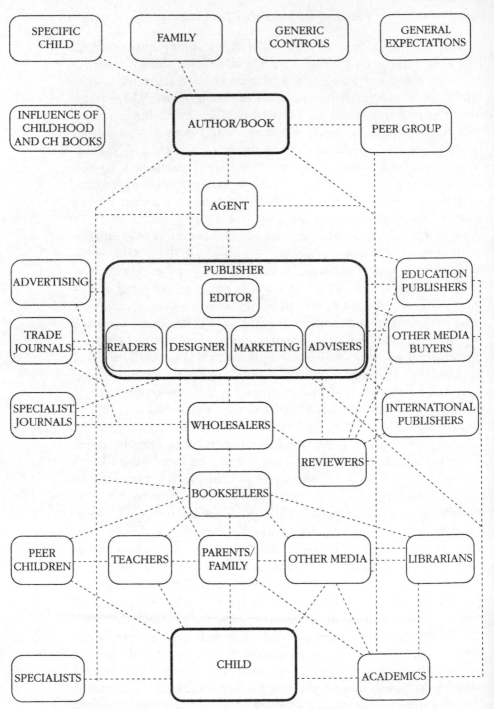

Figure 2 *Feedback in the transmission process*

paths, suggests the pressure that, ultimately, is brought to bear on the author and the publisher. It is hardly surprising that there is a confusion in the minds of buyers as well as producers as to what constitutes, and what should constitute, a children's book.

Writers *about* children's books, who occupy a somewhat ambivalent position at the edges of the flow-charts, have a tendency to identify one or two influences on texts and to elaborate cultural-poetic theories based on those few. Who, for example, determines the *style* of the contemporary children's book? Could it be the international publishers or the educationalists, the two, ironically, most concerned? Who determines the content (if such a concept can be entertained in post-deconstructive days)? Is it the child or the marketing person? In her recent survey, Michele Landsberg observes that librarians have become 'cogs in the consumer machine', and quotes Randall Jarrell that 'professional users of words process their product as if it were baby food and we babies'.[14] But why is this so?

It may well be that none of the items included in the diagrams in fact determines the progress of the children's book. Maybe it is some, as it were, third-dimensional force which controls all these. This could be cultural politics, or it could be sexual-textual politics, or, more likely a dependent of these – economics. In a brilliant survey for *The Signal Approach to Children's Books* in 1980, Elaine Moss reviewed the 1970s in publishing, and pointed out such oddities as the fact that

> Economics dictated that more and more new titles should be published to meet the reduced demand for books generally; the reason for this was the shortage of cash and the desperate need for quick return on investment ... In the brave new world of decisions led by sales forecasts ... the battle between the editor-with-flair and the sales-department-with-figures appears to be shaking some of the edifices of good children's book publishing.[15]

In all this, it may seem that the author is indeed dead, and that the restraints of genre (including style, structure, and content) in terms of what is acceptable in the market-place dominate over the original and the individual. The massive influence of feedback from influential groups not only changes the attitudes of authors directly, but alters general and generic expectations. This may always have been so; but in a world in which the hardback book is fast disappearing and it is extremely difficult for experimental work to be published, it seems likely that societal restraints are overriding the literary norm of growth and experiment. None the less, whatever the macro-influences, they will always be expressed in the micro-systems. Equally, both are capable of subversion.

It is clear that to attempt to chart these influences in detail, while entertaining perhaps, is impossible; while to chart their influence on a single text is, in effect, to write another novel. The only privilege that authors have in describing the process by which their books emerge is that of involvement – which may well equate with bias, if not bitterness (to judge from the amount of historical abuse levelled by authors at publishers). Self-analysis is, in any case, one of the least useful of analytical techniques, for as Chambers said with regard to reading his own books, 'I speak only as one reader among many, whose reading is no more important than any other's.'[16]

However, in pursuit of those influences, literary and, as well as versus, societal, which affect the text-as-printed (rather than as read), it may be useful to record, as objectively as possible, the modifications that may need to be made to a children's book if it is to be published.

Producing Children's Books: A Personal Report

Elaine Moss commented in her *Signal* survey that 'It seems doubtful, in this economic climate, that we shall see many publishers embarking on small select lists with an individual flavour such as Julia MacRae books.'[17] I see it as my immense good fortune to be included on that list, because Julia MacRae represents, the subversion, as it were, of the system that I have outlined in the second section of this chapter, and thus provides an excellent place from which to view that system.

Since 1983 Julia MacRae Books has published four of my novels and two short books for 'younger' readers. *The Maps of Time* (1983), *A Step off the Path* (1985), and *Backtrack* (1986) are all novels designed broadly for fluent, intelligent readers, and centred on children. They are all experimental, designed to confront, rather than confirm, expectations. The first two attempt to do something original with the camping/fantasy genres, the third with the detective story. In all three, I have used a dense, elliptical style, based on three beliefs: first, that the child-reader is capable of highly sophisticated understanding of texts (which is, after all, no more than writers would have us believe, and no more than educators have proved);[18] second, that if the book is to survive in the face of highly sophisticated alternative media, it cannot afford to be simple-minded, but must use all the resources available to it; and third, that the form of the classical-realist novel, for all its dominance, should be challenged.

As I have already said, I have been fortunate in my publisher. Julia MacRae's company has a very high international reputation for both high quality and willingness to experiment,[19] and it is unlikely that three such books would have been published by many other publishers.

As an academic, a writer of both novels for older children and stories for younger children, and the father of four small daughters, I have recently found myself having to confront the issues from several contrasting and, at first sight, conflicting angles, being continually caught between the ideal of freedom ('all censorship is bad') and the ideal of responsibility towards children. It is hardly a new problem. For every worried reader who would stamp out what he or she sees as irreligion or sex or violence in children's books, there have been, both in Britain and the USA, writers who have maintained that children's texts should be mind-expanding and developmental, that they should be 'open' and should confront, not confirm.

Not long ago, my eldest daughter, before I could stop her, volunteered my services as part of National Children's Book Week, and I spent one morning talking to the whole village school, 59 children from age 4 to 11. The experience taught me two important things. First, it led me re-examine the responsibility of the writer (watching faces of children as they listen to a story is a long way from imagining a child on the other side of a word-processor). Second, it made me acutely aware of my role as a parent.

At the school, I read two things to the children (including my eldest daughter). The first was the dummy of a picture book I have been working on, about a group of small children who go for a walk up a small valley and meet cows and chickens and horses and so on. To make the book 'interactive', I asked the children in the school to decide, for example, on the names of the children in the book, what they had in their sandwiches, and what the new calf was called. Second, I read from the proofs of what I thought was a cheerful little story about two girls who get involved in bee-keeping, *Sue and the Honey Machine*.[20] No sex, no drinking or swearing. Yet I found myself cutting and changing and censoring both books – not because the children's response showed incomprehension, but because they understood too well. Should I, for example, let the small children in the picture book go off by themselves without telling their parents where they are going? Should I let them wander among horses (last week my neighbour was bitten by one), or climb walls and fences or walk beside a stream without pointing out that these things could be dangerous? Should I show two young girls doing something so potentially lethal as dealing with bees? More positively, should I have pointed a moral? Or should I have made sure that the group of children in the book included children of different or mixed races, like the group sitting in front of me? All of a sudden, I wasn't so sure that I could do as I pleased.

It has always seemed obvious to me that children are basically cleverer than adults like to think, and can very well tell the difference between fiction and real life, and so children not telling their mother where they are going, encountering unknown horses, or sledging at night are not things that they are likely to suppose are legitimized by fiction.

Watching the children's faces as I read, and edited, and watching the older ones watch me edit, I became aware of what is probably an obvious fundamental truth, albeit one I had evaded for years, that *it is not children I am protecting, but myself*.

And does this also apply to Peter Hunt the author for young adults? I cannot claim that texts do not have an effect, or I would not bother to write them. Texts must contain a message of some kind; no text is neutral. (The same disingenuous arguments revolve around TV violence. If TV does not have an effect, what would be the point of TV advertising, and advertising (generally) declares itself as such?). We cannot object, as Thomas Hardy did when his novels were censored, that the author is not responsible for effects on a few deviant minds. If we create a believable, affective world, which, as in my case, purports to reflect the real world, with a view to presenting this to developing readers who do not have the perspectives to make fully informed judgements, then we have to take responsibility.

With my fourth novel, *Going Up*, my intention was to make use of material which had been 'needing to be written' for some years – which, as we have seen, is a very long way from writing what anyone needs to read or what anyone would be prepared to publish. It is a novel which provides, as setting and theme, an introduction to university life, specifically for the undergraduate going to a university other than Oxford or Cambridge. The vast majority of 'campus' novels published in Britain have either been about Oxbridge or about the teaching staff/faculty at provincial universities. I have taught at provincial universities all my working life, and so I find these novels, from Amis through to Lodge and Bradbury, generally accurate (and, as such, not particularly interesting) renditions of life. My conscious purpose, then, was to confront the genre and to produce an original novel that looked at student life.

I can identify certain basic conscious decisions, such as to aim for non-sexism, humour, and entertainment; but the two most important for our purposes here were, first, to aim for truthfulness – that is, the book should show life as I saw it, and, to the best of my ability, as current undergraduates see it; thus the staff were not going to figure greatly, if at all (I scarcely remember the staff at my first university – other things were far more interesting – and I do not flatter myself that undergraduates I have stood in front of remember me any better) – and, second, to continue my post-modernist/post-structuralist experiments. The audience I envisaged, in general terms, was of intelligent fifteen-year-olds (and onwards) requiring (and deserving) a stimulating style and density of reference. All this attempts to relate to the elements of the first group in Figure 2, although it is almost all in opposition to what I perceived as the norm.

After several years of sporadic writing and many partial drafts, I produced a complete novel of around 75,000 words. But it was turned down. Of course, I reflected (bitterly), Julia MacRae should know what she is talking about. After all, she had taken on my three previous, experimental novels. Now she seemed to be suggesting that I was not maintaining my writing standards. But there was also a problem of content. I had wanted to make *Going Up* a 'realistic' book, a book which would accurately portray what it is really like to go to university today. I did not want to make it an autobiography, largely because I spent most of my first year at university in a state that was a combination of terror and loneliness; so the two main characters are a lot more forceful and confident than I was. But neither did I want to duck the truth, and so, although it is not dwelt upon, there is a description of the loneliness of leaving home, as well as the excitement. I also wanted to pinpoint other key aspects of university life. Looking back, and looking sideways at students today, the most memorable things were (and are) the often terrible accommodation (about 50 percent of students live in university dormitories) and the exploration of what for most students is a new freedom, which, for very many, includes an exploration of sex, and drinking too much. Usually this is fairly harmless; and I suspect – and surveys show – that students are perhaps rather more circumspect in their sexual activities than they were in the 'swinging sixties' when I was an undergraduate. None the less, it would be to give an untruthful picture not to acknowledge that this is what university life is like, whether parents like it or not. Like Garner, I am not promoting these activities, merely reporting them.

So the first draft of the novel had scenes in slum accommodation and scenes involving drunken students. It didn't have any 'sex' scenes, partly because I find them difficult to write, and partly because they wouldn't have been relevant to the story. However, I did not make a conscious decision *not* to include any reference to sex – it is, after all, relevant to young adults – and it was certainly there by implication. Similarly, the book did not contain any reference to drugs (other than alcohol), because in the 21 years that I have been teaching at universities, I have never myself come across drug-taking, and have only heard of two (unsubstantiated) cases (which may be only to say that I have been very lucky).

The difficulty was that, enshrined in a book, the males who

drank too much beer, the girls with loose morals, and the scruffy of both sexes were what stuck in the mind. For me to argue that in fact that *is* what sticks in the mind (rather than the wisdom of the faculty members) was to be, like Garner, ingenuous. Readers without any counter-balancing material might have been attracted to university life for the wrong reasons, or repelled by it. The fact that I was trying to mirror life, and that this produced a distortion of emphasis, reminded me of something we are too prone to forget, that fiction is not life, nor is it *like* life. (Proof of this was another problem with the first draft of *Going Up*. I had tried to make it 'like life' in its narrative style; so it was fragmentary, impressionistic, rambling, and inaccurate – and, like life, ultimately incomprehensible to the reader. The most striking character in that original version was someone whom I had entirely 'made up'.)

But we live in a world in which innocence is at a premium. If there is no 'bad' language in a book about school or university, might it not be accused, by the child or young adult reader, of being unreal? After all, children's vocabularies have very few gaps.

Here is a sample from the first draft of *Going Up*. Tom, one of the central characters, has just arrived at the university town. He is sharing lodgings with a rather eccentric student called Anthony B. The two other students who will be living there have not yet arrived. Mrs Evans is the landlady.

The eating room of the Evans' emporium was the back room; well, not quite the back, because there was a door out into a kitchen, where you could glimpse a child of some kind, and occasionally a neanderthal figure we assume to be Mr Evans. That bit, it is clear, is forbidden territory. A dining table with chairs, the table covered permanently by a plastic cloth; bits of green suite jammed in; a dead tiled fireplace.

And here we are; six o'clock, mealtime. Tom coming downstairs, fearing even worse, and there is Anthony B. sitting at a table set for four, each plate having two tomato-halves, and a circular slice of a pale pink flabby substance. Anthony B. sitting to attention, apparently in rapt anticipation. I appeard to have lost the use of my brain, or why am I sitting here opposite this twit? After a while, Anthony B. appeared to register Tom's presence.

'I trust you had a pleasant walk.'

'Fine,' said Tom.

'Looks good, doesn't it,' Anthony B. said. Tom at a loss for a moment. I can't see anything that looks good. Easeful death, perhaps, and then, with a certain incredulity, it appears that the oaf is referring to the stuff on his plate. I'm certainly getting through the emotions today. He can't be serious. Do you know how they make this stuff? Steam-stripped carcasses; a slurry of bones and eyeballs: mechanically recovered meat. Yeugh. However, if I open my mouth, there's a strong possibility that I'll be sick. Brings to mind what the shopkeeper said [in the first version Tom always referred to his father as 'the shopkeeper'], last time they were presented with liquefied sprouts for lunch. 'You'll appreciate her cooking once you get out there. You'll soon learn not to be fussy.' Not that he was right about either thing. But if Anthony B. actually thinks this is good, it gives you a new perspective on the way other people eat. You see, education working already; trouble is, it's on things I don't want to know.

Tom saved from trying to assemble a response by Mrs Evans wobbling unsmilingly up out of the kitchen, preceded by a dish of chips, and greeted by a werewolf smile from Anthony B.

'Ah, chips.'

Anthony B. has a positive genius for stating the blindingly obvious, and although I'm a peaceful soul, I can see myself smashing a plate of luncheon meat over his head fairly shortly. The two empty chairs not holding out much hope.

'Can't go wrong with chips.'

Well there, A. B., I'm afraid you've made a mistake. These chips disproved another great truism. Tom looked at them. Things *have* got worse. These are quite distinctly chip-shop chips; not your home-cooked chunks, nor yet your slim golden evenly-graded hamburger-chain chips. These are faintly grey and soggy, and quite obviously made from unhappy potatoes and cooked in horse grease. A slight smell of disinfectant exuding from A.B. who is shovelling these disgraces to the name of chip onto his plate. Mrs Evans gives him a lot of teeth, and the empty chairs a disapproving look, and wobbles away. Tom dispiritedly spooned some of the objects onto his round pink animal sludge, which began to melt slightly. This must be the most desolate plate in the whole space-time continuum.

My stylistic debts to my literary mentors, J. P. Donleavy and P. G. Wodehouse, will be obvious. (The material may also seem to owe something to the boarding-house breakfasts of John Wain or Kingsley Amis, but this is merely cognate.) The comments by Julia MacRae and her editors were more direct.

They felt that, stylistically, the attempt to collapse the consciousness of author and characters was unsuccessful in practice, although not in principle. They also felt that sustaining this mixture of tenses and viewpoints, participial constructions and disjunctures, for 70,000 words dissipated its effect, and limited its appeal. It was not the innovation *per se*, but its application; and the derivation from other authors showed.

There were also matters of content. The book as it stood seemed to the readers at Julia MacRae Books to emphasize the negative, by leaving in the mind the discomfort, the loneliness, and the less estimable habits of students. It might, both for moral and for melancholic reasons, dissuade people from going to university – or, at least, disillusion their parents.

As it happened, this view agreed with my own intention. I would not agree with Jean Ure that depression should not be written into books for teenage readers – although I myself would not write it, because I happen to prefer a more positive, forward-looking approach to life. Had my wish been to write a negative book, I probably would have argued, and the book might not have been published at all. Nor would I think it any business of the writer to encourage or discourage university entrance. But that would be a case of wilful authorial egoism: a book *has* influence; the audience most likely to read it is one that is likely to be influenced. No publisher of any kind overlooks this; this publisher and the author for children are expected by both society and the market-place to account for their actions. The debate over *Going Up* is an example of the publisher having, if not quite autocratic rights, at least equal rights with the author. Unlike with most publishers, sales were not basically at issue, only principles.

The balance of characters was more troublesome. If I were to be completely truthful, I would have to admit that the people who stay in my mind from college days were the drunken men and the girls of dubious moral character; for they did make an impression on an impressionable 18-year-old. But I was reminded that fiction is not fact. As Mark Twain said, 'Why *shouldn't* truth be stranger than fiction? Fiction, after all, has to make sense.'[21] Fiction and the censorship of fiction are controlled on the society/literature interface by the *fact of the book*. The status of the book *qua* book changes what is said in it; its contents have the force of respectability. Hence to *write* a swear-word in some sense legitimizes it. To draw a character who stays in the mind is not the same as to encounter such a character in real life, where he is absorbed and balanced by the whole continuum of life.

After thinking it over, I came to the conclusion that a compromise over *Going Up* would not be dishonourable. Because the book is not like life, it was my responsibility – to myself – to structure and balance the book so as to give the reader the *best* chance of feeling the *real* connotative meaning, the atmosphere I wanted to pass on. And so I rewrote *Going Up* (all 75,000 words of it!), partly to make it more coherent and partly to provide a more balanced view and a more positive outcome. The unpleasant, or questionable, elements are still there, but they are debated and contextualized. Now that may smack of commercialism versus art: another liberal bites the dust. I hope not, but it remains perplexing. How far were the changes really self-censorship? And how far were they real censorship applied subtly?

In short, my original conception was modified, in both style and shape, both of which became 'more conventional'. In the good judgement of a publisher in daily contact with all those layers of expertise, a message is only a message if it is read. With a lesser publisher, that might, and does, lead to market-led publishing, competition with other media on the lowest level. Marshall McLuhan is reported to have said that 'A successful book cannot afford to be more than ten percent new'[22] and that seems to me to be true, even in the context of the fluid role of the reader. The reader will make individual meanings from text, but there is certainly a point all which societal norms will control perception, just as they control literary norms and, hence, new texts.

Whether it is possible to usefully refine the model of societal and literary conflict – it would certainly be possible to add to it – in view of the larger forces which control it, is difficult to say.

Certainly a micro-analyis is useful for authors, and may be of help to those concerned with the formulation of larger concepts. But we are left, I think, with personal decisions, as author or parent. Who is to decide? And who, in effect, is to censor? For one should not under-estimate the complexity of the influences on the author – from foreign-rights buyer to specific child. (These influences are among those that lead to, in that most misleading phrase, 'the death of the author'.) The (live) writer begins with a freight of societal restraints, and so, if I have to accept inexplicit restraints, why should I not accept explicit ones?

The conclusion of all this, which places me thoroughly in the eighteenth-century liberal camp, is that we are left with individual responsibility. If we want to influence others, it must be by education and with consent. The book, and especially the children's book, cannot be used as a weapon.

Now, this is all very well, and highly principled, but, regrettably, it leads not to freedom, but to freedom for zealots to restrict freedom. People with simple, strongly held convictions have an in-built advantage in this struggle: they care. To the zealot, the 'liberal', who can work only by hope and example, must seem hopelessly weak and confused; I must seem to want freedom without revolution and responsibility without authority.

As member of society, the answer, for me, is simple. Censorship is bad. Period. We can advise people on what is good or bad in our opinions, but the reading material should be available to us, regardless. If this seems positively irresponsible, I would merely cite the quotation from Jonathan Swift given at the beginning of Chapter 8. In a passage in *Gulliver's Travels*, the King of Brobdingnag, the land of the giants, debates the issue of liberty with Gulliver. His logic, which appears at first to be liberal, is in fact autocratic; the decision about what is poison and what is cordial is not one I would leave to a king.

The answer, as a parent, is very local. I can advise and educate my own family, and it does not seem to be sensible to crusade against the rest of the world. This is not only because I could not succeed against everyone who disagrees with me, but because, leaving aside some (to me) obvious villains, most writers are following their own principles. That I disagree with people does not make me right – or give me any rights. (An excellent exploration of personal versus popular principles in children's books, with special reference to writers such as Roald Dahl and Judy Blume, can be found in Michele Landsberg's *The World of Children's Books*.)[23]

So far so good – or bad – for my own daughters. But what about the rest? Can I simply, in good conscience, leave the majority of children to the less-than-responsible devices of their parents? This is the classic liberal double-bind, perhaps, but I have to face it. I *would* do good for others, but I can never be sure of *what* is good for the others.

But what about the situation of a writer for *young* children? Here I would argue that the existence of multiple meanings generated, potentially and unknowably, by the child-reader makes prescription a very dubious business. At the very least, it suggests that not only are the 'visible' targets of sex, race, and class quite likely to be invisible to the child-readers, unless we *want* them to be visible, but also that the apparently innocent and desirable text may carry corrupting meanings that we are unable to see.

In the face of that massive, and perhaps overwhelming, insight, which amounts to a lack of faith in language as a communicative instrument, I am quite happy to say that, as parent, citizen, writer, and academic, I have different standards – and that they are all compatible. They are all controlled and resolved in a central faith in humanity (despite all the evidence); but, in the normal course of life, because we have to be different things at different times, they are bound sometimes to conflict. We spend our lives – as our children will – constantly processing, weighing, and balancing a phenomenal range of knowledge and perceptions and feelings. We cannot be simplistic about them, and we do not expect our children to be. It should be obvious that the same is true of our approaches to children's books and our relationships to them.

But, to conclude, here is the segment of *Going Up* which, in the published version, replaced that quoted earlier. It has been made more conventional and more accessible, a victim – or a benefactor – of the system that controls the poetics of texts for children.

The eating room at Mrs Evan's house was the back room of the two. The front room was stuffed with what seemed to be several three-piece suites, and gave the impression of not having any air in it. Beyond the eating room was a glass door leading into forbidden territory, a kitchen, and beyond it, presumably, the Evan's living area. It didn't seem to be very big. A stocky figure, presumed to be Mr Evans, could occasionally be glimpsed. Otherwise, there was a dining table and chairs, the table permanently covered by a plastic cloth, an armchair, and a dead, tiled fireplace. The smell of jam was pervasive.

At six o'clock, the appointed mealtime (although it fitted fairly neatly between any late-day mealtimes that Tom was familiar with), he came downstairs, having been waiting in his room for half-an-hour, rather unsure of what to do.

Anthony B. was sitting at a table set for four, and each place had a plate between the knives and forks. Each plate had two tomato-halves, and a thin, circular slice of a pink substance. Anthony B. was sitting to attention, apparently in rapt anticipation. Tom felt as though he had lost the use of his brain. Anthony B. looked around.

'I trust you had a pleasant walk.'

'Yes, fine, thanks,' Tom said, his eyes on the plates.

'Looks good, doesn't it, 'Anthony B. said. Tom was at a loss for a moment. He nearly said: 'You can't be serious,' but he sat down, and thought: I know how they make this stuff. They steam-strip carcasses and mix it with a slurry of bones and eyeballs: mechanically recovered meat. Yeugh.

But he didn't say any of that, largely because he thought that he might throw up if he opened his mouth. His father, who had a fairly un-husbandly view of his wife's cooking, had once said, after a particularly soggy serving of Brussels sprouts: 'One day, you'll learn to appreciate cooking like this. Once you get out there, you'll soon learn not to be fussy.' Not that he was right about either thing, so far. But, Tom thought, if Anthony B. actually thinks this is good, it gives you a new perspective on the way other people eat. More education.

Mrs Evans wobbled unsmilingly in from the kitchen and glanced witheringly at the empty chairs. She was carrying a bowl of chips.

'Ah, chips,' A. B. said, displaying a penchant for stating the blindingly obvious. 'Can't go wrong with chips.'

Tom looked at them, and thought, you're wrong there, A. B. They were quite distinctively chip-shop chips; not home-cooked chunks like his mother produced, nor yet the slim, golden, evenly-graded hamburger-chain chips. They were faintly grey and smelled of disinfectant.

A. B. shovelled chips onto his plate. Tom, whose spirits had returned to zero, spooned some of them onto the round of pink animal sludge, which began to dissolve slightly. Tom stared at his plate, thinking that this must be the most desolate place in the whole space-time continuum.[24]

10

Criticism and the Picture Book

'And what is the use of a book,' thought Alice, 'without pictures or conversation?'
Lewis Carroll, Alice's Adventures in Wonderland

Children's literature borrows from all genres. But there is one genre that it has *contributed*, that of the picture book, as opposed to the illustrated book. This distinction is largely organizational, yet, if we bear in mind that the fact of illustration alters the way we read the verbal text, this is even more true of the picture book.

Faced with this difference in the mode of reading both illustrated and picture books, criticism and theory have been very limited, tending to resort to figurative platitudes. As the illustrator Celia Berridge has observed, 'the real reason picture books get such cursory reviewing treatment is not that they are seriously evaluated and found wanting, but that they are *all* regarded as being the least important part of the book world'.[1] As an American commentator has also noted, the downgrading of the picture book results from the simplicity of the language; for 'Much of the complexity, the use of metaphor for example, is expressed by the visual elements: the size and shape of the book, the thickness of the paper, the type....'[2]

In short, we need a critical language for this new area, an area in which many things are possible. 'The complexity of interplay between picture-meaning and text-meaning ... [and] what that interplay allows', writes Philip Pullman 'is the greatest storytelling discovery of the twentieth century: namely, counterpoint.'[3] Pullman points out the central difficulty for commentators:

A different kind of seeing is involved: the sort of simultaneity that we get in cinema ... In a comic strip we can see several things happening together, and it doesn't matter which we read first. In the frame of the comic strip, the stream of time breaks up into little local eddies – and this loosening of the tyranny of the one-way flow makes counterpoint possible, releasing the most extraordinary virtuosity in storytelling.[4]

Picture books can exploit this complex relationship; words can add to, contradict, expand, echo, or interpret the pictures – and vice versa. Picture books can cross the boundary between the verbal and the pre-verbal worlds; they can be allies of the child-reader, as we have seen in the cases of *How Tom Beat Captain Najork and his Hired Sportsmen* and *Rosie's Walk*. As Margaret Meek put it:

[W]e can say that a page in a picture book is an icon to be contemplated, narrated, explicated by the viewer. It holds the story until there is a telling. So in the beginning the words are few; the story happenings are in the pictures which form the polysemic text. The reader has to learn which of the pictorial events carries the line of the story, while each rereading shows that other things can also be taken into account. The essential lesson of *Rosie's Walk* depends on there being no mention of the fox, but the reader knows there would be no story without him. Nowhere but in a reader's interaction with a text can this be learned.[5]

Picture books, then, can develop the difference between reading words and reading pictures: they are not bound by linear sequence, but can orchestrate the movement of the eye. Most important, as Sonia Landes has said, is that 'What today's illustrators understand is that picture books really deal with two story lines, the visual and the verbal; and each can be separately phased so as to reinforce, counterpoint, anticipate or expand, one the other.'[6] They have a great semiotic/semantic potential; they are emphatically *not* simply collections of pictures, 'books of paintings sewn together carelessly or craftily'.[7] This is a medium in which the pages can be seen in terms of openings and of free explorations of the interactions of two media; for, as Nicholas Tucker has said, 'the art of the picture book ... rests on the interactions between illustration and the text'.[8]

But – and this is sadly true in the majority of cases – they can also fix the words into a restrictive, mundane interpretation. Obviously there is no way in which pictures can 'simply' illustrate what the words say; they must interpret them, but the interpretation may be bland or conform to commercial/popular visual stereotypes of shape or colour or visual-verbal patterns. This is despite Brian Alderson's rare slip, where, talking of early picture books, he remarks that 'One of the characteristics of the great illustrated books is, of course, the working together of text and image *seriatim*',[9] in itself an improbability. He suggests that many examples are 'representational: literal portrayals of what the text says ... [The illustrator] seeks to give an unadorned account of phenomena *as he sees them*.'[10] This same view is found in Sonia Landes: 'One role of pictures in a picture book is to enhance the meaning of a story by illustrating the words. But good picture book artists go well beyond that by inventing and developing additional story material.'[11]

Such books ignore the *possibilities* of a complex medium. I suspect that with those books whose worthy purpose (overt or otherwise) is to teach the reading of words rather than the reading of words-and-pictures, there has to be a deliberate poverty in the pictures so that children will use them only to guess the meanings of the words. This is no criticism of the use of pictures for this purpose; it is just that such books are not picture books, but illustrated books. To add a 'reading score' to a book, as has been done quite often in recent picture books in Britain, only serves to degrade the picture book still further, to an illustrated book that has no richness of words.

But what is the relationship of this theory to real children? It is clear, as we have seen, that, even at a fairly advanced stage of socialization, children perceive things differently from adults; yet it may be, paradoxically, that with the picture book, adults and children are at their closest. Nicholas Tucker quotes Maurice Sendak, author-illustrator of some of the most successful and influential of modern picture books, who after being accused of grotesquerie, for drawing child-figures with large heads said: '"I know the proportions of a child's body. But I am trying to draw the way children *feel* – or rather, the way I imagine they feel."'[12]

There is a good deal more empirical evidence from children themselves. Joan Cass has noted that

Children also tend at this age (2.6–3.6) to recognise objects in pictures whatever their position in space; this means that they will sometimes look at their picture books upside-down and still be able to name the things that are there. This tendency to ignore spatial organisation means that they do not always analyse what they see and so do not separate the important from the unimportant ... [they] do not, until about 4 to 4.6, recognise a series of action in different pictures; they see each one as separate from the rest.[13]

This is a very long way from the adult's perception, and it is rare that an author-illustrator is able to address just this problem. The illustrations by Henry Holiday for Lewis Carroll's *The Hunting of the Snark* are a case in point. Although it can be argued that these are illustrations of a text, rather than the work of an equal or dominant partner, there is just this distortion of part of the picture; as Carroll said, 'If *only* he can draw grotesques.'[14]

Most strikingly, there are the books by David McKee, whose *Not Now Bernard* was discussed earlier. This *I Hate My Teddy Bear*[15] might be described by an adult reader as an exercise in surrealism. The text is quite coherent. It begins: 'On Thursday, Brenda's mother came to visit John's mother. Brenda came to play with John. "Why don't you go outside and play with your teddy bears?" said John's mother. John and Brenda took their teddies outside. "I hate my teddy bear," said John. "I hate my teddy bear," said Brenda. "But my teddy is better than yours," said John. "No it isn't, my teddy's better than yours," said Brenda', and so on.

In the first three pictures, there is a direct reflection of the words: Brenda and her mother are shown at the door of John's flat; Brenda meets John; they are sent outside to play. In subsequent pictures, Brenda and John are seen quarrelling. Thus far, coherence. But, even in the first picture, there are some unanswered questions. There are various adult characters outside a door, one holding chocolates, one holding flowers, one writing on a pad. Two old women point at them. And, more notably, three men are carrying a huge hand down the stairs. All these present immediate questions of narrative. Are we going to find out what the men are doing with the hand or who the others are visiting? Even more disturbing is the fact that the perspectives are wrong; the landing and stairs are not in the same plane as the characters.

In the second picture, where Brenda meets John, we find that the flat is sparsely furnished: there is a sofa, a sun bed, bare boards, and tea-chests, one of which contains tea-things, another many letters. Brenda's mother is crying; John's mother is looking at a letter and a photograph. A huge foot is being lowered past the window.

By the third picture, the page has three dimensions flattened to two, so that three rooms and three sets of actions are presented simultaneously – and then Brenda and John go out into a staggeringly bizarre world in which there are hundreds of fragments of narrative: women palm-reading, a dropped glove (which a woman bemoans several pages later), a man clutching his brow and throwing away a newspaper, a woman painting a rainbow, crowds of people looking in the same direction, an old couple with ice-creams looking at each other suggestively, people following each other through a strange arch, lines of identically dressed women – all of them involving adults doing unresolved things. In almost every picture huge hands are carried past.

For the adult reader, it is a lesson in the extent to which we attempt to make sense of what we see by applying generic expectations. What do these things symbolize and predict? Where are the other ends of the predictions? And why, at the end of the book, is John's flat carpeted and comfortable, with the mothers on their knees drinking china tea? The mystery of the huge hands and foot is resolved on the last page, where it turns out that there is a hand- and foot-sculpture open-air exhibition. But that is about the extent of the coherence.

I would argue that, like *Alice in Wonderland* or John Masefield's *The Midnight Folk*[16] or Ellen Raskin's *The Westing Game*,[17] *I Hate My Teddy Bear* is a genuine children's book in so far as it is definitely not an adult's book. It is easier to find examples of lateral thinking in children's books, where, in a sense, the words are superseded by the pictures, which provide their own coherence and depth of reference. This is in addition to the way in which familiar objects may be re-seen or the way in which sets of colours and tone-moods (within the book or with external references) can replace or expand or counterpoint verbal semantic sets.

Thus Joan Cass's comment that 'Children under six or seven tend to see "wholes", so figures in pictures need to be strong and clear in outline, otherwise they may appear just as a lot of unrelated detail'[18] suggests a somewhat prescriptive view. She suggests, citing M. D. Vernon's classic *The Psychology of Perception*, that for children under 11, words are necessary to explain the pictures and sequences, and that 'Studies of children's preferences tend to show that they enjoy realistic, stylised, near abstract and caricature, provided there is unity and harmony between the story and the picture.'[19] On the one hand it is good to see an acknowledgement that children can appreciate all types of art; on the other, depressing to find an acceptance of socialization, of conventionalization of children's responses, as admirable.

A more constructive approach is that of Frederick Laws. He suggests that children have a

> severely literal visual imagination. The thing imagined for them is not of another order of reality from the thing seen. After all, you can see it in your head. They are willing to accept flexible conventions in imagining ... yet their fancy has hard edges ... Until corrupted by whimsical elders, they prefer what they know or can see to fanciful inventions.[20]

The difficulty here, of course, is establishing quite what they can see. The distinguished illustrator Roger Duvoisin pinpoints the difference between children and adults which adult readers and prescribers of picture books should always keep in mind: 'With their uninhibited vision, children do not see the world as we do. While we see only what interests us, they see everything. They have made no choice yet ... the child also has the tendency to enjoy this detailed world of his in terms of happenings, of things being done, in other words, in terms of stories.[21]

Again, we have to appreciate just what is meant by 'story' in this context, and it is that which differs from adult concepts. Whereas images are perceived holistically, words are perceived linearly. The grammarian James Muir quotes Randolph Quirk on the image of a boy patting a dog:

We could not readily assign an order to the boy, the patting, the dog, the boy's stoop, the dog's tail. On the other hand, as soon as you try to report what you have seen, you find that you not only can, but *must*, assign an order to it and *must* break up your impression into pieces of your own choosing and present them, not simultaneously, but one by one.[22]

Thus linearity is a feature of verbal text, but not necessarily of pictures. To force pictures into the same mould as words seems to be potentially unproductive, except in terms of establishing conventions, when, of course, it is, by definition, necessary.[23] Words may suggest a much more precise indication of what things mean, but not necessarily a more precise overall impression. Words are necessarily semantic empty vessels: they limit meaning, but do not prescribe it. Pictures can do the same; the classic British example is Edward Ardizzone, whose pictures contain much that is half hidden in the shadows, and whose *forte* was drawing the backs of people. As Ardizzone said himself, *Little Tim and the Brave Sea Captain*[24] was written for, and with the help of, his children. This has the advantage that the verbal text reads well, since his children made suggestions as the book grew. He says of children: 'They will add those wonderful inconsequential details which only children can think of and which, if incorporated in a tale, so greatly enrich the narrative.'[25] Note here the word 'inconsequential' in apposition to the word 'enriches'; the judgement here is clearly on two levels, levels that do not necessarily sit well together. Brian Alderson's view, that 'The force of a text may be diluted or even lost, behind artistic bravura; the mind ceases to attend to narrative implications in the appreciation of visual distrations or cleverness'[26] would thus be seen as adultist.

As with other forms of texts, it may be piously said that we should not restrict children; but, equally, if we are going to keep from restricting them, we need some appreciation of what we are liberating them to. John Rowe Townsend writes: 'Picture books are often a child's first introduction to art and literature ... To give him crude, stereotyped picture books is to open the way for everything else that is crude and stereotyped ... even if children do not always appreciate the best when they see it, they will have no chance of appreciating it if they don't see it.'[27]

This is all well and good, but it still contains the concept of 'best'. What makes a picture book good? Is there any way of reading it that will allow us to make this value-judgement? I myself am rather suspicious of panaceas, because the world seems full of exceptions.

The Australian artist Ray Reardon has suggested that the basic tenets of *Gestalt* theory are also the characteristics of a naturally appealing work of art: good figure background (positive-negative) relationships, clear organizational principles, the persistence or recurrence of the illustration, and the fact that the illustration is dynamic. These tend to produce pleasing artwork, artwork that inclines towards symmetry, balance, and simplicity.[28]

If, as Patricia Cianciolo suggests, 'There is little agreement among critics of children's literature about the criteria one should use to evaluate the illustrations that appear in books read by children',[29] where can we begin?

Descriptive approaches seem most profitable, such as those of William Moebius and Jane Doonan. Moebius in 'Introduction to picture book codes',[30] notes the variables at work in picture books: the layout, the concept of openings rather than pages (a concept of Barbara Bader)[31] the size of frame (the most commonly cited example is Maurice Sendak's *Where the Wild Things Are*,[32] in which the frame correlates to the character's imaginative development), and the overall design of the page. From this, Moebius proposes codes of position, size, diminishing returns (more than once on the page), perspective, frame, line and capillarity, and colour. All these can be symbolic, allusive, referential within texts, joking, or can metafictionally stand outside the text, commenting on it, or representing intertextuality. For example, a character shown on the left of a page is more *likely* to be secure than one on the right. Consequently, there are conventional codes of dominance and completion. In terms of frame, we might be given a glimpse or a selective part of a scene; in terms of layout and colour, there maybe a preponderance of white space. In a sense, the page-break becomes a significant quasi-grammatical unit. The effect of not making text and picture congruent in some way is illustrated by *Make Way for Ducklings*.[33] Sonia Landes makes a similar point: the book stands as a whole, and so the layout of the whole text from the title-page or before (as with

Where the Wild Things Are or *Rosie's Walk* or the complete map of the book at the beginning of *Each, Peach, Pear, Plum*[34] is significant. There are leitmotifs carried by purely illustrative elements, such as the vulture in Robert Lawson and Munro Leaf's *The Story of Ferdinand*[35] and the robin in *The Tale of Peter Rabbit*.[36] Then there are extra-textual symbols such as the flowers and trees in *The Story of Ferdinand* (which so much annoyed Ernest Hemingway that he began a story in 1951 with the words 'One time there was a bull and his name was not Ferdinand and he cared nothing for flowers.')[37] Landes also cites the changes in size of Ping and Peter Rabbit and Max according to success or failure.[38]

Similar points have been made by Jane Doonan, who points out that where artists choose to place the eye-level has a strong effect on the viewer, and that 'tactile space is not only created by artificial perspective, but also by equivalences of texture'.[39] Celia Berridge notes that the flattening of perspectives, depths, and shallows changes the relationship of picture and reader in *Each, Peach, Pear, Plum*; thus 'shallow picture depth [gives] the viewer a feeling of intimacy with the picture, of being right up in front of it'.[40] The modern picture book consequently has much room for experimentation of various kinds, from cartoon to pop-up. Equally, as Moebius points out, 'intertextuality is more common in the picture book than might appear'.[41]

'Since comprehending a picture is not the same process as reading a text [the new breed of] picturebooks can intrigue any non-reader, child or adult.'[42] (In this, picture books are like poetry.) This is not simply the case with texts where the words are as densely loaded as the pictures (a notable example is Raymond Briggs's *Fungus the Bogeyman*).[43] It is also the case in books featuring the work of artists such as Michael Foreman, Charles Keeping, and John Burningham, who go in for multiple experimentation. Most notable among these is probably John Burningham, who, in several of his books, has pushed back the boundaries of the picture book vocabulary by encapsulating the relationships between childhood, adulthood, and fantasy. Of these, the most successful – and controversial – has been *Granpa*,[44] in which the relationships between the fragmentary text and between the full-colour pictures and the sepia pictures (reality and fantasy or memory, perhaps) are as important as whether the book is read in a conventional sequence or not. His *Come Away from the Water, Shirley* and its successor, *Time to get out of the Bath, Shirley* contrast, on facing pages, the mundane, colourless world of adults, with their workaday words, and the bright, imaginative world within the child's head, which is wordless.[45] (These books are discussed further in Chapter 11.)

In a sense, this may be a confrontation that appeals to adults. Much more subtle is *Where's Julius?*[46] As the parents produce a succession of meals, they take them to Julius, who is at first building a house 'out of three chairs, the old curtains and the broom', but more and more is found in exotic places: the pyramids, the frozen wastes of Russia, and shooting rapids in South America. The blend of bland reality – meals – and fantasy – the parents intrepidly trudging through the snow or the desert with loaded trays – indicates the possibilities of the picture book.

Burningham generally refers only to 'real' objects. Anthony Browne goes further in demonstrating the possibilities of allusiveness. There are recurring images and allusions within his *oeuvre*; allusions to the surrealist painters and common motifs. His *A Walk in the Park*[47] is made up of visual jokes. His *Hansel and Gretel*[48] which starts out as an 'illustrated text' gradually takes on the status of a picture book because of his repetition of motifs, of bars and birds. The stepmother and the witch are identified with each other in purely visual terms. Browne also makes great use of the 'opening', as Jane Doonan notes: 'Passing from one [image] to another, the effect is kinetic. But where the film camera would need a succession of frames to present such a sequence, [Browne's] double-page opening gives us simultaneous images which we can look at, choosing our own speed.'[49]

This is a basic point about illustration, and Doonan expands her view of this.

> Directly we see shapes on a canvas (or illustrated page) take on spatial properties and represent something, the abstract repetition of shapes and proportions and patterns in the scheme of the painting ... takes on a new power. The same shape repeated in different objects ... and in negative shapes left between, on the same scale, provides links which make associations and affinities

between objects and events and areas of painting. The metaphorical link is both formal and psychological, and it owes its power to ambiguity.[50]

Hence we can have visual allusion, by blending symbolic shapes and colours of anxiety and pleasure. Doonan notes that Browne delights in detailed patterning, but that 'such patterning does not create a naturalistic world, for the eye does not perceive the natural world in this way'. This is partly the result of outlining, for 'outlines insist on the separateness of things, which is rarely as we find them when we look about us'.[51]

This suggests that the picture book crosses boundaries (as is shown in the pioneering work of Elaine Moss dealing with picture books for older children, 'Them's for the infants, Miss' and *Picture Books for Young People. 9–13*,[52]) although there is a certain encroaching danger of blandness. Bettina Hurlimann has noted the paradoxes inherent in the concept of 'Europrinting': 'Pictures speak a universal language ... but the risk lies in a tendency towards uniformity – the different national characteristics becoming submerged for the sake of "the European market." '[53]

The multi-media aspect of the picture book is nothing new. As early as 1920 Rupert Bear was using four elements of the story: picture, couplet, prose, headline.[54] Margery Fisher points out that the 'wise writer for this [early] age (Beatrix Potter is one shining example) reserves adjectives, as it were, for the illustrations, where innumerable small points, some of them sophisticated, can be stressed'.[55]

In any one year, there is little of what Pullman called the 'release of the most extraordinary virtuosity in storytelling'.[56] Rather, there are missed opportunities: books that do not make *any* use – let alone full use – of the medium. It is not always clear, for example, why the words are there. While I sympathize with the view that the wordless picture book deprives children of words, the words-because-there-ought-to-be-words concept is just as 'closing' as a mundane illustration. Sometimes an absence of words would have provided a 'gap' which takes intelligence and imagination to fill. There is a case for the 'pure' picture book – but that does not mean that the portfolio of paintings counts.

Such a portfolio is static. The same might be said of 'manufactured' pieces, tours around farms under the pretext of a cat finding its supper or the like. Words and pictures must do things together.

The yardstick must be the interactive book, which, because it *is* interactive, cannot be easily fitted into (or excluded from) any age-bracket. In *Granpa*, the relationship between the two characters is not comfortable or sentimental, and the relationship between the words and the pictures reflects this in being highly ambiguous. Burningham sets a standard for interatcive narrative which avoids the visual cliché – and there is a lot of that about, too. What is the point of having families of hippos or bears doing essentially human things? There are some good reasons, admittedly: animism, avoiding racist stereotypes (although in certain commercial exercises the 'naughty' teddies are less 'pure' in colour than the virtuous ones), universalizing, allowing children to empathize with, say, misbehaviour, while recognizing (as with cartoons) that this is not reality. But very often, no real use is made of the possibilities. Mary Rayner's books about the Pig family are a good example. Whereas *Mrs Pig's Night Out*[57] made a sharp (and even notorious) point (the babysitter is a wolf), its successor[58] involves only ordinary domesticities, helped only a little way from blandness by the piggishness. There are hundreds of books of the same type, and only occasionally does one rise above the rest. One example is Margaret Gordon's 'Wilberforce' books. Margaret Gordon exploits the contrast between the deadpan text and the visual mayhem created by the (also deadpan) bear Wilberforce.[59] Both adults and children can appreciate the discrepancies. In addition, Wilberforce is the quintessential child; the story has shape and point; and the meticulous drawings contain many minor observations on family life. A similar exercise in charm and nostalgia is *Angelina Ballerina*, where there is nothing particularly mouse-like about the activities, but the mouse pictures by Helen Craig have sufficient detail to stand alone, as well as an elusive, hard-to-describe quality of commitment and affection.[60]

Many books use pictures to complement the words by showing things that are difficult to imagine or by mixing fantasy and reality. The best of these sustain the idea right through the book.

We have already mentioned Felix Pirani's *Abigail at the Beach*.[61] What is not described in the text is the close relationship between father and daughter and the practical application of fantasy to warding off the perils of the real world. While her father reads his own fantasy novel and drinks real beer, Abigail preserves her real sand-castle from other, bigger children and their bikes and dogs, while the pictures also *show* the way her imagination is treating the world. Another classic father-daughter relationship is in Anthony Browne's *Gorilla*, in which there is a complex visual and psychological relationship between the fantasy gorilla and the remote father.[62]

Many of the classic picture books – for example, Edward Ardizzone's 'Little Tim' books and Quentin Blake's books – interweave text and pictures physically on the page. The most ingenious contemporary exponent of this technique is Bob Wilson. The highly competent 'Lion-and-Albert'-type verses are woven in among the cartoon strips, using, for example, notices on the hospital walls as part of the verses, while a secondary text is carried in the word-balloons.[63] Wilson's work raises the question of whether the relationship between words and pictures can be like that of a singer and an orchestra: a balanced partnership in which, when one is foregrounded, the other assumes a supporting role. The obvious difficulty is that the sophistication may become such that the interaction of text and picture exceeds the limit in terms of age-acceptability. A classic case of this is Graham Oakley's 'Church Mouse' series, with its great detail not only in the pictures but also in the text.[64]

Pushing at the boundaries in trying to exploit the possibilities of the picture book brings us close to the book as game, and perhaps none the worse for that. An interesting example is Phillipe Dupasquier's *The Great Green Mouse Disaster*, in which a hotel is reduced to chaos by a mass of green mice.[65] But every room is seen simultaneously, so you must choose between reading several narratives at the same time or following the happenings in one room through the whole book, then going back and doing the same for another room. Rather like the 'choose your own adventure' binary-choice books, this demonstrates the visual/narrative possibilities of the picture book.

But, for all the conventionally excellent artwork in evidence, books which take advantage of the form remain in a minority. What may have emerged here is the immense potential of the type. Clearly, any judgement of books will remain local, if not actually personal; what we have seen is a way of investigating whether a book is reaching towards the potential of the form.

As Jane Doonan concludes:

> Whether the illustration is congruent or deviates from the text, the reader-viewer will be able to make more meanings if it is not assumed that illustrations merely reinforce the subject matter of the words, and the pictures are allowed to do their own talking. We miss much in any work of art if we only look for what we expect to find, instead of opening ourselves to what it has to offer.[66]

Indeed, as Perry Nodelman has noted, 'picture books have unique rhythms, unique conventions of shape and structure, a unique body of narrative techniques.'[67] Both criticism and publishing could perhaps take more note of this fact.

11

Criticism for Children's Literature

In this book I have tried to avoid three things: value-judgements, universalizing judgements, and speculative criticism – that is, a kind of psychoanalysis of either the author, as found for example, in Humphrey Carpenter's *Secret Gardens*[1] or the characters, as in Margaret and Michael Rustin's *Narratives of Love and Loss*.[2] For many readers, this may seem to be evading the very aim of criticism; but I hope I have shown that it is helpful simply to examine just what we are doing and why when we approach a book or start to talk about it.

In this chapter, I would like to go one stage further and suggest that we need to recognize, at least in the interim, a distinctive kind of criticism, one that I have called 'childist', which we should adopt when working in this area. Second, I would like to propose a radical rethinking of the ends of criticism itself and, by implication, the subject-matter before us.

As we have seen, there is a complex interaction not just between child and book, but between child and the idea of the book, which could to some extent be called a 'counter-reading'. If we take counter-reading seriously – and the evidence of reading teachers, as well as of psychologists, suggests that we should – then we will find much current judging of children's books suspect, whether it is of the 'children *might* like', 'children *should* like', 'children *do* like', or 'children *will* like' variety. Obviously the academic 'might likes' are solidly in the adult, or adultist, world, while the 'should likes' speak with the voice of the indoctrinator – but what of the others? 'Do like' and 'will like' judgements are based on observation, very often on years of loving, committed, skilled observation. There is, of course, a problem with the observer influencing what is to be observed, as well as with interpretation. A good example is the writer Roald Dahl, who may seem to produce books which reflect the child's viewpoint. Michele Landsberg says of him: 'Like Blyton, Dahl wins his young readers' affection in part by allying himself with their instinctive drives. She provided patterns of adventurous autonomy in which youngsters triumphed without adult help; he seems to subvert adult strictures by endorsing children's impulses to aggression and vengeance.'[3] Nor does he under-estimate his reader's capacity to handle sophisticated narrative devices. It may seem that his books are not merely in contact with the child culture, but as Sarland puts it, 'part of an oppositional culture'.[4] But although this may account for both opposition to Dahl in bookish circles and support for him in non-bookish circles, is it actually true? Is Dahl really throwing his skills onto the side of *what children see as the adults' idea of their culture*? What John Rowe Townsend has called 'urchin verse' is, like Dahl's writing, the 'acceptable face' of childhood, a mildly anarchic rebellion allowed by the ruling adult culture.

At best, a story is not merely entertainment – should such a thing be conceivable. As Arthur Applebee has pointed out, in what, I hope, was not intended as a sinister statement:

The stories they hear help them to acquire expectations about what the world is like – its vocabulary and syntax as well as its people and places – without the distracting pressure of separating the real from the make-believe. And although they will eventually learn that some of this world is only fiction, it is specific characters and specific events which will be rejected; the recurrent patterns of values, the stable expectations about the roles and relationships which are part of their culture, will remain. It is these underlying patterns ... *which make stories an important agent of socialization, one of the many modes by which they are taught the values and standards of their elders.*[5]

But is any of this the child's view of the world or of the book? For example, does the child's culture automatically comprehend the prejudices of the adult culture: male versus female, black versus white, left versus right, dirty versus clean, acceptable versus unacceptable? Such things have to be learned, along with language, along with story-shapes. Although recently he has been seen as only 'being on his own side', Dahl, by defining the acceptably unacceptable, is simply part of the regulatory system, part of the learning process – which may account for his support among adults who might have been expected to criticize his material. The supposed contract with the child, ('the story's sugar-coating may lull adult apprehensions'),[6] distracts attention from what might be seen as the books' covert, anti-child (and perhaps anti-human) purposes.

One rewarding way of approaching these difficulties would involve a total re-reading of texts from the 'childist' point of view. Simply to invite adults to read as children is scarcely novel, and it is likely not only to revive old prejudices, but, as we have seen, to prove remarkably difficult. Rather, we have to challenge all our assumptions, question every reaction, and ask what reading as a child actually means, given the complexities of the cultural interaction.

Until very recently, talk about books has been based on general assumptions about meaning, value, and acceptability – tacitly taking the norm of the WASP male – that are rooted in the very structure of the language. As Jonathan Culler puts it in *On Deconstruction*: 'If the experience of literature depends upon the qualities of a reading self, one can ask what difference it would make to the experience of literature if this self were, for example, female rather than male'[7] or, one might add, a child. At first sight, this may seem to be stating the obvious: women readers must read as women. What else can they do? Well, the answer is that they read as women as defined by men; for the value-systems and the ways of perceiving prevalent in our culture are determined by males, even to the point of the way the language names things that are neutral.

The parallel between the situations of women and children has been well stated by Lissa Paul:

There is good reason for appropriating feminist theory to children's literature. Both women's literature and children's literature are devalued and regarded as marginal or peripheral by the literary and educational communities. Feminist critics are beginning to change that.... Children, like women, are lumped together as helpless and dependent; creatures to be kept away from the scene of the action, and who otherwise ought not to be seen or heard. But women make up more than half the population of the world – and all of us once were children. It is almost inconceivable that women and children have been invisible and voiceless for so long.[8]

To transpose the arguments for 'feminist' reading to the area of children's books, we need a new word. 'Childish' and 'child-like' already have layers of accumulated meaning and association. 'Childist' may serve our purpose. We have seen that the problem of defining what we mean by 'reading as a child' is not a small one. As Annette Kolodny noted, the problems are deep-seated: 'What is crucial is that reading is a *learned* activity which like many other learned interpretive strategies in our society is inevitably sex-coded and gender-inflected.'[9] It is quite possible, then, that in playing the literary/reading game, children are progressively forced to read against themselves as children. And this is rarely taken into account in reading children's books. (Given the fact that most children's book practitioners are women, the possibilities of 'skewed' readings is compounded.)

How do we cross the gap, to see what is really happening on the child's terms, rather than continue dealing in ingrained assumptions about children's perceptions and competences? Are we trapped in our own formulations? As Perry Nodelman, writing about how typical children read typical Books, observes: 'The important question is, why do so many children demand identification with the characters they read about? A distressing answer to that question is that we work hard at teaching them to do it.'[10]

Certainty storying is, in Barbara Hardy's phrase, 'a primary act of mind',[11] and the child makes sense of the world by telling him or herself stories. But there are differences between the stories of childhood and the stories of the book. Patterns of story have to be learned, as we have seen; and intertextuality and the non-specificity of the text make a great deal of difference. Written language is about itself, and is more reflexive and allusive than oral language. As D. R. Olson has noted, written and spoken modes represent differences in cultures. 'Oral language ... is a universal means of sharing our understanding of concrete situations and practical actions. Moreover, it is the language children bring to school.'[12]

In teaching language, we are teaching children word-games, ways of partitioning experience:

> Narrative, the sequencing of events in time, is a fundamental way of organizing the recounting of personal experience in both speech and writing, but the successful production of 'stories' of this kind in either situation requires knowledge of different concepts of language use; and it is the development of an awareness of such differences that is crucial for the successful growth of a child's writing abilities.[13]

Thus interaction is a matter of shared rules, and children play our game because it is the only game we allow them to play. But that is only in response. Within themselves they may be reacting differently, making something different. For example, consider genre.

> The producer [of a story] must either conform to the general principles of a story and operate within a genre, create and 'sell' her own new genre, or risk banishment from the hall of the storyteller. And the consumer must have general expectations of what a story is like, knowledge of how certain genres look, and sufficient acquaintance with the real world so that the details, as well as the overall organization of the narrative, can be appropriately apprehended.[14]

Thus we are in danger of confusing competence with conformity and reaction with skill. As we have seen, we abstract linguistic characteristics and story-shapes according to our adultist norms, and then test the child's reaction against this. But is our reading a 'true' one? Is it useful or relevant to children? The answer must be, developmentally and sociologically, yes; personally, probably no. The meaning that a child makes of a book is likely to be the result of a collision.

In *With Respect to Readers* Walter Slatoff sums up the positions we tend to take when talking about books:

> Most aestheticians and critics ... speak as though there were only two sorts of readers: the absolutely particular, individual human being ... and the ideal or universal reader whose response is impersonal and aesthetic. Most actual readers, except the most

naive, I think, transform themselves as they read into beings somewhere between these extremes.[15]

Thus the child-reader's interpretation of a text, given that there
is, by both common sense and 'deconstruction', no single or
stable meaning in a text, is inferior only in terms of the game
imposed from outside. As Hugh Crago has pointed out, adults
tend to cheat when comparing children's responses with their
own: 'Children's responses to literature probably do not differ in
any significant way from adults' responses, given that the comparison is made between individual children and adults whose
articulacy and sophistication are roughly equivalent'.[16]

Childist criticism is something that we have seen in practice. It
is based on possibilities and probabilities, not in the absence of
empirical data, but in the face of the immense difficulty of dealing
with that data. It is thus no different from adult criticism, except
that in adult criticism it is rarely, if ever, admitted that there *is* a
problem with the data.

Good examples of the way childist criticism works can be
given by looking at picture books and poetry for children.
To begin with, let us look again at the work of John Burningham.
In his *Come Away from the Water, Shirley*,[17] the adult-oriented
and child-oriented versions of the same time-span are presented
on facing pages. On the left-hand pages, in muted colours, Shirley's parents settle in their chairs on the beach and conduct a
one-sided conversation (full of adult evasions and peremptory
commands) with Shirley, who remains offstage. Although there is
considerable fragmentation of the 'conversation', there is no discontinuity in the time-sequence. Shirley's adventures, with pirates
and buried treasure, wordless and (literally) highly coloured, take
place on the facing pages. The point may be obvious, but the
contrast of codes is interesting. The 'adult' pages rely for their
comprehensibility on reference to extra-textual experience,
whereas Shirley's (imagined?) adventures are based on intertextual reference and reflect the performative patterns of the
counter-culture of childhood, and perhaps allow some inter-
change between child and adult culture.

Burningham moves closer (in structural terms) towards what

might be called a true children's book in *Granpa*.[18] The broad
pattern of this book is of a full-colour picture on the right
opening, usually featuring various encounters between a small girl
and a man whom we may assume to be her grandfather, (with no
particular sequence suggested). On the facing pages are fragments
of dialogue, and below these, in sepia, outline drawings which
variously decorate or elaborate or comment on the pictures opposite, by showing details or flashbacks or fantasies. Thus the first
opening has the dialogue ' "There would not be room for all the little
seeds to grow." "*Do worms go to heaven?*" ' facing a picture of the
girl and Granpa in a greenhouse. The sketch beneath the text adds
details of the greenhouse. The third opening shows Granpa nursing
a female doll and a teddy bear; facing is the line ' "I didn't know
Teddy was another little girl" ', above a sketch of a female teddy
bear applying make-up in a mirror. Another has Granpa skipping
and the little girl inquiring, ' "Were you once a baby as well,
Granpa?" ' and the sketch gives us a box of old sports equipment.
Even the ending is ambiguous and unpredictable. In successive
openings, the girl and Granpa walk in the snow; Granpa is unwell
(' "Granpa can't come out to play today" '); they watch TV together
(' "Tomorrow shall we go to Africa, and you can be Captain?" ');
and in the penultimate opening, the girl sits looking at Granpa's
empty chair. The final page, in very bold colours, shows a little girl
pushing a baby energetically in a very old-fashioned pram. Does life
go on? Or is this Granpa's childhood?

This fragmentation, the possibility of reading on several different planes, with, if anything, under-coding of conventional
elements (like dialogue), may seem to be over-sophisticated for its
audience. But I would argue that its very complexity, together
with the relinquishing of any authorial control in the verbal text,
makes *Granpa* closer to the comprehension patterns of an orally
based reader than the vast majority of texts that set out to be 'for
children'. As such, it contains serious challenges for critics.

Similar questions are raised by children's poetry. This is one of
the most questionable areas of writing for children: is there such a
thing? The conventional answer might be that *poetry* for children
is a contradiction in terms; that children, by virtue of being
children, are unable to appreciate the depth and subtlety that go
to make up poetry. On the other hand, verse, which plays with

words and has attractive rhythms, *is* acceptable. Eleanor Grahame
noted in the Preface to the significantly titled *A Puffin Book of
Verse* that 'I have had a simple standard in compiling this anthology for children, namely to find verses which sing in the ear and
catch in the mind . . . [that have] clear appeal to the simplicity of
youth.'[19] This is clearly imposing firm 'adultist' limitations; but at
least it is more positive than what Janet Adam Smith says in her
introduction to the *Faber Book of Children's Verse*, which does
not discriminate at all. '[It] seems reasonable to give children
poems to read at this age (8–14) that they will like to find in their
heads twenty or thirty years later.'[20] The resulting collection does
not differ noticeably from any 'general' anthology – except,
perhaps, for a greater emphasis on light verse, narrative verse, and
'childhood' subjects. The same might be said of more recent
collections, such as Roger McGough's *Strictly Private*, in which
the ostensible subject-matter of many of the poems is childhood
or adolescence, although the viewpoint is noticeably 'adult', or,
when the viewpoint is that of a child, the implied readership is
adult.[21]

Poetry is not necessarily verse, and verse is not necessarily
poetry. Like the word 'literature', the word 'poem' suggests a
value-judgement. Certainly it requires a different approach to
narrative; it does not necessarily have to be related to a probability or set within a generic framework which has anything referential in it. The poem is allowed to communicate more directly to
the reader; it is legitimate, post-romantically, for mind to speak
to mind, for the words to 'foregrounded' – to be, as it were,
noticeable for their own sake. Benton and Fox quote L. A. G.
Strong's stricture on teaching: 'Remember, the object at every
stage is to keep and develop the child's liking for the music of
words. Explanations and annotations do not matter. A child's
misconception may be of much greater value to him than the
explanation which destroys it.'[22]

That in itself could be seen as a highly adultist remark, which
reserves to itself 'understanding' even if it also implies freedom,
or privateness, of interpretation. Clearly, if education = socialization, one can have no quarrel with such a remark; let us decide
the limits of misunderstanding and teach within them. But let us

not confuse this with any absolute. The concept of letting go here is most important; and it is only at the more extreme edges of poetry that one can confidently make the point that a child's reading may be as valid as an adult's. Janet Adam Smith's principle of selection: 'I shall not be worried if anybody criticizes me for including poems which children cannot "understand". The poems are here for pleasure: the understanding will grow with the reader'[23] is not one that could be lightly applied to prose. Further, with poetry, as Iona and Peter Opie commented in their introduction to the *Oxford Book of Children's Verse*, 'Naturally, the more pure the poetry, the more difficult it is to say for whom the poet is writing.'[24] This idea of 'pure' poetry, of something that bypasses the intellect and challenges or defies interpretation, is a very liberating one for children's literature.

Take a famous example from Walter de la Mare's *Peacock Pie* (1913), subtitled 'A Book of Rhymes'. John Rowe Townsend suggests that de la Mare's 'special quality as a poet is ... an ability to recapture the childlike vision, to show things in words as they feel to a child'.[25] But is this so? 'The Song of the Mad Prince',[26] seems at first to be non-sensical, to have no concrete referents. But this may be only as far as the adult is concerned. The adult mind, it seems to me, is far less likely than the mind of a child to accept images and atmosphere and undirected allusions. There is a tendency (probably educated into us) to interpret, to 'make sense', to find a single transferable meaning. If you are unaware of *Hamlet* as a *key* to this poem, does it diminish or improve the reading?

There is thus a reluctance on the part of the adult world to appreciate that it is only in the least important area of poetry, the ostensible subject-matter, that any distinction (should one be deemed administratively desirable) can be made between what is appropriate for children and what for adults. Thus Roger McGough, whose flippancy is very often a mask worn to keep despair at bay, is able to include poems from his 'adult' collections such as *Holiday on Death Row* and *Melting into the Foreground*[27] in his collections marketed for children, *Strictly Private* and *Nailing the Shadow*.[28] Much less successful has been Ted Hughes, whose collections specifically for children, such as *The Earth-Owl and Other Moon*

People,[29] are largely adult-based (and therefore demeaning) doggerel. On the other hand, his *Under the North Star*[30] is indistringuishable from his 'mainstream' work.

Poetry (and verse) is unforgiving, fortunately, so it is very obvious when poetry has been 'manufactured' specifically for a child audience. The bulk of original verse for children published today is scarcely competent even on its own terms; it is striking evidence of the need for adult readers to become more skilled readers. But this also points to the need for a radical rethinking of the approach to children's literature generally.

Thus far I have suggested reading, as far as possible, from a child's point of view, taking into account personal, sub-cultural, experiential, and psychological differences between children and adults – in short, allowing the reader precedence over the book. There are several major implications of this, which, I think, are increasingly being faced in literary studies generally, but which are particularly pertinent to children's literature. We have got ourselves into the peculiar situation in which the 'privileged' way of reading (in terms of cultural status and educational assessment, both potent sources of power) is a way that is demonstrably abnormal or unnatural, in that it ignores the context of reading. This is not only in terms of the immediate, physical impact of the book-as-object. Things that make the text only *part* of the experience of making meaning – biography, authorial comment, social background, and so on – are either ignored or regarded as secondary. Clearly, vast amounts of project-work are done with literature in schools which addresses exactly this objection; yet the book, totem-like, remains central.

As I have already said, at conferences people flock to sessions addressed by authors. It is not clear, from a literary point of view, why this should be so; after all, the book is a multiple-communicator, the author only a single person. The author is already dead, in a sense. Yet the live author exerts a fascination which, like biography, seems to betray a basic lack of faith, in *fiction itself*. The tendency has been to react against this; but I feel that we should accept this, and thus de-centre and de-privilege the text as such. To do so, immediately places the book in the real world, as part of a larger context in which the (live) author is one element. Any value placed on the text must then be seen to be

bother about the children, Mrs Parker will love it.' As an artist one might genuinely prefer that one's novel should be praised by a single critic, whose opinion one valued, rather than be bought by 'the mob'; but there is no artistic reward for a book written for children other than the knowledge that they enjoy it. For once, and how one hates to think it, *vox populi, vox Dei.*[33]

The second is from W. H. Auden, discussing the 'Alice' books; and it is a quotation that, I think, all of us concerned with children and books should ponder very seriously:

In assessing their value, there are two questions one can ask: first, what insight do they provide as to how the world appears to a child?; and, second; to what extent is the world really like that?[34]

Notes

Introduction: A Map of Criticism

1   Alan Garner, *The Stone Book Quartet* (Collins, London, 1977), p. 31.
2   Anita Moss, 'Structuralism and its critics', *Children's Literature Association Quarterly*, 6, 1 (Spring 1981), p. 25.

Chapter 1: Criticism and Children's Literature

1   For critiques of post-structuralist criticism, see, for example, Raymond Tallis, *In Defence of Realism* (Arnold, London, 1988).
2   See, for example, Roland Barthes, *The Pleasure of the Text*, trans. Richard Miller (Cape, London, 1965; repr. 1976).
3   See, for example, Lissa Paul, 'Intimations of imitations: mimesis, fractal geometry, and children's literature', *Signal*, 59 (May 1989), pp. 128–37.
4   See, for example, Tessa Rose Chester, *Sources of Information about Children's Books* (Thimble Press, South Woodchester, 1989), and Tony Ross, *I Need a Book! The Parent's Guide to Children's Books for Special Situations* (Thorsons, Wellingborough, 1987).
5   *Touchstones: a list of distinguished children's books* (Children's Literature Association, West Lafayette, n.d. [1986?]).
6   Elaine Moss, *Part of the Pattern* (Bodley Head, London, 1986), pp. 207–8.
7   Cited by John Rowe Townsend, 'Standards of criticism for children's literature', in *The Signal Approach To Children's Books*, ed. Nancy Chambers (Kestrel (Penguin), Harmondsworth, 1980), pp. 193–207,) at p. 199.
8   Aidan Chambers, *Booktalk* (Bodley Head, London, 1985), p. 90.
9   Hugh Crago, 'Children's literature: on the cultural periphery', *Children's Book Review*, 4, 4 (1974), p. 158.

10 See Jacqueline Rose, *The Case of Peter Pan, or, the impossibility of children's fiction* (Macmillan, London, 1984).
11 See Lissa Paul, 'Enigma Variations: what feminist theory knows about children's literature', *Signal*, 54 (September 1987), pp. 186–201.
12 Malcolm Bradbury, *Mensonge. My strange quest for Mensonge, structuralism's hidden hero* (Arena (Arrow), London, 1987), pp. 22–3.
13 'Tell me: are children critics?' in Chambers, *Booktalk*, pp. 138–64; Michael Benton and Geoff Fox, *Teaching Literature, nine to fourteen* (Oxford University Press, London, 1985); Michael Benton et al., *Young Readers Responding to Poems* (Routledge, London, 1988); Diana Kelly-Byrne and Brian Sutton-Smith, *The Masks of Play* (Leisure Press, West Point, NY. 1984); Marilyn Cochran-Smith, *The Making of a Reader* (Ablex, Norwood, NJ, 1984); Hugh Crago, 'The roots of response', *Children's Literature Association Quarterly*, 10, 3 (Fall 1985), pp. 100–4.
14 Hugh Crago, 'Cultural categories and the criticism of children's literature', *Signal*, 30 (September 1979), pp. 140–50, at p. 148. See also Hugh and Maureen Crago, *Prelude to Literacy: a preschool child's encounter with picture and story* (Southern Illinois University Press, Carbondale, 1983).
15 Frank Smith, *Reading*, 2nd edn (Cambridge University Press, Cambridge, 1985), p. 83.
16 See Margaret Meek et al., *The Cool Web; the pattern of children's reading* (Bodley Head, London, 1977); Crago and Crago, *Prelude to Literacy*; Benton et al., *Young Readers*.
17 Cf. Terry Eagleton, *Literary Theory: an introduction* (Blackwell, Oxford, 1983), and Catherine Belsey, *Critical Practice* (Methuen, London, 1980).
18 See, for example, Wallace Hildick, *Children and Fiction* (Evans, London, 1970), pp. 76–114.
19 Chambers, *Booktalk*, p. 123.

CHAPTER 2: THE SITUATION OF CHILDREN'S LITERATURE

1 Brough Girling, 'Children's books – toys or medicine?' *Woodfield Lecture XII* (Woodfield and Stanley, Huddersfield, 1989), p. 7.
2 Janet and Allan Ahlberg, *The Jolly Postman, or other people's letters* (Heinemann, London, 1986).
3 Nancy Chambers (ed.), *The Signal Selection, 1986* (Thimble Press, South Woodchester, 1987), p. 2.

4 See Clifton Fadiman, 'The case for children's literature', *Children's Literature*, 5 (Temple University Press, Philadelphia, 1976), pp. 9–21.

5 *Children's Book Review*, 5, 3 (1975).

6 Neil Philip, *A Fine Anger* (Collins, London, 1981), p. 7.

7 Humphrey Carpenter and Mari Prichard, *The Oxford Companion to Children's Literature* (Oxford University Press, London, 1984).

8 John Rowe Townsend, *A Sounding of Storytellers* (Kestrel, Harmondsworth, 1979), pp. 9–10.

9 See Aidan Chambers, 'Letter from England: three fallacies about children's books', repr. in *Signposts to Criticism of Children's Literature*, Robert Bator ed. (Chicago, American Library Association, 1982), pp. 54–60.

10 See, for example, S. Bolt and R. Gard, *Teaching Fiction in Schools* (Hutchinson Educational, London, 1970) p. 25; Margaret Meek et al. (eds), *The Cool Web: the pattern of children's reading* (Bodley Head, London, 1977), p. 180; Virginia Haviland (ed.), *Children and Literature, views and reviews* (Bodley Head, London, 1973), p. 306; Arthur N. Applebee, *The Child's Concept of Story: ages two to seventeen* (University of Chicago Press, Chicago, 1978); Aidan Chambers, *Introducing Books to Children* (Heinemann, London, 1973); Jim Trelease, *The Read-Aloud Handbook* (Penguin, Harmondsworth, 1984).

11 Peggy Heeks, *Choosing and Using Books in the First School* (Macmillan Educational, London, 1981), p. 50.

12 Eleanor Cameron, *The Green and Burning Tree* (Atlantic, Little, Brown, Boston 1969), p. 90; Selma G. Lanes, *Down the Rabbit Hole* (Athenaeum, New York, 1971), pp. vii–viii; Sheila Egoff et al. (eds), *Only Connect. Readings on children's literature* (Oxford University Press, Toronto, 1980), p. xv.

13 Geoff Fox et al. (eds), *Writers, Critics, and Children* (Agathon Press, New York; Heinemann Educational, London, 1976), p. 139.

14 Gillian Avery and Julia Briggs (eds), *Children and their Books* (Clarendon Press, Oxford, 1989), p. 2.

15 Quoted in Edward Blishen (ed.), *The Thorny Paradise* (Kestrel, Harmondsworth, 1975). p. 10.

16 Margaret Meek, *Symbolic Outlining: the academic study of children's literature* (Woodfield and Stanley, Huddersfield, 1986), p. 2.

17 Brian Alderson, 'The irrelevance of children to the children's book reviewer', *Children's Book News*, January/February 1969, pp. 10–11; repr. in *Children's Literature: the development of criticism*, ed. Peter Hunt (Routledge, London, 1990), p. 55.

18 Stephanie Nettell, 'Escapism or realism? The novels of Jean Ure' *Children's Books, British Book News* supplement, March 1985, p. 3.

19 Quoted in *Children's Literature in Education*, 12 (September 1973), p. 63.

20 Carolyn Field, *Special Collections in Children's Literature* (American Library Association, Chicago, 1982); Tessa Rose Chester, *Sources of Information about Children's Books* (Thimble Press, South Woodchester, 1989).

21 Edward B. Jenkinson, *Censors in the Classroom: the mind benders* (Avon, New York, 1982), p. 75.

22 Beatrix Potter, *The Tale of Peter Rabbit*, illustrated by Allen Atkinson (Bantam, New York, 1983).

23 Beatrix Potter, *The Tale of Peter Rabbit* (Warne, London, 1902), pp. 9–10.

24 David Hately (adaptor), *The Tale of Peter Rabbit* (Ladybird, Loughborough, 1987), unpaginated.

25 Potter, *Peter Rabbit*, pp. 18–22.

26 Hately, *Peter Rabbit*.

27 See Lance Salway (ed.), *A Peculiar Gift, nineteenth century writings on books for children* (Kestrel (Penguin), London, 1976).

28 See J. S. Bratton, *The Impact of Victorian Children's Fiction* (Croom Helm, London, 1981); Robert Leeson, *Reading and Righting; the past, present, and future of children's books* (Collins, London, 1985).

29 Potter, *Peter Rabbit*, pp. 56–59.

30 Hately, *Peter Rabbit*; my emphasis.

31 Edward Ardizzone, 'Creation of a picture book', repr. in *Only Connect*, ed. Egoff et al., p. 293.

32 Rumer Godden, 'An imaginary correspondence', in *Children and Literature*, ed. Haviland, pp. 136–7.

33 Potter, *Peter Rabbit*, p. 33.

34 Godden, 'Imaginary correspondence', p. 138.

35 Hately, *Peter Rabbit*.

36 Felix Pirani, *Abigail at the Beach*, illustrated by Christine Roche (Collins, London, 1988), unpaginated.

37 Craig Brown, 'Once upon a perfect time', *The Times*, 25 December 1988. See also Rosemary Sandberg, 'Who censors?' *Books for Keeps*, 58 (September 1989), p. 23.

38 Brown, 'Once upon a perfect time'.

39 See Keith Barker, *In the Realms of Gold: the story of the Carnegie Medal* (MacRae/Youth Libraries Group of the Library Association, London, 1986); Marcus Crouch and Alec Ellis (eds),

Chosen for Children, 3rd edn (The Library Association, London, 1977).

40 Dominic Hibberd, 'The Flambards trilogy: objections to a winner', *Children's Literature in Education*, 8 (July 1982); repr. in *Writers, Critics, and Children*, ed. Fox et al., pp. 125–37, at pp. 126–8.

41 Ibid., p. 136.

42 Ibid., p. 128.

43 Ibid., p. 136.

44 Ibid., p. 137.

45 Colin Ray, '"The edge of the cloud" – a reply to Dominic Hibberd', *Children's Literature in Education*, 9 (November 1972), repr. in *Writers, Critics and Children*, ed. Fox et al., pp. 138–9, at p. 139.

46 Crouch and Ellis (eds), *Chosen for Children*, p. 164.

47 Quoted in Peter Hunt, 'The good, the bad, and the indifferent', in *The Signal Approach to Children's Books* Nancy Chambers ed. (Kestrel (Penguin), Harmondsworth, 1980), p. 227.

48 Frank Eyre, *British Children's Books in the Twentieth Century* (Longman, London, 1971), p. 158

49 Benjamin Disraeli, *Sybil, or the two nations* (1845; Penguin, Harmondsworth, 1954), pp. 90–1. I have shortened the original text slightly.

50 William Mayne, *Ravensgill* (Hamish Hamilton, London, 1970), pp. 162–3.

51 Cameron, *The Green and Burning Tree*, pp. 141–2;

52 Peter Hollindale, *Choosing Books for Children* (Elek, London, 1974), p. 157.

53 I. A. Richards, *Practical Criticism* (Routledge and Kegan Paul, London, 1929).

54 Aidan Chambers, 'The reader in the book', *Signal*, 23 (May 1977), p. 206.

55 John Rowe Townsend, *A Sense of Story* (Kestrel, Harmondsworth, 1971), p. 130.

56 Arthur Ransome, *We Didn't Mean to Go to Sea* (Cape, London, 1937), p. 319.

57 Dennis Wheatley, *To the Devil, a Daughter* (Arrow, London, 1956), p. 99.

CHAPTER 3: DEFINING CHILDREN'S LITERATURE

1 W. H. Auden, 'Today's "wonder world" needs *Alice*', in *Aspects of Alice*, ed. Robert Philips (Penguin, Harmondsworth, 1974), p. 37.

2 C. S. Lewis, 'On three ways of writing for children'; repr. in *Only Connect, readings on children's literature* ed. Egoff, et al., 2nd edn (Oxford University Press, Toronto, 1980), p. 210.

3 Rebecca Lukens, *A Critical Handbook of Children's Literature* (Scott, Foresman, Glenview, Ill., 1976), p. v; see also Lilian H. Smith, *The Unreluctant Years, a critical approach to children's literature* (American Library Association, Chicago, 1953), p. 7.

4 James Steele Smith, *A Critical Approach to Children's Literature* (McGraw Hill, New York, 1967), p. 13.

5 Isobel Jan, *On Children's Literature*, trans. and ed. Catherine Storr (Allen Lane, London, 1973), pp. 142–3.

6 Egoff et al., *Only Connect*, p. x.

7 Lance Salway (ed.), *A Peculiar Gift, nineteenth century writings on books for children* (Kestrel (Penguin), London, 1976), p. 11.

8 Nicholas Tucker, *Suitable for Children? Controversies in children's literature* (Sussex University Press, London, 1976), pp. 18–19.

9 Marcus Crouch, *The Nesbit Tradition* (Benn, London, 1972), p. 8.

10 Jill Paton Walsh, 'The Rainbow Surface', in *The Cool Web: the pattern of children's reading*, ed. Margaret Meek et al. (Bodley Head, London, 1977), pp. 192–3.

11 Patricia Wright, 'Usability: the criterion for designing written information', in P. A. Kolers et al., *Processing of Visible Language*, vol. 2 (London, Plenum, 1980), p. 186.

12 Dorothy Parker, *The Penguin Dorothy Parker* (Penguin/Viking, New York, 1973), p. 437.

13 Pat Hutchins, *Rosie's Walk* (Bodley Head, London, 1968).

14 Rosemary Wells, *Stanley and Rhoda* (Kestrel, Harmondsworth, 1980).

15 Michael Benton et al., *Young Readers Responding to Poems* (Routledge, London, 1989).

16 Stanley Fish, *Is there a text in this Class? The authority of interpretive communities* (Harvard University Press, Cambridge, Mass., 1980).

17 See also Rhonda Bunbury, 'Can children read for inference?' in *The Power of Story* (Deakin University, Victoria, 1980), pp. 149–57; Michael Benton, 'Children's responses to stories', *Children's Literature in Education*, 10, 2 (1975), pp. 68–85.

18 See Zohar Shavit, *Poetics of Children's Literature* (University of Georgia Press, Athens, GA. 1986), pp. 33–42.

19 Quoted in Raman Selden (ed.), *The Theory of Criticism* (Longman, London, 1988), pp. 500–1.

20 See F. R. Leavis, 'Literary criticism and philosophy: a reply', in *Scrutiny*, 6, 1 (June 1937), pp. 59–70.

208 *Notes*

21 Quoted by Felicity A. Hughes, 'Children's literature: theory and practice', *English Literary History*, 45 (1978), pp. 542–61; repr. in *Children's Literature: the development of criticism*, ed. Peter Hunt (Routledge, London, 1990), pp. 71–89, at p. 75.
22 Howard Felperin, *Beyond Deconstruction. The uses and abuses of literary theory* (Oxford University Press, London, 1985), p. 8.
23 Ibid., p. 9.
24 Jeremy Tambling, *What is Literary Language?* (Open University Press, Milton Keynes, 1988), pp. 8–9.
25 Elaine Moss, 'Selling the children short', *Signal*, 48 (September 1985), p. 138.
26 C. S. Lewis, 'On stories', in *Essays Presented To Charles Williams* (Oxford University Press, London, 1947); repr. in Meek et al., *Cool Web*, pp. 76–90, at pp. 78–89.
27 E. M. Forster, *Aspects of the Novel* (1927; repr. Penguin, Harmondsworth, 1976), p. 40.
28 René Wellek and Austin Warren, *Theory of Literature*, 3rd edn (Penguin, Harmondsworth, 1963), p. 212.
29 John M. Ellis, *The Theory of Literary Criticism, a logical analysis* (University of California Press, Berkeley, 1974), p. 41.
30 Ibid., p. 42.
31 Ibid., p. 44.
32 Raymond Williams, *Keywords*, rev. edn (Fontana, London, 1988), pp. 183–8.
33 Terry Eagleton, *Literary Theory, an introduction* (Blackwell, Oxford, 1983), p. 202; see also the Introduction, pp. 1–16, and pp. 194ff.
34 Leeson, *Reading and Righting: the past, present, and future of books for the young* (Collins, London, 1985), p. 144.
35 Peter Dickinson, 'In defence of rubbish', repr. in *Writers, Critics, and Children*, ed. Geoff Fox et al. (Agathon Press, New York; Heinemann Educational, London, 1976), p. 74.
36 Ibid., pp. 75–6.
37 Shavit, *Poetics of Children's Literature, passim*.
38 Nicholas Tucker, *What is a Child?* (Fontana/Open Books, London, 1977).
39 Nicholas Tucker, *The Child and the Book* (Cambridge University Press, Cambridge, 1981); Jean Piaget, *The Child's Conception of the World* (Routledge and Kegan Paul, London, 1929).
40 See Diana Kelly-Byrne, 'Continuity and discontinuity in play conditioning: the adult-child connection', in *The Masks of Play*, ed. Brian Sutton-Smith and Diana Kelly-Byrne (Leisure Press, West

Point, NY, 1984); idem, 'The 1984 conference of the Children's Literature Association ... a participant's response', *Children's Literature Association Quarterly*, 9, 4 (1984–5), pp. 195–8; R. and S. Scollon, *Narrative Literacy and Inter-ethnic Communication* (Ablex, Norwood, NJ, 1981); Marilyn Cochran-Smith, *The Making of a Reader*, (Ablex, Norwood, NJ, 1984).

41 See Arthur N. Applebee, *The Child's Concept of Story: ages two to seventeen* (University of Chicago Press, Chicago, 1978).

42 J. R. R. Tolkien, *Tree and Leaf* (Allen and Unwin, London, 1970), p. 34.

43 Brian Alderson, 'Lone voices in the crowd: the limits of multiculturalism' in *Cross Culturalism in Children's Literature*, ed. Susan R. Gannon and Ruth Anne Thompson (Pace University, Pleasantville, NY, 1988), p. 8.

44 Pierre Machery, *A Theory of Literary Production* (Routledge and Kegan Paul, London, 1978), p. 70.

45 Quoted in Selma G. Lanes, *Down the Rabbit Hole* (Athenaeum, New York, 1971), p. 152.

46 Gillian Adams, 'The first children's literature? The case for Sumer', *Children's Literature*, 14 (1986), p. 1.

47 Lee A. Jacobus, 'Milton's *Comus* as children's literature', *Children's Literature*, 2 (1973), p. 67.

48 Geoffrey Summerfield, *Fantasy and Reason; children's literature in the eighteenth century* (Methuen, London, 1984), p. 86.

49 J. R. R. Tolkien, *The Hobbit* (Allen and Unwin, London, 1937); idem, *The Lord of the Rings* (Allen and Unwin, London, 1954–5).

50 John Rowe Townsend, *A Sense of Story* (Longman, London, 1971), p. 9.

51 Myles McDowell, 'Fiction for children and adults: some essential differences', *Children's Literature in Education*, 10 (March 1973); repr. in *Writers, Critics, and Children*, ed. Fox et al., pp. 141–2.

52 Jan, *On Children's Literature*, pp. 142–3.

53 Neil Philip, 'Children's literature and the oral tradition', in *'Further Approaches to Research in Children's Literature*, ed. Peter Hunt (University of Wales, Cardiff, 1982), p. 20.

54 Shavit, *Poetics of Children's Literature*, pp. 63–9.

55 A. A. Milne, *Winnie-the-Pooh* (Methuen, London, 1926).

56 Anthony Browne, *Bear Goes to Town* (Hamish Hamilton, London, 1982); idem, *A Walk in the Park* (Hamish Hamilton, London, 1977).

57 John Burningham, *Granpa* (Cape, London, 1984).

58 Russell Hoban and Quentin Blake, *How Tom Beat Captain Najork and his Hired Sportsmen* (Cape, London, 1974).

CHAPTER 4: APPROACHING THE TEXT

1 Barbara Hardy, 'Towards a poetics of fiction: an approach through narrative', in *The Cool Web: the pattern of children's reading*, (Bodley Head London, 1977), ed. Margaret Meek et al. p. 12.
2 D. W. Harding, 'Psychological processes in the reading of fiction', in ibid., p. 72.
3 Jonathan Culler, *The Pursuit of Signs* (Routledge and Kegan Paul, London, 1981), p. 50. See also Mary Louise Pratt, *Towards a Speech Act Theory of Literary Discourse* (Indiana University Press, Bloomington, 1977).
4 Quoted in Lewis Carroll *The Annotated Snark*, ed. Martin Gardner, rev. edn (Penguin, Harmondsworth, 1973), p. 22.
5 Laurence Sterne, *Tristram Shandy* (1759–67), vol. 2, ch. 11.
6 Michael Stubbs, 'Stir until the plot thickens', in *Literary Text and Language Study*, ed. Ronald Carter and Deirdre Burton (Arnold, London, 1982).
7 Jonathan Culler, 'Prologomena to a theory of reading', in *The Reader in the Text*, ed. Susan R. Suleiman and Inge Crosman (Princeton University Press, Princeton, 1980), p. 50.
8 Susan R. Suleiman, 'Introduction: varieties of audience-oriented criticism', in ibid., p. 37.
9 Rudyard Kipling, *Stalky and Co* (Macmillan, London, 1899).
10 Margaret Meek, *How Texts Teach what Readers Learn* (Thimble Press, South Woodchester, 1988), p. 11.
11 Ibid., p. 31.
12 Ibid., p. 20.
13 Ibid., p. 13. See also Aidan Chambers et al., 'Tell me: are children critics?' in Aidan Chambers, *Booktalk* (Bodley Head, London, 1985), pp. 138–174; Michael Benton et al., *Young Readers Responding to Poems* (Routledge, London, 1989).
14 Hugh Crago and Maureen Crago, *Prelude to Literacy: a preschool child's encounter with picture and story* (Southern Illinois University Press, Urbana, 1983), *passim*.
15 Hugh Crago, 'The roots of response', *Children's Literature Association Quarterly*, 10, 3 (Fall 1985); repr. in *Children's Literature: the development of criticism*, ed. Peter Hunt (Routledge, London, 1990), pp. 118–129, at p. 128.

16 Walter Nash, *The Language of Humour* (Longman, London, 1985), p. 74.

17 Rick Rylance (ed.), *Debating Texts, a reader in 20th century literary theory and method* (Open University Press, Milton Keynes, 1987), p. 113.

18 Arthur Ransome, *Swallows and Amazons* (Cape, London, 1930).

19 Janni Howker, *Isaac Campion* (MacRae, London, 1986).

20 Meek et al. (eds), *Cool Web*, p. 74.

21 Stanley Fish, *Is there a Text in this Class? The authority of interpretive communities* (Harvard University Press, Cambridge, Mass., 1980), p. 267.

22 Shirley Brice Heath, *Ways with Words: language, life, and work in communities and classrooms* (Cambridge University Press, Cambridge, 1983), p. 184.

23 Heather Dubrow, *Genre* (Methuen, London, 1982), p. 107.

24 Margaret Meek, *Learning to Read* (Bodley Head, London, 1982), p. 37.

25 E. D. Hirsch, *Validity in Interpretation* (Yale University Press, New Haven, 1967), p. 93.

26 J. D. Salinger, 'Seymour, an introduction', in *Raise High The Roofbeam, Carpenters and Seymour, an introduction*, (Penguin, Harmondsworth, 1964), p. 156.

27 Walter Ong, *Orality and Literacy* (Methuen, London, 1982), p. 171.

28 Ibid., p. 142. Compare W. Labov, *Language in the Inner City* (University of Pennsylvania Press, Philadelphia, 1974), p. 363; A. K. Pugh, 'Construction and reconstruction of text', in *The Reader and the Text*, ed. L. John Chapman (Heinemann Educational, London, 1981), pp. 70 – 80; Nancy Stein, 'The comprehension and appreciation of stories, a developmental analysis', in *The Arts: cognition and basic skills*, ed. S. S. Madeja (Cemrel, St Louis, 1978), pp. 231–49.

29 Ong, *Orality and Literacy*, p. 142.

30 See Shlomith Rimmon-Kenan, *Narrative Fiction: contemporary poetics* (Methuen, London, 1983), p. 118, and Jeffery Wilkinson, 'Children's writing: composing or decomposing?' *Nottingham Linguistic Circular*, 10, 1 (June 1981), pp. 85–99; M. A. K. Halliday and R. Hasan, *Cohesion in English* (Longman, London, 1976), pp. 32–3; Arthur N. Applebee, *The Child's Concept of Story: ages two to seventeen* (University of Chicago Press, Chicago, 1978), pp. 56–70.

31 Suzanne Romaine, *The Language of Children and Adolescents: the acquisition of communicative competence* (Blackwell, Oxford, 1984), pp. 149–50.

32 Howard E. Gardner et al., 'Children's literary development: the realms of metaphors and stories', in *Children's Humour*, ed. Paul E. McGee and Anthony J. Chapman (John Wiley, Chichester, 1980), pp. 98, 111.

33 Seymour Chatman, *Story and Discourse: narrative structure in fiction and film* (Cornell University Press, Ithaca, 1978), p. 27.

34 See Jan Nicholas, 'The case for reading schemes', and Jill Bennett, 'Reading, but what?', in *Books for your Children*, 23, 3 (Autumn/ Winter 1988), pp. 16–17, 19.

35 Quoted in Suleiman and Crosman (eds), *Reader in the Text*, p. 227.

36 Hugh Crago, 'The readers in the reader: an experiment in personal response and literary criticism', *Signal*, 39 (September 1982), pp. 172–82.

37 Mark Roberts, *The Fundamentals of Literary Criticism* (Blackwell, Oxford, 1964), p. 3.

38 Elaine Moss, 'The dream and the reality: a children's book critic goes back to school', *Signal*, 34 (January 1981), pp. 22–36.

39 Betsy Byars, *The Eighteenth Emergency* (1971; Puffin (Penguin), Harmondsworth, 1981).

CHAPTER 5: THE TEXT AND THE READER

1 Christine Brook-Rose, *A Rhetoric of the Unreal* (Cambridge University Press, Cambridge, 1981), p. 41.

2 See Raman Selden, *A Reader's Guide to Contemporary Literary Theory* (Harvester, Brighton, 1985), p. 17.

3 Ann Digby, *First Term at Trebizon* (Granada, London, 1980), pp. 8–9.

4 Betsy Byars, *The Eighteenth Emergency* (Puffin (Penguin), Harmondsworth, 1981), p. 59.

5 Jacqueline Rose, *The Case of Peter Pan, or, the impossibility of children's fiction* (Macmillan, London, 1984), pp. 1–2.

6 Michelle Magorian, *Goodnight Mr Tom*, (Penguin, Harmondsworth, 1983), p. 192.

7 Shlomith Rimmon-Kenan, *Narrative Fiction: contemporary poetics* (Methuen, London, 1983), pp. 86–116.

8 A. A. Milne, *Winnie-the-Pooh* (1926; repr. Methuen, London, 1970), pp. 16–17.

9 Robert Leeson, *Reading and Righting: the past, present, and future of books for the young* (Collins, London, 1985), pp. 15–109.

10   Ruth Park, *Playing Beattie Bow* (Penguin, Harmondsworth, 1982), pp. 96–7.

11   Adapted from Robert Protherough, *Developing Response to Fiction* (Open University Press, Milton Keynes, 1983), p. 30.

12   Robert Cormier, *After the First Death* (Gollancz, London, 1979).

13   C. S. Lewis, *The Lion, the Witch, and the Wardrobe* (1948; repr. Collins, London, 1950, 1982).

14   Roger Fowler, *Linguistic Criticism* (Oxford University Press, London, 1986), p. 27.

15   Ibid., p. 69.

16   Frank Smith, *Writing and the Writer* (Heinemann Educational, London, 1982), pp. 95–6.

17   See Margaret Meek, *How Texts Teach what Readers Learn* (Thimble Press, South Woodchester, 1988).

18   Frank Smith, *Reading*, 2nd edn (Cambridge University Press, Cambridge, 1985), p. 83.

19   Janni Howker, *Isaac Campion* (MacRae, London, 1986), p. 1.

20   Berke Breathed, *'Toons For Our Times: Bloom County* (Little, Brown, Boston, 1984), p. 91.

21   Smith, *Writing and the Writer*, pp. 88–9, 94–5.

22   Howker, *Isaac Campion*, p. 1.

23   Richard C. Anderson, 'Schema-directed processes in language comprehension', in *The Psychology of Written Communication*, ed. R. Hartley (Kogan Page, London, 1980), p. 37.

24   Catherine Belsey, *Critical Practice* (Methuen, London, 1980), p. 109.

25   Howard Felperin, *Beyond Deconstruction. The uses and abuses of literary theory* (Oxford University Press, London, 1985), p. 131.

26   Frank Hatt, *The Reading Process. A framework for analysis and description* (Clive Bingley, London; Linnet, Hamden, Ct, 1976), p. 71.

27   Michael Benton et al., *Young Readers Responding to Poems* (Routledge, London, 1988), p. ix.

28   Hatt, *Reading Process*, pp. 66, 74.

29   Harold Rosen, *Stories and Meanings* (National Association for the Teaching of English, London, 1985), p. 38.

CHAPTER 6: STYLE AND STYLISTICS

1   Quoted in Terry Eagleton, *Literary Theory, an introduction* (Blackwell, Oxford, 1983), p. 79.

2 Ibid., pp. 79–80.

3 See Justine Coupland, 'Complexity and difficulty in children's reading material', unpublished Ph. D. thesis (University of Wales, Cardiff, 1983).

4 Cynthia Harnett, *The Woolpack* (1951; repr. Penguin, Harmondsworth, 1981), p. 211.

5 Ian Watt, 'The first paragraph of *The Ambassadors*: an explication'; repr. in *Twentieth Century Literary Criticism*, ed. David Lodge (Longman, London, 1972), p. 59.

6 Geoffrey N. Leech, *A Linguistic Guide to English Poetry* (Longman, London, 1969), p. 225.

7 Henry Widdowson, 'Stylistics', in J. B. R. Allen and S. Pit Corder, *The Edinburgh Course in Applied Linguistics*, vol. 2 (Oxford University Press, London, 1973), p. 204.

8 See Stanley Fish, *Is there a Text in this Class? The authority of interpretive communities* (Harvard University Press, Cambridge, Mass., 1980), pp. 68–96.

9 Roger Fowler, *Literature as Social Discourse* (Batsford, London, 1981), p. 19.

10 Anne Cluysenaar, *Introduction to Literary Stylistics* (Batsford, London, 1976), p. 16.

11 See Raman Selden, *A Reader's Guide to Contemporary Literary Theory* (Harvester, Brighton, 1985; 2nd edn 1989), pp. 16–19.

12 Horst Ruthrof, *The Reader's Construction of Narrative* (Routledge, London, 1981), p. 123.

13 David Crystal and Derek Davy, *Investigating English Style* (Longman, London, 1969), pp. 15–19; Geoffrey Leech and Michael Short, *Style in Fiction* (Longman, London, 1981), pp. 75–82.

14 M. Cummings and R. Simmons, *The Language of Literature* (Pergamon, London, 1983), p. 218.

15 Fowler, *Literature as Social Discourse*, p. 28.

16 Eleanor Cameron, *The Green and Burning Tree* (Atlantic, Little, Brown, Boston, 1969), p. 87.

17 Joan Aiken, 'Purely for love', in *Children's Literature, views and reviews*, ed. Virginia Haviland (Bodley Head, London, 1974), p. 148.

18 E. B. White, 'On writing for children', in ibid., p. 140.

19 Janice Dohm, 'On Enid Blyton', in *Young Writers, Young readers*, ed. Boris Ford (Hutchinson, London, 1963), pp. 99–106, at p. 99.

20 See, for example, Carol Chomsky, *The Acquisition of Language in Children from 5 to 10* (MIT Press, Boston, 1969); David McNeill, *The Acquistion of Language* (Harper and Rowe, New York, 1970).

21 David Holbrook, *The Secret Places* (Methuen, London, 1964); idem, *The Exploring World* (Cambridge University Press, Cambridge, 1967).
22 John Holt, *How Children Learn* (Penguin, Harmondsworth, 1970).
23 James Britton, *Language and Learning* (Penguin, Harmondsworth, 1972).
24 Connie and Harold Rosen, *Language of Primary School Children* (Penguin Education, Harmondsworth, 1973).
25 Geoffrey Summerfield, *Topics in Education for the Secondary School* (Batsford, London, 1965), pp. 16–17.
26 Enid Blyton, *Tricky the Goblin* (Macmillan, London, 1950), pp. 138–9.
27 Dohm, 'On Enid Blyton', p. 100. See also Sheila Ray, *The Blyton Pheonomenon* (André Deutsch, London, 1982), pp. 111–31.
28 Jean Roberton, *Hans Christian Andersen's Fairy Tales* (Pan Books (Piccolo), London, 1974), p. 7.
29 Fiona French, *Snow White in New York* (Oxford University Press, London, 1986).
30 Alan Garner, *A Bag of Moonshine* (Collins, London, 1988).
31 C. S. Lewis, *The Lion, the Witch, and the Wardrobe* (1948; repr. Collins, London, 1950, 1982), pp. 17–19.
32 Eagleton, *Literary Theory*, p. 178.
33 Wayne Booth, *The Rhetoric of Fiction* (University of Chicago Press, Chicago, 1961). pp. 2ff.; Shlomith Rimmon-Kenan, *Narrative Fiction: contemporary poetics* (Methuen, London, 1983), pp. 106–8.
34 See, for example, Seymour Chatman, 'The structure of narrative transmission', in *Style and Structure in Literature*, ed. Roger Fowler (Cornell University Press, Ithaca, 1975), p. 230; idem, *Story and Discourse: narrative structure in fiction and film* (Cornell University Press, Ithaca, 1978), p. 201; Helmut Bonheim, *The Narrative Modes: techniques of the short story* (D. S. Brewer, Cambridge, 1982), p. 51; Roger Fowler, *Linguistics and the Novel* (Methuen, London, 1977), pp. 102ff.; Rimmon-Kenan, *Narrative Fiction* pp. 108–16; David Young, 'Projection and deixis in narrative discourse', in *Styles of Discourse*, ed. Nikolas Coupland (Croom Helm, Beckenham, 1988), pp. 20–49.
35 Leech and Short, *Style in Fiction*, pp. 323–4.
36 Rimmon-Kenan, *Narrative Fiction* pp. 110–11.
37 Fowler, *Linguistics and the Novel*, p. 103.
38 Bonheim, *Narrative Modes*, p. 52.
39 Leech and Short, *Style in Fiction*, p. 324.

40 Ibid., p. 344.

41 Ibid., p. 345.

42 'Carolyn Keene', *The Invisible Intruder* (Collins, London, 1972), pp. 332–3.

43 Alan Garner, *Red Shift* (London, Collins, 1975), p. 130.

44 Neil Philip, *A Fine Anger* (Collins, London, 1981), p. 106.

45 Chatman, *Story and Discourse*, p. 200.

46 Chatman, 'Structure of narrative transmission', pp. 244–5.

47 Joan G. Robinson, *When Marnie Was There* (Collins, London, 1967), p. 200.

48 Malcolm Bradbury, *The History Man* (Hutchinson, London, 1977); idem, *Rates of Exchange* (Hutchinson, London, 1984).

49 Alan Garner, *The Stone Book* (Collins, London, 1976), p. 11.

50 Fish, *Is there a Text?*, p. 267.

CHAPTER 7: NARRATIVE

1 C. S. Lewis, 'On stories,' in *Essays Presented to Charles Williams* (Oxford University Press, London, 1947); repr. in *The Cool Web*, ed. Margaret Meek et al. (Bodley Head, London, 1977), pp. 76–90, at p. 87.

2 Vladimir Propp, *The Morphology of the Folk Tale* (University of Texas Press, Austin, 1968).

3 See Arthur N. Applebee, *The Child's Concept of Story: ages two to seventeen.* (University of Chicago Press, Chicago, 1978).

4 Seymour Chatman, *Story and Discourse: narrative structure in fiction and film* (Cornell University Press, Ithaca, 1978), pp. 47–8.

5 Jacqueline Rose, *The Case of Peter Pan, or, the impossibility of children's fiction* (Macmillan, London, 1984), pp. 63–4.

6 Wayne Booth, *The Rhetoric of Fiction* (University of Chicago Press, Chicago, 1961).

7 Shlomith Rimmon-Kenan, *Narrative Fiction: contemporary poetics* (Methuen, London, 1983).

8 Quoted in Jonathan Culler, *The Pursuit of Signs* (Routledge and Kegan Paul, London, 1981), p. 171.

9 Chatman, *Story and Discourse*, pp. 18–19.

10 See, for example, Ronald Carter and Walter Nash, *Discourse Stylistics* (Routledge, London, 1989).

11 Rimmon-Kenan, *Narrative Fiction*, pp. 118, 119.

12 Robert L. Caserio, *Plot, Story, and the Novel* (Princeton University Press, Princeton, 1979), p. 8.

13 Ibid., p. 169.

14 Michael Zeraffa, 'The novel as literary form and as social institution', in *Sociology of Literature and Drama*, ed. Tom and Elizabeth Burns (Penguin, Harmondsworth, 1973), p. 32.

15 Jane P. Tompkins, 'An introduction to reader response criticism', in *Reader Response Criticism: from formalism to post-structuralism*, ed. Jane P. Tompkins (The Johns Hopkins University Press, Baltimore, 1980), p. xxi.

16 Kenneth Grahame, *The Wind in the Willows* (1908; Methuen, London, 1975).

17 See Elspeth Grahame (ed.), *First Whisper of 'The Wind in the Willows'* (Methuen, London, 1944).

18 Jonathan Culler, 'Defining narrative units', in *Style and Structure in Literature*, ed. Roger Fowler (Blackwell, Oxford, 1975), pp. 138–41.

19 Grahame, *Wind in the Willows*, pp. 236–7.

20 Michael Stubbs, 'Stir until the plot thickens', in *Literary Text and Language Study*, ed. Ronald Carter and Deirdre Burton (Arnold, London, 1982), p. 51.

21 See Nicholas Tucker, *The Child and the Book: a psychological and literary exploration* (Cambridge University Press, Cambridge, 1981), pp. 14–16, 97.

22 A. A. Milne, *Toad of Toad Hall* (Methuen, London, 1940), pp. v–vii.

23 See Humphrey Carpenter and Mari Pritchard, *The Oxford Companion to Children's Literature* (Oxford University Press, 1984), pp. 274–5.

24 Grahame, *Wind in the Willows*, p. 106.

25 Rudyard Kipling, *Puck of Pook's Hill* (Macmillan, London, 1906).

26 Grahame, *Wind in the Willows*, p. 83.

27 See Applebee, *Child's Concept of Story*, pp. 62–3.

28 Pat Hutchins, *Rosie's Walk* (Bodley Head, London, 1968).

29 Hugh and Maureen Crago, *Prelude to Literacy: a preschool child's encounter with picture and story* (Southern Illinois University Press, Urbana, 1983).

30 J. R. R. Tolkien, *The Hobbit*. (Allen and Unwin, London, 1937).

31 E. Nesbit, *The Wouldbegoods* (Fisher Unwin, London, 1901); idem, *The Railway Children* (Wells Gardner, London, 1906).

32 David McKee, *Not Now Bernard* (Andersen Press, London, 1980).

33 Florence Parry Heide, *The Shrinking of Treehorn* (Holiday House, New York, 1971; Kestrel, Harmondsworth, 1976).

34 Fish, *Is there a Text in this Class? The authority of interpretive*

communities (Harvard University Press, Cambridge, Mass., 1980), pp. 303–4.

35 Russell Hoban and Quentin Blake, *How Tom Beat Captain Najork and his Hired Sportsmen* (Cape, London, 1974).

36 Lissa Paul, 'Enigma Variations: what feminist criticism knows about children's literature', *Signal*, 54 (September 1987), pp. 198–9.

37 J. R. R. Tolkien, *The Lord of the Rings* (Allen and Unwin, London, 1978), p. 1069.

38 Ibid., p. 9.

39 Arthur Ransome, *Swallowdale* (Cape, London, 1931; repr. 1936), p. 448.

40 Arthur Ransome, Peter Duck (Cape, London, 1932).

41 Arthur Ransome, Winter Holiday (Cape, London, 1933).

42 Arthur Ransome, *Pigeon Post* (Cape, London, 1936).

43 Arthur Ransome, *We Didn't Mean to Go To Sea* (Cape, London, 1937).

44 Arthur Ransome, *Great Northern?* (Cape, London, 1948).

45 Frank Smith, *Writing and the Writer* (Heinemann Educational, London, 1982), pp. 88–9, 94–5, 95–6.

46 Roger Fowler, *Linguistic Criticism* (Oxford University Press, London, 1986), p. 69.

47 M. A. K. Halliday and R. Hasan, *Cohesion in English* (Longman, London, 1982).

48 Eric S. Rabkin, *Narrative Suspense* (University of Michigan Press, Ann Arbor, 1973), p. 121.

49 Janni Howker, *Isaac Campion* (MacRae, London, 1986), pp. 1–2.

50 Rabkin, *Narrative Suspense*, p. 47.

51 Ibid.; my emphasis.

52 Frank Kermode, *The Genesis of Secrecy: on the interpretation of narrative* (Harvard University Press, London, 1979), p. 144.

CHAPTER 8: POLITICS, IDEOLOGY, AND CHILDREN'S LITERATURE

1 Aidan Chambers, 'An interview with Alan Garner', in *The Signal Approach to Children's Books,* ed. Nancy Chambers (Kestrel (Penguin), Harmondsworth, 1980), p. 327.

2 Sarah Trimmer, 'Observations on the changes which have taken place in books for children and young persons' (1802), in *A Peculiar Gift: nineteenth century writings on books for children,* ed. Lance Salway (Kestrel (Penguin), London, 1976), p. 21.

3 Patrick Shannon, 'Unconscious censorship of social and political

ideas in children's books', *Children's Literature Association Quarterly*, 12, 2 (1987), p. 105.

4 Ibid., p. 139.

5 Robert Leeson, *Reading and Righting: the past, present, and future of books for the young* (Collins, London, 1985), p. 170.

6 Nicholas Tucker, *The Child and the Book: a psychological and literary exploration* (Cambridge University Press, Cambridge, 1981), p. 20.

7 Terry Eagleton, *Literary Theory, an introduction* (Blackwell, Oxford, 1983), p. 194.

8 Bob Dixon, *Catching them Young: 1: Sex, Race, and Class in Children's Books* (Plenum, London, 1977), pp. xv, xiv.

9 Jill Paton Walsh, 'The language of children's literature', *Bookquest*, 8, 1 (1985), pp. 4–9, at p. 9.

10 Nicholas Tucker (ed.), *Suitable for Children? Controversies in Children's Literature* (Sussex University Press, London, 1976), p. 11.

11 Leeson, *Reading and Righting*, p. 142.

12 Ibid.

13 Ibid.

14 Aidan Chambers, *Booktalk* (Bodley Head, London, 1985), pp. 14–15.

15 Leeson, *Reading and Righting*.

16 Humphrey Carpenter, *Secret Gardens; the golden age of children's literature* (Allen and Unwin, London, 1985).

17 Leeson, *Reading and Righting*, p. 171.

18 Carpenter, *Secret Gardens*, p. ix.

19 Carpenter, *Secret Gardens*, p. 83.

20 Leeson, *Reading and Righting*, p. 104.

21 Carpenter, *Secret Gardens*, p. 113.

22 Richard Jefferies, *Bevis*, ed. Peter Hunt (London, Oxford University Press, 1989), p. 10.

23 Carpenter, *Secret Gardens*, p. 221.

24 Leeson, *Reading and Righting*, p. 171.

25 Ibid., p. 185.

26 Ibid., pp. 186–7.

27 Charles Sarland, 'False premises', *Signal*, 37 (January 1982), pp. 12–13.

28 Walter Ong, *Orality and Literacy* (Methuen, London, 1982), *passim*.

29 Susan Dickinson, letter in *Signal*, 14 (May 1974), p. 106.

30 Jacqueline Rose, *The Case of Peter Pan, or, the impossibility of children's fiction* (Macmillan, London, 1984), pp. 1–2.

31   Aidan Chambers, *Breaktime* (Bodley Head, London, 1978); idem, *Now I Know* (Bodley Head, London, 1987).
32   Ellen Raskin, *The Westing Game* (Dutton, New York, 1978; London, Macmillan, 1979).
33   William Mayne, *Salt River Times* (Nelson, Sydney, 1980).
34   William Moebius, 'Introduction to picture book codes', *Word and Image*, 2, 2 (April–June 1986), pp. 141–58, at p. 151.
35   John Burningham, *Granpa* (Cape, London, 1984).
36   Janet and Allan Ahlberg, *The Jolly Postman or other people's letters* (Heinemann, London, 1986).
37   Raymond Briggs, *Fungus the Bogeyman* (Hamish Hamilton, London, 1977).
38   David McKee, *I Hate My Teddy Bear* (Scholastic, London, 1983).
39   Peter Hollindale, 'Ideology and the children's book', *Signal*, 55 (1988), pp. 3–22, at p. 7.

CHAPTER 9: PRODUCING CHILDREN'S LITERATURE

1   Pierre Machery, *A Theory of Literary Production* (Routledge, London, 1978), p. 70.
2   Peter Hunt, *Going Up* (MacRae, London, 1989).
3   Barbara Harrison and Gregory Maguire (eds), *Innocence and Experience: essays and conversations on children's literature* (Lothrop, Lee and Shepard, New York, 1987), p. 231.
4   For example, Justin Wintle and Emma Fisher, *The Pied Pipers* (Paddington Press, New York, 1974); Jonathan Cott, *Pipers at the Gates of Dawn: the wisdom of children's literature* (Random House, New York, 1983).
5   Quoted in Margaret Meek et al. (eds), *The Cool Web, the pattern of children's reading* (Bodley Head, London, 1977), p. 180.
6   See Geoffrey Trease, 'The revolution in children's literature', in *The Thorny Paradise*, ed. Edward Blishen (Kestrel, Harmondsworth, 1975), pp. 13–24; Aidan Chambers, *Booktalk* (Bodley Head, London, 1985); Wallace Hildick, *Children and Fiction* (Evans, London, 1970).
7   Julia MacRae, 'Amateur joys', in *The Signal Approach to Children's Books*, ed. Nancy Chambers (Kestrel (Penguin), Harmondsworth, 1980), p. 100.
8   Elspeth Grahame, *The First Whisper of 'Wind in the Willows'* (Methuen, London, (1936).
9   See Jacqueline Rose, *The Case of Peter Pan, or, the impossibility of*

children's fiction (Macmillan, London, 1984); Robert Leeson, *Reading and Righting: the past, present, and future of books for the young* (Collins, London, 1985).

10 Quoted by Stephanie Nettell, 'Escapism or realism? The novels of Jean Ure', *Children's Books (British Book News supplement)*, March 1985, pp. 3–4.

11 Heather Dubrow, *Genre* (Methuen, London, 1982), p. 31.

12 See Roger Lancelyn Green, *Authors and Places* (Batsford, London, 1963).

13 Tony Bradman, *I Need A Book! The parent's guide to children's books for special situations* (Thorsons, Wellingborough, 1987), p. 12.

14 Michele Landsberg, *The World of Children's Books* (Simon and Schuster, London, 1988), p. 209.

15 Elaine Moss, 'The seventies in picture books', in *The Signal Approach*, ed. Chambers, pp. 56–7.

16 Aidan Chambers, *Booktalk* (Bodley Head, London, 1985), p. 93.

17 Moss, 'Seventies in Picture Books', p. 57.

18 Michael Benton et al., *Young Readers Responding to Poems* (Routledge, London, 1988); Michael Benton and Geoff Fox, *Teaching Literature, Nine to Fourteen* (Oxford University Press, Oxford, 1985).

19 See Amanda Holloway, 'The great Walker shake-up', *The Bookseller*, 10 March 1989, pp. 846–8.

20 Peter Hunt, *Sue and the Honey Machine* (MacRae, London, 1989).

21 Quoted by Jon Winokur, *Writers on Writing* (Headline, London, 1988), p. 47.

22 Quoted by Winokur, *Writers on Writing*, p. 34.

23 Landsberg, *World of Children's Books*.

24 Hunt, *Going Up*, p. 26.

CHAPTER 10: CRITICISM AND THE PICTURE BOOK

1 Celia Berridge, 'Taking a good look at picture books', *Signal*, 36 (September 1981), pp. 152–8, at p. 157.

2 Kenneth Marantz, 'The picture book as art object: a call for balanced reviewing', *Wilson Library Bulletin*, October 1977, pp. 148–51; repr. in *Signposts to Criticism of Children's Literature*, ed. Robert Bator (American Library Association, Chicago, 1983), p. 155.

3   Philip Pullman, 'Invisible pictures', *Signal*, 60 (September 1989), pp. 160–86, at p. 171.
4   Ibid., p. 172.
5   Margaret Meek, *How Texts Teach what Readers Learn* (Thimble Press, South Woodchester, 1988), pp. 12–13.
6   Sonia Landes, 'Picture books as literature', *Children's Literature Association Quarterly*, 10, 2 (Summer 1985), p. 52.
7   Elaine Moss, 'W(h)ither picture books? Some tricks of the trade', *Signal*, 31 (January 1980), pp. 3–7, at p. 3.
8   Nicholas Tucker, *The Child and the Book: a psychological and literary exploration* (Cambridge University Press, Cambridge, 1981), p. 47.
9   Brian Alderson, *Sing a Song for Sixpence* (Cambridge University Press in association with the British Library, London, 1986), p. 9.
10 Ibid., p. 17; my emphasis.
11 Landes, 'Picture books as literature', p. 51.
12 Quoted in Tucker, *The Child and the Book*, p. 49.
13 Joan E. Cass, *Literature and the Young Child*, 2nd edn (Longman, London, 1984), p. 5.
14 Lewis Carroll, *The Annotated Snark*, ed. Martin Gardner, rev. edn (Penguin, Harmondsworth, 1973), p. 17.
15 David McKee, *I Hate My Teddy Bear* (Andersen Press, London, 1982).
16 John Masefield, *The Midnight Folk* (Heinemann, London, 1927).
17 Ellen Raskin, *The Westing Game* (Dutton, New York, 1978; London, Macmillan, 1979).
18 Cass, *Literature and the Young Child*, p. 7.
19 Ibid., p. 11.
20 Frederick Laws, 'Randolph Caldecott', *The Saturday Book*, 16 (1956); repr. in *Only Connect, readings on children's literature* ed. Sheila Egoff et al., 2nd edn (Oxford University Press, Toronto, 1980), p. 317–25, at p. 322.
21 Roger Duvoisin, 'Children's book illustration: the pleasures and problems', *Top of the News*, 1965; repr. in *Only Connect*, ed. Egoff et al., pp. 299–318, at p. 314.
22 Randolph Quirk, *The Use of English* (Longman, London, 1962), pp. 176ff.; quoted in James Muir, *A Modern Approach to English Grammar* (Batsford, London, 1972). p. 1.
23 See Margaret Donaldson, *Children's Minds* (Collins, London, 1978), pp. 100–1.
24 Edward Ardizzone, *Little Tim and the Brave Sea Captain* (Oxford University Press, London, 1936; rev. edn, 1955).

25 Edward Ardizzone, 'Creation of a picture book', *Top of the News*, 1959; repr. in *Only Connect*, ed. Egoff et al., pp. 289–98, at p. 290.
26 Alderson, *Sing a Song for Sixpence*, p. 18.
27 John Rowe Townsend, *Written for Children*, new edn (Penguin, Harmondsworth, 1983), p. 321.
28 Ray Reardon, 'The art of illustration in children's literature', in *Children's Literature: the whole story*, ed. Rhonda Bunbury (Deakin University, Victoria, 1980), p. 167.
29 Patricia Cianciolo, *Illustrations in Children's Books* (William C. Brown, Dubuque, Iowa, 1970); quoted in *Children's Literature*, ed. Bunbury, p. 137.
30 William Moebius, 'Introduction to picture book codes', *Word and Image*, 2, 2 (April – June 1986), pp. 141–58.
31 Barbara Bader, *American Picturebooks: from Noah's ark to the beast within* (Macmillan, New York, 1976).
32 Maurice Sendak, *Where the Wild Things Are* (Bodley Head, London, 1981).
33 Robert McCloskey, *Make Way for Ducklings* (Blackwell, Oxford, 1944).
34 Janet and Allan Ahlberg, *Each, Peach, Pear, Plum* (Kestrel, Harmondsworth, 1978).
35 Robert Lawson and Munro Leaf, *The Story of Ferdinand* (Viking, New York, 1936).
36 Beatrix Potter, *The Tale of Peter Rabbit* (Warne, London, 1906).
37 Quoted by Jean Streufert Patrick, 'Robert Lawson's *The Story of Ferdinand*, death in the afternoon or life under the cork tree', in *Touchstones: reflections on the best in children's literature*, vol. 3 (Children's Literature Association, West Lafayette, Ind., 1989), pp. 74–84, at p. 83.
38 Landes, 'Picture books as literature', p. 53.
39 Jane Doonan, 'The object lesson: picturebooks of Anthony Browne', *Word and Image*, 2, 2 (April – June 1986), pp. 159–72, at p. 168.
40 Berridge, 'Taking a good look at picture books', p. 156.
41 Moebius, 'Introduction to picture book codes', p. 147.
42 Doonan, 'Object lesson', p. 159.
43 Raymond Briggs, *Fungus the Bogeyman* (Hamish Hamilton, London, 1979).
44 John Burningham, *Granpa* (Cape, London, 1984).
45 John Burningham, *Come Away from the Water, Shirley* (Cape, London, 1977); idem, *Time to Get Out of the Bath, Shirley* (Cape, London, 1978).

46 John Burningham, *Where's Julius?* (Cape, London, 1986).
47 Anthony Browne, *A Walk in the Park* (Hamish Hamilton, London, 1977).
48 Anthony Browne, *Hansel and Gretel* (MacRae, London, 1988).
49 Doonan, 'Object lesson', p. 160.
50 Ibid.
51 Ibid., p. 164.
52 Elaine Moss, 'Them's for the infants, Miss', *Signal*, 26 (1978), pp. 66–72; idem, *Picture Books for Young People, 9 – 13* (Thimble Press, South Woodchester, 1981).
53 Bettina Hurlimann, *Three Centuries of Children's Books in Europe*, trans. and ed. Brian Alderson (Oxford University Press, London, 1967), p. 213.
54 See Philip Pullman, 'Invisible pictures'.
55 Margery Fisher, *Intent upon reading*, 2nd ed. (Brockhampton, Leicester, 1974), p. 21.
56 Pullman, 'Invisible pictures', p. 172.
57 Mary Rayner, *Mrs Pig's Night Out* (Macmillan, London, 1976).
58 Mary Rayner, *Mrs Pig Gets Cross and Other Stories* (Collins, London, 1986).
59 See, for example, Margaret Gordon, *Wilberforce Goes to Playgroup* (Viking Kestrel, London, 1987).
60 Katharine Holabird and Helen Craig, *Angelina Ballerina* (Arum Press, London, 1983).
61 Felix Pirani, *Abigail at the Beach*, illustrated by Christine Roche (Collins, London, 1988).
62 Anthony Browne, *Gorilla* (MacRae, London, 1983).
63 Bob Wilson, as in *Stanley Bagshaw and the Rather Dangerous Miracle Cure* (Penguin, London, 1989).
64 Graham Oakley, *The Church Mouse* (Macmillan, London, 1972).
65 Phillipe Dupasquire, *The Great Green Mouse Disaster* (Walker, London, 1987).
66 Doonan, 'Object lesson', p. 169.
67 Perry Nodelman, *Words about Pictures*, (University of Georgia Press, Athens, 1988), p. viii.

CHAPTER 11: CRITICISM FOR CHILDREN'S LITERATURE

1 Humphrey Carpenter, *Secret Gardens* (Allen and Unwin, London, 1986).

2 Margaret and Michael Rustin, *Narratives of Love and Loss* (Verso (New Left Books), London, 1987).

3 Michele Landsberg, *The World of Children's Books* (Simon and Schuster, London, 1988), p. 88. See also Charles Sarland, 'The Secret Seven vs the Twits: cultural clash or cosy combination?' *Signal*, 42 (September 1983), pp. 155–71.

4 Sarland, 'Secret Seven', p. 100.

5 Arthur N. Applebee, *The Child's Concept of Story: ages two to seventeen* (University of Chicago Press, Chicago, 1978), p. 53, my emphasis.

6 Landsberg, *World of Children's Books*, p. 88.

7 Jonathan Culler, *On Deconstruction* (Routledge, London, 1983), p. 42.

8 Lissa Paul, 'Enigma Variations: what feminist theory knows about children's literature', *Signal*, 54 (September 1987), pp. 186–201, at p. 181.

9 Quoted by Culler, *On Deconstruction*, p. 51.

10 Perry Nodelman, ' "I think I'm learning a lot". How typical children read typical books about typical children on typical subjects', *Proceedings of the 7th Annual Conference of the Children's Literature Association*, Baylor University, Texas, 1980, p. 148.

11 Barbara Hardy, 'Towards a poetics of fiction: an approach through narrative', in Margaret Meek et al., *The Cool Web: the pattern of children's reading* (Bodley Head, London, 1977), pp. 12–23, at p. 12.

12 Quoted in Jeffery Wilkinson, 'Children's writing: composing or decomposing?' *Nottingham Linguistic Circular*, 10, 1 (June 1981), p. 73.

13 Ibid., pp. 78–9.

14 Howard Gardner, quoted in Paul E. McGee and Antony Chapman (eds), *Children's Humour* (John Wiley, Chichester, 1980), p. 104.

15 Quoted in Culler, *On Deconstruction*, p. 41.

16 Hugh Crago, 'Cultural categories and the criticism of children's literature', *Signal* 30 (September 1979), p. 148.

17 John Burningham, *Come Away From the Water, Shirley* (Cape, London, 1977).

18 John Burningham, *Granpa* (Cape, London, 1984).

19 Eleanor Grahame (ed.), *A Puffin Book of Verse* (Penguin, Harmondsworth, 1953), prefatory page.

20 Janet Adam Smith (ed.), *Faber Book of Children's Verse* (Faber, London, 1953), p. 20.

21 Roger McGough, *Strictly Private* (Penguin, Harmondsworth, 1982).

22 Quoted in Michael Benton and Geoff Fox, *Teaching Literature: nine to fourteen* (Oxford University Press, London, 1985), p. 32.

23 Smith (ed.), *Faber Book of Children's Verse*, pp. 20–1.

24 Iona and Peter Opie, *Oxford Book of Children's Verse* (Oxford University Press, Oxford, 1973), p. ix.

25 John Rowe Townsend, *Written For Children*, 2nd edn (Penguin, Harmondsworth, 1983), p. 194.

26 Walter de la Mare, *Peacock Pie* (Faber, London, 1980), pp. 118–9.

27 Roger McGough, *Holiday on Death Row* (Cape, London, 1979); idem, *Melting into the Foreground* (Viking, London, 1986).

28 Roger McGough, *Strictly Private* (Penguin, London, 1982); idem, *Nailing the Shadow* (Viking Kestrel, London, 1987).

29 Ted Hughes, *The Earth-Owl and other Moon People* (Faber, London, 1963.

30 Ted Hughes, *Under the North Star* (Faber, London, 1981).

31 McGough, *Strictly Private*, p. 174.

32 Catherine Belsey, 'Literature, History, Politics', repr. in David Lodge (ed.), *Modern Criticism and Theory, a reader* (Longman, London, 1988), pp. 400–10. See also Peter Widdowson, *Re-reading English* (Methuen, London, 1982).

33 A. A. Milne, *It's Too Late Now* (Methuen, London, 1939), p. 238.

34 W. H. Auden, 'Today's "wonder-world" needs Alice', in *Aspects of Alice*, ed. Robert Philips (Penguin, Harmondsworth, 1974), p. 7.

Select Bibliography

This bibliography lists the most useful and most accessible books (and some articles) in the fields of criticism, critical theory, and the criticism (rather than the history, surveys, or specific studies) of children's literature. Volumes marked with an asterisk have particularly useful bibliographies.

GUIDES TO MODERN CRITICISM AND THEORY

The most accessible single-author studies are:

Eagleton, Terry, *Literary Theory, an introduction*, Blackwell, Oxford, 1983.*

Hawthorn, Jeremy, *Unlocking the Text. Fundamental issues in literary theory*, Arnold, London, 1987.

Selden, Raman, *A Reader's Guide to Contemporary Literary Theory*, Harvester, Brighton 1985; 2nd edn, 1989.

Selden, Raman, *Practising Theory and Reading Literature: an introduction*, Harvester Wheatsheaf, Hemel Hempstead, 1989.

There are many anthologies of modern criticism. The following is selection of the most useful:

Lodge, David (ed.), *Modern Criticism and Theory, a reader*, Longman, London, 1988.

Newton, K. M. (ed.), *Twentieth-Century Literary Theory, a reader*, Macmillan, London, 1988.

Rice, Philip and Waugh, Patricia (eds), *Modern Literary Theory, a reader*, Arnold, London, 1989.*

Rylance, Rick (ed.), *Debating Texts, a reader in 20th century literary theory and method*, Open University Press, Milton Keynes, 1987.*

ASPECTS OF CRITICISM DISCUSSED IN THIS BOOK

General

Birch, David, *Language, Literature and Critical Practice. Ways of analysing text*, Routledge, London, 1989.

Burns, Tom and Elizabeth (eds), *Sociology of Literature and Drama*, Penguin, Harmondsworth, 1973.

Felperin, Howard, *Beyond Deconstruction. The uses and abuses of literary theory*, Oxford University Press, London, 1985.

The Reader

Ong, Walter, *Orality and Literacy*, Methuen, London, 1982.

Suleiman, Susan R. and Crosman, Inge (eds), *The Reader in the Text*, Princeton University Press, Princeton, 1980.

Tompkins, Jane P. (ed.), *Reader Response Criticism: from formalism to post-structuralism*, The Johns Hopkins University Press, Baltimore, 1980.

Stylistics

Crystal, David and Davy, Derek, *Investigating English Style*, Longman, London, 1969.

Fowler, Roger, *Linguistic Criticism*, Oxford University Press, London, 1986.

Leech, Geoffrey N. *A Linguistic Guide to English Poetry*, Longman, London, 1969.

Leech, Geoffrey N. and Short, Michael, *Style in Fiction*, Longman, London, 1981.

Narrative

Booth, Wayne, *The Rhetoric of Fiction*, University of Chicago Press, Chicago, 1961.

Carter, Ronald and Nash, Walter, *Discourse Stylistics*, Routledge, London, 1989.

Chatman, Seymour, *Story and Discourse: narrative structure in fiction and film*, Cornell University Press, Ithaca, 1978.

Fowler, Roger, *Linguistics and the Novel*, Methuen, London, 1977.

Kermode, Frank, *The Genesis of Secrecy: on the interpretation of narrative*, Harvard University Press, London, 1979.

Illustration

Alderson, Brian, *Sing a Song for Sixpence*, Cambridge University Press in association with the British Library, London, 1986.

Doonan, Jane, 'The object lesson: picturebooks of Anthony Browne', *Word and Image*, 2, 2 (April–June 1986), pp. 159–72.

Landes, Sonia, 'Picture books as literature', *Children's Literature Association Quarterly*, 10, 2 (Summer 1985), pp. 51–4.

Moebius, William, 'Introduction to picture book codes', *Word and Image*, 2, 2 (April–June 1986), pp. 141–58.

Pullman, Philip, 'Invisible pictures', *Signal*, 60 (September 1989), pp. 160–86.

Nodelman, Perry, *Words About Pictures*, University of Georgia Press, Athens, 1988.

CRITICISM AND CHILDREN'S LITERATURE

General

There is an indispensable guide to current critical and bibliographical works:

Chester, Tessa Rose, *Sources of Information about Children's Books*, Thimble Press, South Woodchester, 1989.

Useful bibliographies can be found in:

Chester, Tessa Rose, *Children's Books Research: a practical guide to techniques and sources*, Thimble Press, South Woodchester, 1989.

Hunt, Peter (ed.), *Children's Literature: the development of criticism*, Routledge, London, 1990.

Salway, Lance (compiler), *Reading about Children's Books. An introductory guide to books about children's literature*, National Book League, London, 1986.

See also:

Bator, Robert (ed.), *Signposts to Criticism of Children's Literature*, Chicago, American Library Association, 1982.

Cameron, Eleanor, *The Green and Burning Tree*, Atlantic, Little, Brown, Boston, 1969.

Carpenter, Humphrey and Pritchard, Mari, *The Oxford Companion to Children's Literature*, Oxford University Press, London, 1984.

Chambers, Aidan, *Booktalk*, Bodley Head, London, 1985.

Chambers, Nancy (ed.), *The Signal Approach to Children's Books*, Kestrel (Penguin), Harmondsworth, 1980.

Dixon, Bob, *Catching them Young: 1: sex, race, and class in children's books*, Pluto Press, London, 1977.

Egoff, Sheila et al. (eds), *Only Connect. Readings on Children's Literature* 2nd edn, Oxford University Press, Toronto, 1980.

Fox, Geoff et al. (eds), *Writers, Critics, and Children* Agathon Press, New York: Heinemann Educational, London, 1976.

Harrison, Barbara and Maguire, Gregory (eds), *Innocence and Experience: essay and conversations on children's literature*, Lothrop, Lee and Shepard, New York, 1987.

Haviland, Virginia (ed.), *Children's Literature, views and reviews*, Bodley Head, London, 1973.

Hollindale, Peter, 'Ideology and the children's book', *Signal*, 55 (1988), pp. 3–22; repr., *Ideology and the Children's Book*, Thimble Press, South Woodchester, 1989.

Fred, Inglis, *The Promise of Happiness. Value and meaning in children's fiction*, Cambridge University Press, Cambridge, 1981.

Leeson, Robert, *Reading and Righting: the past, present, and future of books for the young*, Collins, London, 1985.

Meek, Margaret et al. (eds), *The Cool Web: the pattern of children's reading*, Bodley Head, London, 1977.

Moss, Elaine, *Part of the Pattern*, Bodley Head, London, 1986.

Paul, Lissa, 'Enigma Variations: what feminist theory knows about children's literature', *Signal*, 54 (September 1987), pp. 186–201.

Rose, Jacqueline, *The Case of Peter Pan, or, the impossibility of children's fiction*, Macmillan, London, 1984.

Rustin, Margaret and Michael, *Narratives of Love and Loss*, Verso (New Left Books), London, 1987.

Townsend, John Rowe, *Written for Children*, Penguin, Harmondsworth 1974; rev. ed., Kestrel/Penguin, Harmondsworth, 1983.

Tucker, Nicholas, *The Child and the Book: a psychological and literary exploration* Cambridge University Press, Cambridge, 1981.

Tucker, Nicholas (ed.), *Suitable for Children? Controversies in children's literature*, Sussex University Press, London, 1976.

Zipes, Jack, *Fairy Tales and the Art of Subversion. The classical genre for children and the process of civilization*, Wildman, New York, 1983.

EDUCATION, PSYCHOLOGY, AND RELATED DISCIPLINES

Applebee, Arthur N., *The Child's Concept of Story: ages two to seventeen* University of Chicago Press, Chicago, 1978.

Benton, Michael et al., *Young readers Responding to Poems*, Routledge, London, 1988.

Chambers, Aidan, *Introducing Books to Children*, Heinemann, London, 1973.

Crago, Hugh and Maureen, *Prelude to Literacy: a preschool child's encounter with picture and story*, Southern Illinois University Press, Urbana, 1983.

Heeks, Peggy, *Choosing and Using Books in the First School*, Macmillan Educational, London, 1981.

McGee, Paul E. and Chapman, Anthony J. (eds), *Children's Humour*, John Wiley, Chichester, 1980.

Meek, Margaret, *Learning to Read*, Bodley Head, London, 1982.

Protherough, Robert, *Developing Response to Fiction*, Open University Press, Milton Keynes, 1983.

Romaine, Suzanne, *The Language of Children and Adolescents: the acquisition of communicative competence*, Blackwell, Oxford, 1984.

Rosen, Harold, *Stories and Meanings*, National Association for the Teaching of English, London, 1985.

Smith, Frank, *Reading*, 2nd edn, Cambridge University Press, Cambridge, 1985.

Smith, Frank, *Writing and the Writer*, Heinemann Educational, London, 1982.

Tucker, Nicholas, *What is a Child?*, Fontana/Open Books, London, 1977.

Index